When you've found your greener grass - Part 1

Graham Field

Leaving Essex to live in Eastern Europe

A diary

Published by Little m Press

littlempress.co.uk

For more copies of this book, please email:

graham@grahamfield.co.uk

Copy editing and typeset by Ross Dickinson

perfectenglishonline.co.uk

Layout, cover and map by John Hepburn

jhepburn.co.uk

Spine photo by Heliana Haralanova

Printed in Great Britain

This book is dedicated to anyone
who has had the courage and conviction
to set out in search of greener grass.

Acknowledgements

Firstly, I'd like to thank Horizons Unlimited for giving me somewhere to go and Motocamp for finding me somewhere to stay.

A friend of mine messaged me to say he was stuck in pissing rain on his bike in the Lake District (is there any other kind of weather there?) and that, due to limited choice on his Kindle, he was rereading *In Search of Greener Grass*. Then, he later told me, to keep continuity he was going to reread *Eureka* (I must find out who made his tent and battery, they're clearly both resilient). I suggested he should now complete the trilogy, to which I got 'Bastard' as a reply, but he knew I was right. It occurred to me there wasn't anyone better qualified on the planet at this moment in time to proofread the first draft of this, my fourth book. So, in the order in which they helped with this project, I would like to thank Paul Chamberlin for keeping the secret, correcting and suggesting changes to all that I submitted to him. To Galena Tsvetkova for concurring that the initial opening was way too harsh, and later for proofing the final draft. I'd like to say thanks to Antonia Bolingbroke-Kent, her contributions to the book in the form of walk-on parts in my life were not worthy of a mention in these acknowledgements, but in my contrary ways I thought I would anyway – then she sealed the deal by putting me in touch with Ross Dickinson of perfectenglishonline.co.uk, the impeccable and punctual copy editor for which and to whom I am very grateful. As always, to John Hepburn for his skill on the Mac with graphics and stuff I don't understand, designing the cover which was a concept by Radost Georgieva, and his ePub talents, as well as all the work he does on my website. Once again, to Galena for the final proofread – yeah, I know I've said that, but I'm a diarist and like to keep things chronological.

I've changed many names in this book but not all, I don't lie to my diary so this is the truth as it occurred to me. Others may have another side to tell, but they probably don't keep diaries so are less able to recall the moments with such clarity, having only vague memories tainted by the present. During periods away from the keyboard, I listened to Leonard Cohen for his inspirational and beautiful wordsmithing, and to Marillion: *Clutching at Straws* it seemed to be the soundtrack to this book. I would also dip into Dan Walsh's *These Are The Days That Must Happen To You*, which helped me up my game, stopped me from describing in lazy, thoughtless clichés, and drove me to actually relive the moment I was telling, hopefully taking you to the places I write of and actually feeling it – because, if you can't feel it, I didn't do my job.

And, while I'm talking about you, let me end by thanking you for your trust, your following, encouraging comments, five years' patience waiting for the publication of this book and, ultimately, for buying it. I do hope you enjoy this forbidden and tantalising insight into my soul. If I can't tell you how my life occurred in the order in which it happened then the content is fiction and that's a waste of life and time, and those ingredients for me are the most integral of our existence. Oh, and alcohol of course, obviously.

Preface

I can think of four – OK, maybe 5 – reasons why people travel. The popular one is to seek out new lands, scenery, cultures and sights.

Another, maybe, is to escape the rat race: the drudgery of alarm clock, commute, work, commute, pay mortgage, repeat until death.

The third might be that life has thrown you a painful blow, the loss of a loved one – be it by death or dishonour. Travel can be a way of trying to outrun the pain, of hiding and hoping a different location will bring relief. However, generally those people take the pain with them, as the road rarely heals. It may appear to, although it's actually the passage of time that eases the pain, not the distance travelled.

Then there is the gap-year crowd, who infest their fashionable destinations to indulge in whatever drug is in abundance on that particular part of the planet: the Asian opium, South American marching powder, Indian charas, or hallucinogenics from the hot and humid. The Hooray Henry is an easy target for the dealer, the tour operator and the travel writer – and now I've got it out the way we can move on.

The other traveller (and I have to confess I've travelled in all of the styles above) is the one who is looking for contentment: in climate, culture, lifestyle, landscape and love. A relocation that will meet all needs. And that is why I always said I was happiest while I was searching for happiness …

And then I found it.

Introduction

I don't really have holidays, because I don't have paid leave. I've been self-employed for close to twenty years, first as a freelance truck driver and later as a handyman – in my account book an expense column was changed from *Tolls* to *Tools*. Then I became a writer and all my books became accounts of my life. Work is what happens when I don't travel, but prolonged independent travel is what I write about so it might be work. For this reason, I try to avoid situations where I'm asked what I do for a living, because my reply is either pretentious or evasive – I make my dreams come true … and then I have a different dream … *twat*!

However, what I'm about to embark on definitely falls into the category of holiday. At least, I think it's a holiday. I'm not going to call it an overland journey, and it's certainly not an adventure. I'm attending two events which happen to be one week and just over 2,000 miles apart. I'm getting to them by riding my KTM Adventure 950 because I want speed – the KTM is not the only horse in the stable, but it's the most suitable for this course of events.

I'm leaving my house in Essex and riding to Enniskillen in Northern Ireland and then back to Essex to get a ferry to Holland for my ride to Bulgaria. The event at both locations is a Horizons Unlimited overland travel meeting. A place where people who have travelled travel to, to tell of their experiences, give advice, inspire and encourage. Not me, I like to speak last in the evening, not for any prestigious headline recognition, but because what I have to say is best heard with alcohol. I'm not about to teach or preach, I just love to talk bollocks to an appreciative audience. Seems like a happy little plan: ride across ten borders, see some familiar faces and maybe sell a book or two. Yeah, it's a book promotion tour, that's what it is. Cool, now I have a name for it.

I don't think I've ever had a motorcycle breakdown policy before – strange really, when, for the last thirty-five years of my life I've had motorcycles which have all broken down. However, none of them were shrouded in bright orange plastic, and diagnosing, locating and fixing the problem was far easier when the engine didn't have a cloak of inaccessibility.

Also, in the past my journeys were longer, deadlines were visa-expiry dates and not ferry departure times, frontiers were no more flexible than a rising loading ramp, and yet somehow the pressure was less based on punctuality – time moves slower when you ride to the beat of a ticking visa than it does when racing to a scheduled departure.

So, for this adventure (no, wait, it's a promotional book tour, isn't it?) I choose to bask in the luxury of support in the form of breakdown assistance – it's a tax write-off, I suppose, because this is a working holiday. The dream job. The motorcycle travel author is hitting the road, or at least that's the image I'm projecting over social media. In actual fact, all I'm doing is a European ride with some heavy ballast at the bottom of my panniers. It's always hard to know the starting point of the journey because preparation is a vital part of the trip, but not always the most enjoyable to recount or read. We all want to get going. Are we nearly there yet?

—

Good evening, I'm from Essex in case you couldn't tell.
Ian Dury, 'Billericay Dicky'

—

I may not have gone where I intended to go, but I think I have ended up where I needed to be.
Douglas Adams

Integrity is everything to me. I will not die ashamed. I will lie on my deathbed knowing that I gave it my best shot, and everything else is meaningless to me.
Lemmy Kilmister, Motörhead

Just for the record I'm gonna put it down
Marillion, 'Just For The Record'

From A to eX

I'm up at 4 a.m. Team Rock is playing 'Child in Time' on the radio. I only discovered the station by accident. After a power cut my digital radio reboots itself and its new default setting rocks. I love this station; the DJs are annoying but the mix of music had me discovering much-needed new bands, as my iPod is well and truly stuck in the last millennium. It was hit by flying Led Zeppelin at its conception and the songs remain the same. Still, this ageless song about time seems to be as auspicious a song as any to start my day, my trip, this book, wait for the ricochet.

Today is Midsummer Day and, of the lines drawn between the centre of the planet and the one that depicts the Arctic Circle, Essex is closer to the upper. In midsummer it may not be the land of the midnight sun, but the darkness doesn't last as long as your average shut-eye.

That said, after some intense dawn packing, by 7 a.m. I decide it's time for a snooze, because the shops aren't open yet and the inevitable last-minute supplies have to be purchased.

One particular last-minute purchase is, however, a vanity-based need. I've got another appointment at the optician to once more attempt to learn how to put a contact lens into my eye. If I can't get one in and out three times in the half-hour appointment, they won't let me have them. I fail again, I'm sure the problem is based on the structure of my face, I've got this bone beneath my eye and moving my fingers like I'm trying to expand a photo on a phone does nothing to increase the surface area and expose more sclera. My eye waters, my blink reaction accelerates to strobe levels and the assistant runs out of patience with me. Other patients are waiting. So, looks like I'll be wearing glasses for the seeable future.

Still, it's said that where one sense fails another compensates, and I buy a new voice recorder to speak my thoughts and experiences of the upcoming trip into, because one day I might write about it.

My first stop will be Anglesey, where I have an ex-girlfriend. In the history of my relationships, she is possibly my second-biggest disaster. I don't rate every girl I've been out with, only the very best, and the biggest mistakes that I've ever made are worthy of grading. It was never intentional to have a rating system, but it's helpful for evaluation purposes, so as not to keep making the same mistake – even though I still do. I expect they do too.

The problem with the Anglesey ex is that the incompatibility wasn't evident under the sheets. It was a long-distance relationship so most of it was spent in bed. Celibate, sober and absent, she'd keep us connected with her all-consuming addiction to handbags – as her habit outgrew her apartment, she would have the seller send them to me. I have a pile of them in the loft, designer names. They have value, but not to me. I stuff them all in a drybag and bungee it angrily onto the pillion seat. I'm trying to declutter. I'm supposed to be moving out of my house next month.

I came back from a bike trip in the Americas this spring to find a note through my door.

'Sir, I would like to buy your house, I viewed it when it was for sale but can no longer see it listed. Please call me.'

Much as I would have loved to have done a deal directly with the writer of the note, an implicating signature on an expired contract meant I was obliged to call my old estate agent and let them take a commission for co-ordinating the sale.

I'd given up on trying to sell it, tired of people traipsing through my home with their shoes on, before entering the garage of motorbikes, covered from envious eyes to avoid predictable conversations. The inevitable summing of the guided tour was invariably, 'It's quirky isn't it?' Say *quirky* one more time, I dare you. The feedback from the estate agent a few days later was equally expected, they felt the driveway was a bit narrow. They could have seen that before they made an appointment to view and certainly without invading my home with their precious, 4x4-back-seat progeny. It's been on and off the market for seven years and it turns out the best way to sell it is to ride off round Central America for the winter.

The problem with a journey like that is the culture shock always occurs on the return, the re-entry into western society is never easy. I find Tesco's car park epitomises everything I dislike about my life, my town, my country, the state of the planet, the unsustainable growth combined with the paradoxical lack of infrastructure. So why would I want to buy another house here when prices are so inflated, the country so crowded and the rest of the world so wondrous? I'd looked at houses for sale on Rightmove wearing an expression like I'd found a felching site. The prices are extortionate and I loathe estate agents, with their 'comprising of' descriptions. I cast judgement like a grammar Nazi; I despise these wideboys in suits who think they are essential but are actually as unnecessary as a string on a teabag. We can buy and sell every other commodity in our lives without an agent, so why do they still exist? Anyway, with that attitude I was destined to be homeless. So my dream lifestyle seems to have become infested with a plague of irritations and a motorcycle trip generally rids me of them.

So now, I ride, but after twenty minutes I realise I've left my waterproofs behind, and I'm heading for north-west Wales and then Ireland. I'll be getting wet then. As I settle into the rhythm of riding a familiar road with a heavier load, I realise I'm not wearing my bike boots. All those miles, all those countries, all that experience – well, I'll be passing back through Essex on my way to Bulgaria, I'll pick up then what I don't have now. Although I'm going to need waterproofs sooner rather than later.

I quickly grow tired, and struggle to keep my eyes open. I've not been riding two hours yet, but I have to pull into a service station. With my helmet on, I lay on a grassy bank and the sun's warmth sends me to sleep. An hour passes. I don't mind missing the daylight hours, but the prolonged dawns and dusks that happen this time of year I find unmissable. Yet I can't sustain it. I need more sleep.

So, it would seem, does the bike, as approaching Northampton it dies in the fast lane. With panic, imposing persistence and what little momentum is left, I force myself through the unforgiving and incredulous traffic to the hard shoulder. I try the starter. Nothing. An electrical component somewhere has malfunctioned. Buried behind orange plastic, it's going to be laborious to unearth the bad connection. *Well*, I think, *I've got breakdown cover, may as well make the call.* While I wait for assistance, I press the starter again – obviously, what else am I going to do? It starts and I spend twenty minutes on hold to cancel the roadside assistance.

It's 4 p.m. now. I'd wanted to take the A5 to scrub in my new tyres – Continental TKC 70s, I'm supposed to be reviewing them – but I think I'll opt for a faster route now. So much for my scenic and enjoyable ride. I stop for a wee in a lay-by of the A55 and the bike won't start again. A police car pulls up. The officer had a KTM like mine and he knows more about them than I do. I've figured out the problem is the fuel pump; he recommends an aftermarket one and a KTM dealership nearby. Not that it's going to help now – it's 7.30 p.m. I do what I did last time but without the phone call, and without reason I hear the fuel pump whirr into life and the bike starts. I ride hard to Anglesey. It's taken me eight hours to do a five-and-a-half-hour journey.

My ex looks good. She's got the biggest boobies I've ever encountered, or at least the biggest I've been free to have a close encounter with. I would no more describe myself a fan of big boobies than I would of jumbo jets, but, still, they turn my head and get my attention by the pure unfathomable size of them. How do they stay up there? I've known her since she was twenty-nine, she's pushing forty now, and perhaps like an old plane, with the passage of time, gravity has won the fight. Or, at least, that was the case when our paths last crossed. Tonight, however, there is a firmness that somehow seems natural. I find out later she's pregnant again, not sure by whom, not me, I've been firing blanks for a decade.

She's living back at home for now. We have a curry and her mother takes over the conversation but has no idea where to steer it. The radio is on in the background, the DJ bragging as she broadcasts from Glastonbury. Either the festival has lost its aura or she's not feeling it because the atmosphere is lost across the airwaves.

When I've had enough food, beer and monologuing from the mother, I wait for an intake of breath and announce I'm going to bed. Her daughter follows and I fire a few more blanks into the night. Well, I've come a long way.

Pumps and waterproofs

I wake up and make love ... *probably, didn't I? I think I must have, why wouldn't I have? The bike was definitely on my mind, it's how my diary entry starts, hence the shag uncertainty.*

I try to get Wi-Fi and then reception, but neither are available with any consistency. I can see the mountains of Snowdonia from the landing window but there is no signal here. I don't get much of a reception from mother either. I'm not the nervous boyfriend I once was, anxious to make a good impression. We all know there are lies and deceit in the air. Perhaps that's what is blocking the phone signal.

It turns out the bike is already fitted with an aftermarket fuel pump: a replacement is £55. The KTM shop only has factory pumps in stock and they are twice the price. My dislike for dealerships continues. I email some eBay sellers. Mother leaves for work and daughter has never got up before midday, so I ride into town. I try six shops to find waterproofs. Why didn't I just turn around and pick mine up?

Nevertheless, I get plenty of help with my bike issue – I now have an address in Northern Ireland I can have a pump sent to and a lovely girl in Bristol says she will send one out with next-day delivery. Everyone from the Horizons Unlimited meeting are rallying round to help me. What a truly honourable community this is. I end up getting some high-visibility Day-Glo waterproofs from Jewson. They cost me £20. It's annoying, but not as annoying as getting wet.

Despite all this, I'm not particularly stressed. If I don't make it to Ireland or even Bulgaria, it doesn't really matter. This apathy is perhaps caused by the overwhelming and daunting need to find somewhere to live. It's an interesting mindset, a thin line between indifference and a *que sera sera* attitude, and I'm not sure if I'm balancing on it or tripping over it. I opt for the comfort of a bacon-and-egg bap from a burger van and realise there is now nothing else I can do, the bike problem is out of my hands and the fuel pump is in the hands of the helpful.

I go back to the house. It's 2 p.m. and she's just getting up. That was good timing – back to bed then. We get up at 4 p.m., have a shower and lunch and then I have a beer. Well, I am on holiday, and to prove it I have a ferry to catch tomorrow morning. I should probably get an early night, but then I'm woken by rain on the skylight window. It reminds me of living in a van. She's not asleep. It's rarely dry here.

Shut up and get off

Friday 26th June

It's early, it's light, it's wet. Her long auburn hair would complement the colour of the KTM, but her company is not conducive to the journey I have planned. Leaving her pale, leggy body in bed is best for both of us. She's a bad habit I've had for too long. The willpower I summon to leave this room I manage to sustain, and this time I leave her life completely. I'm never to see her again, that is definitely best for both of us. A friend or hers once described us as a car crash. I wasn't about to argue. As of today, I'm steering my life in a direction away from her. There are only two things I'm going to miss, and they are not her Welsh accent or her well-shagged scent.

No time to boil the kettle. I don the bright waterproofs: at 90mph down the A55 they flap like frustration. The road splashes and my colour co-ordination clashes, but I make the ferry.

I came last year too. Back then, as I entered the ferry terminal, I met some people I knew and the weekend continued in that vein. This morning there are no familiar faces and the bikes have already boarded, so no one gets to be dazzled by my waterproofs. I'm the brightest beacon on the dock in this damp morning.

I find a space on the ferry to be alone and eat breakfast. I consider the last thirty-six hours and why I went back to the chaos of her life and let it infect mine. It's not a negative recollection, just a clear perspective and an underlying knowledge that nothing good will ever come of this. I've played with a fiery redhead and not got too burned. I've got away with it this long, remained relatively unscathed. She nearly melted my heart but then gave me the third degree. Now I need to start looking ahead and moving forward. In fact, this is the ideal time and place to start.

As if by magic, a pretty, blonde Polish girl comes over and asks if I have a map of Ireland. She's heading to the Horizons Unlimited event too. We start to chat and I mention I'm off to Bulgaria after this meeting.

'To see Graa ham?' she says.

'Who?'

'Graa ham Filled.'

I shouldn't say anything, but how often does this happen? This is the first time; it will probably be the only time. We can all put ourselves in certain situations where, as they sang in *Cheers*, 'everybody knows your name'. It can be your local pub, yoga class, work environment, school reunion. For me – self-employed, working alone, living alone, riding alone, seventeen years a truck driver, an only child, a soon-to-be nomad – the place I can go and see faces I know is an overland motorcycle travel meeting. So, I have to tell her, 'Actually, that's me.'

'Oh, I am fan,' she says, and that's my day made. Of course, if she was that big of a fan, she might have recognised me in the first place, but this is still the best I've ever got on the recognition stakes and I'll take it because it's rare.

Enough about me, let's talk about you for a minute, I think.

She's off to India soon with her husband. The 'H' word. Both tension and attention subside. He's at home with her child, he doesn't like motorbikes. Well, she's good company, and I'm not looking for a relationship, am I? Am I?

In a token gesture to avoid finding myself homeless after the house sale, I'd considered buying a camper van. It seems a simple solution but is now complicating my plans. There is one I'd seen for sale in Ireland, on eBay, I'd arrange a viewing with the owner, it all sounded a bit dodgy and now as we dock and I have phone reception again I can't get hold of him, which is actually a relief because I've got a new riding buddy, and being on the road again puts the romance back into homelessness.

9

When we disembark, I get fuel and she buys a map. We zigzag through the streets of Dublin and find an Irish pub. It's remarkably easy, much like finding an Indian restaurant in Delhi.

The pub is just opening and she doesn't want alcohol so we have soft drinks, lay the map out on the table and find a route to Enniskillen. It may only be Ireland but it's got a foreign ambience, friendly and fun. Out on the road it feels more European somehow, the distances marked in kilometres, the currency euros. We pass a bike parked by a lake. I know the rider, worked with him at a show last year. So, we have foreign and familiar. It's like a school trip to France. We stop for a sandwich and there is another face I know. It's not that surprising really, we are all on the same road to the same event. The girl in the sandwich shop is so chatty and approachable. Or is that me? You get back what you give and I don't receive such pleasantries in Essex.

There is space here: lots of bungalows, big lawns. Cram any group of animals into a confined space and they will agitate each other. It breeds irritability, and that's what is happening on my crowded island. But there is room to breathe here. We cross into Northern Ireland – the pound is back and signposts display distances in miles once more. It feels more British. That cosmopolitan European feel has been smothered with the familiarity of my homeland. But the hospitality remains.

Last time I came here, I made a massive faux pas. As requested, my presentation was on the Friday evening, and I arrived just an hour before I was due on stage.

'Don't worry, I'm here now, I need a drink.'

'I'm sorry, Graham, the bar isn't open.'

'No, you don't understand, *I need a drink*. I've never done a presentation without one and I'm not about to start now.'

'OK, follow me.'

We went through a door into the bar area – the sliding doors that opened out to the seating area were closed. It was like a backstage VIP drinking area – or, at least, it was in my head. I ordered a Guinness and a Bushmills … obviously. I relaxed immediately and started chatting, and when I turned back to the bar both the drinks had been duplicated. The barmaid had a voice like an audible version of Baileys, it was smooth, rich, intoxicating. The southern Irish accent is one of my favourites. It's so innocuous. They can say 'fuck off' and it's got all the offensive insinuations of *om mani padme hum*. I turned to speak to someone else and the glasses were refilled again. OK, I'm really relaxed now, I set up my PowerPoint display and carefully put my black pint down on the table next to the projector.

The room filled, the lights dimmed and I began. I was getting a good response and occasionally took a sip to lubricate and continue. What I hadn't known was that, to avoid disruption, the bar was not going to open and the food was not going to be served until I had shut up and got off. And there I was, chattering away with a mic in one hand and a pint of Guinness in the other. *Sorry*, I thought, *I'll know next time … if I'm invited back.*

Clearly, my apology was accepted as here I am again and, what do you know, I'm handed a bottle of whiskey. It's like I have a rider, or at least that's what it feels like in my head.

This year the audience don't seem as receptive. I know they can't have a drink until I've finished so I keep the bottle out of sight. I get a few laughs but their reserve holds me back, so I cut it short and let the food and beer upstage me.

At some point I find the time and space to erect my tent. The 'campsite' is actually a sports field and I go to the 'away end': away from noise, disturbance and, annoyingly, the toilet block too. Tonight, Motörhead are playing at the Glastonbury festival – I could have been there, but that's travel for you, you can't do it all.

The evening consists of putting some faces to Facebook names, and then forgetting again. I meet an Essex couple I know, Heather and Rick, but it all goes a bit fuzzy and recall is evading me. I end up stroking the hair of a Kiwi girl at some point – and I only know this as, later, Heather told me how available her body language was. But I didn't see it. In fact, the next thing I see is a polystyrene cup of whiskey that thankfully remains undrunk. It's next to my head, it's light, and I'm safely in my tent.

Keep talking

I don't want to get up, but I don't want to miss breakfast either. I'm revelling in both my ability to stay in my sleeping bag and the fact that I'm not hung-over.

I'm the last person at the buffet. I'm feeling a bit subdued and sit at my display booth at the back of the hall. I say display booth – I have a table where my books, T-shirts and flyers are tantalisingly arranged with a pop-up banner that says 'Book signing today'.

At an outdoor show some years ago, I was setting up one morning and a guy approached me and said, 'Are you signing yet?' Ha! It's funny how a pop-up banner with my face on it turns me into a personality. Yes, of course I was signing. I'll always sign. Bang on the side of my van at 3 a.m. and I'll sign if it means I sell a book. Maybe I'll get that printed on the next pop-up. Anyway, it's generally perceived that the more pop-up banners you have, the more famous and successful you must be. They are also good for hiding behind when you don't like being perceived as famous and cringe with embarrassment at your blatant self-promotion.

I only have one pop-up banner with me today and I sit partially obscured by it as the day passes. From my elevated vantage point (the platform my table is on, not my perceived fame) I get to watch the presentations. None of us are professional presenters and the audience are always forgiving of this. You never hear a boo or hiss and no one heckles. However, for the sake of the audience I think a basic consideration would be to at least have the photos of your PowerPoint presentation in the right order, and the right way up, and to have a vague concept of the time frame you have been allotted. Sometimes I think perhaps a little heckling might not be such a bad thing.

The presentations aren't all 'this is where I went, this is what I saw'. There is variety, including a practical skills demonstration. The tutorial in self-defence has some great little tips. One that sticks with me is this: if you are being threatened with a weapon to hand over your valuables, don't place them in the hand of your extorter, throw them as far as you can and while he goes to retrieve them you can make your escape. I've never found myself even close to such confrontation, but I hope I recall this self-preservation reaction if the situation ever arises.

Over the course of the morning Dermot, whose address I was given, brings my fuel pump. Predictably, the bike hasn't missed a beat since I gave my credit card number to the Bristol retailer. But it's an insurance policy much like my breakdown cover, and hopefully I won't need either.

The books move steadily off my table, but best of all are the conversations that accompany the sales. This is a small and relaxed event and pressure-selling to cover overheads is not necessary. This is not a place of high-volume-footfall anonymity, it's more like a private party, a family gathering, where travellers recharge and continue.

The guy with the camper van calls me. It smells of a scam. I've lost all trust in the seller and interest in the van and, as I've become inspired by presentations about two-wheel travel, l throw my virtual offer away and hope he'll run after it.

I like to watch how people of reputation behave and deliver their performance. Think of how Billy Connolly will laugh as he tells a story or narrates a scene. It's infectious. The other side of the coin is the self-inflated who rest on their reputation. I saw John Cooper Clarke at a Christmas poetry recital once. The young lad who was supporting made such an effort. He'd landed possibly the best gig of his fledgling career and he shone as he ran through his polished performance. When the headliner came on, he hadn't rehearsed and, although he may have seen the audience as a room full of friends, we had still paid to be there. It was all he could do to stumble his way through half-remembered material punctuated with some awkward ad-libbing. Another such act was John Hegley. I'd never heard of him but my date was keen to go. He deliberately played his guitar badly, not with Tommy Cooper incompetence or an Eric Morecombe *all the right notes not necessarily in the right order* kind of way, but in an obnoxious, annoying, inept manner, which any one of the audience could have replicated with equal embarrassment. Well, tonight's headliner reminds me of those past performances, name-dropping newspapers he's written for and publishers and agents he's disobeyed, and incapable of weaving together coherent or articulate anecdotes. His presence alone is supposed to be entertainment enough for us, but it leaves me wanting, either for a better routine or at least a shorter one. The best thing about experiencing such a performance is making sure you never make the same mistakes yourself and come across as self-important and arrogant.

The situation is not helped by the fact that I have heard some quite negative stories about this man. That makes it hard to keep my judgement impartial. Later, when we are introduced, our brief conversation does nothing to convince me the stories are false.

The bar opens and I close down my stall. My raffle number is called but there is nothing on the table of donations I want. What's this book, *In Search of Greener Grass*? No, call another number, I'll pass. I want to ride back with less luggage, not more.

I find myself back in Essex company, and that's when I'm told about the missed opportunity of last night's Kiwi encounter. She's quite perceptive is Heather when it comes to such things. Unfortunately, the irritating Scot who invades our company is less aware of such subtleties. I find my toleration for his company fading and, having had three pints in quick succession, I decide I don't want to suffer him any more than I want to part with fifteen quid for the dinner, so I retreat to my tent for a sausage roll.

The rain patters with a hypnotic rhythm and the manic days ahead play on my mind. I try to slow it all down with positivity – my panniers, I think, will be significantly lighter on the way back.

Perhaps I should be socialising more, but for me these shows are like binge-talking. My weekdays consist of a happy, tranquil solitude. I write, communicate and work in front of a screen these days. The shows *are* my social life and I find the mass input from the conversations quite exhausting. I need time to process all that I've heard and consider how I've responded. Perhaps that's why this weekend I'm not engaging in availability and possibly appear aloof, but that could just be in my head. My eyelids and the rain are getting heavier.

These meetings are not unlike the rally scene of the '80s, but there the main objective was to get wasted, and here's it's how not to waste your life. The age demographic seems to hover around the fifty mark. People are more informed and there is an emphasis on inspiring and on encouraging travel as opposed to escapism. I'm yet to enter the decade of the 'five'-prefix, but that day is looming like a dark cloud as I journey towards it. I still haven't decided if I want to celebrate it openly or let it pass, locked away in a sulky solitude of denial.

I'm happy here, camped at the end of the rugby field. Turns out I was on the right side of the line, because I don't feel indifferent. This was meant to be and I'm meant to be in Bulgaria by next Friday. With that thought, I fall into a premature but apparently much-needed sleep.

16

Broken down and abandoned

My early night has resulted in an early morning, which is foolish considering the long day I have ahead of me. On the plus side, the shower block is empty and there's lashings of hot water. This morning I don't seem to recognise anyone. I've never been good at facial recognition, but you'd think that, this being my third day here, the campsite wouldn't feel like a field full of strangers. I talk to someone who clearly assumes I know who he is and I search our conversation for clues, as evidence of individuality is lacking. He rides a GS, wears the textile uniform and, as I've said, we are all of a similar age group. Everyone has grey highlights, if they have hair at all, and support a middle-age paunch. These shows just don't have the visual diversity of the festival scene, which is ironic because, as travellers, visual diversity is exactly what we yearn for.

I pack up my wet tent and wait in the breakfast line. I'm fine to chat and tell stories when someone else initiates it, but I find it very hard to be the one who approaches and instigates a conversation. When I do and the banter flows, I relish the personal achievement. This morning that doesn't happen, and again I wonder if I'm appearing aloof. Apparently, I missed the Irish dancing last night. I'm quietly pleased.

When I say I can't dance I am not being modest or playing hard to get. I have absolutely no body co-ordination, no sense of rhythm in respect to the beat of the music, and I can't take direction either. Participation in last night's activities would have been frustrating and humiliating for all involved, more *pond erring* than *river dancing*. There are several reasons why I've never got married and one, equal to the fear of commitment, is the fear of the first dance.

17

No bloody way do I want all attention and cameras on me as I drag my bride around the dance floor, stepping on her feet and holding her with all the ease of carrying a split bag of cement.

There is nothing as enticing as last-chance availability. I should have a pop-up saying 'Closing in five minutes'. Because as soon as I start to load my merchandise onto the bike, I get some more sales. I run out of T-shirts and sell the last copy of my most recent book: the slim one; the one that weighs the least; the one that is easiest to transport. I try to sell the customer the thick and heavy slab of printed paper and pictures that is my first published book but they already have that one. Still, it's a bonus end to an excellent weekend.

The sun is out, the clouds don't look too threatening and my damp tent is steaming under the bungees. The goodbye process in such places can be a slow and delaying exercise I do the important ones. Blessed is he who says goodbye and then actually leaves. I wave randomly as my Akrapovič exhausts announce my exit. It's a bit like stepping off the diving board as I pull away and flip the visor down. Thankfully, I'm not immersed in water, but I am instantly in a very different and quiet world. It's just me again, inside my helmet, and the memories of the weekend start to replay. It's a repeat I happily relive. Even when I went to shows in my van, I never played the radio on the way home. It was a time to reflect. There was always a lot of input that had to be processed.

I take tiny lanes to small roads, through undulating farmland on a sleepy Sunday morning in a country that, to my eyes, isn't exactly manic on a Monday. My mania begins when I cross paths with a motorway and ride faster than I'd prefer, getting to the port earlier than I need by paying a toll fee I'd rather have spent on the increased miles of an indirect route.

I'm first on the ferry. The time drags and, as the ferry loads, the internet slows and the noise becomes more intrusive. On deck out of the breeze it's warm enough to doze, and when we dock at 7 p.m. I'm eager and energised to ride into part two of my promotional book tour.

I stay on the A55 out of Anglesey with its fast, smooth dual carriageway. No deviation, no hesitation, no repetition, no car crash. It seems like just minutes before I get to scrub my tyres round Snowdonia's twisting beauty. This is the perfect time of day and year to be here, the scenery is enhanced by the low angle of the sunlight and the road is enhanced by the low angles the bike leans at. The dramatic landscape and recollections recede as I cross back into England. However, there is a crisis looming, and my breakdown company are about to make a drama out of it.

The motorway starts and the fun ends. Almost immediately, the low-fuel light comes on. I have been enjoying the ride too much to stop, but it looks like I'll be stopping soon one way or another. The bike seems to be getting louder, the exhaust sound is coming from beneath me. I'm not going to chance making it to the next motorway services. In the forecourt of an Esso station the orange shroud of the KTM can't hide this problem. The header pipe has sheared away from the flange right as it comes out of the front cylinder. In a less technical terminology, it's a bit fucked.

'European Breakdown, good evening, you are speaking to Inept Boy On The Night Shift. How can I attempt to help you?'

'Yeah, my bike has just broken down on the M6. The exhaust has sheared off at the cylinder head. It's unrideable. I need to be picked up.'

'Can I have your policy number, sir? Please hold.'

I suppose he's checking my location and assistance availability so he can give me an estimated time when help will arrive. And he's back … to tell me that my policy is invalid as my bike is over twelve years old.

'I know how old it is, I told you its age when I bought the policy last week.'

However, even in the darkened corner of this fuel station forecourt, I can see that arguing with stupidity is futile. 'Let me speak to your manager.'

Miss Informed comes on the line and confirms that my bike is over twelve years old and I confirm that in my hand I am holding a piece of paper that says the policy restrictions are for a fourteen-year-old bike and an eighteen-day trip. This is Day 5 of the trip; the bike was built in 2003. The year is 2015. Any fool can see that the bike is less than fourteen years old. But I'm not talking to just any fool. I'm talking to a sadistic, power-crazed, unsympathetic, uncompassionate, erroneous fool. She says there is nothing she can do as my bike is over twelve years old. We are going around in circles and I'm stranded and stationary. European Breakdown are not going to honour their policy, not tonight, and I will have to take responsibility for myself like I did riding in Mongolia, Siberia, Iraq, Mexico and all the other places of dubious reputation which are, in fact, full of good people. Will Wolverhampton shine on this dark night? The Esso station I'm in is not giving me vibes of warmth or security.

What the hell am I going to do now? I consider my options. I'm booked on a ferry to Holland that leaves in thirty hours. I have no one I can think of to call with a van or trailer. I don't want to stop here, sleeping rough on a forecourt. I doubt I will be able to find a room at 10.30 on a Sunday night and, even if I can, it's not in the budget. The bike runs, it's bloody loud but the exhaust can't fall or break any more. How much damage can I do to the engine by running it with a one-inch-long exhaust? You know what, I'm going to find out.

I fill up and, with boy-racer levels of obnoxious noise reverberating round the quiet streets, rejoin the motorway. At 80mph, I head back *daahn sowf*. At this speed it's not *too* loud, but God knows what's happening below me. It's certainly increased my fuel consumption.

I have to stop again on the M25. Now the bloody fuel pump has packed up. I'm feeling a smidge annoyed – *come on you big orange bastard, you've won the Dakar more than any other manufacturer for fuck's sake, are you telling me you're incapable of crossing the wilds of Essex?* It's not a Zen or sympathetic approach to mechanics. It's more an obdurate, fatalistic attitude I learned from European Breakdown. I hit the bike strategically around the relay area, the pump comes back to life and I ride like there's no future into the night, screaming back home for 1.30 a.m.

The kitchen feels warm. That's a pleasant surprise, briefly, until I see the cause of the heat is that the freezer door is open and its little motor has been running like a thief who took the chill out of the night. Now would be a very good time to pack up, unplug and leave – permanently. I have a whiskey and hang the tent on the line. Now what? I still don't know what date I'm supposed to move out of my house.

Dilemmas and decisions

Monday 29th June

I've lost all faith in the reliability of the KTM and now I'm losing time too. I've got too much to do, I just don't actually know what it is. However, I believe that if this manic mood fades, I will be left in the malaise of the malfunctioning and the turmoil of imminent homelessness.

I wheel the KTM into the sun to take a better look. I think the exhaust has been cracked for a while. That would explain the popping I hear when I throttle back. At 9 a.m. I call European Breakdown. Yes, they confirm my policy is valid, they will listen to the phone conversation recordings and their insurance company will be in touch. More apologies follow and the promise of a complimentary policy in the future. I don't want apologies; I want compensation for a valid policy that was not honoured and left me to fend for myself at the side of the road.

Meanwhile, I have a dead bike on my hands and there is no way I can get parts in time for tomorrow's 8 a.m. sailing. I point this out.

'So, you are at home?'

'Yes, I'm at home. Where did you expect me to go?'

He says I have a one-trip policy, and it is now invalid.

'But my house is between Ireland and Holland, I wanted to spend the night here, get a change of underwear and restock the panniers with books. What, you want me to camp in a field behind my house?'

'Well, now you are home your trip is over. Further cover is invalid.'

'You just offered me a complimentary policy. I'll use that if I need to but for now I have a dead bike on my hands. I'm scheduled for a ferry tomorrow. I wrote my entire itinerary on your website before I purchased my policy. You knew my plans.'

My father used to love to fight the unjust. Usually, I'd just rather take flight, but this time I want justice and now. Deprived of the option of flight or ferry, I'll fight for my rights.

I head out to replenish my food supplies and go to the bank.

'Where did you get all these Northern Irish notes from?' asks the suspicious cashier.

Nigeria, I feel like saying.

Back home I do a little KTM research and see there are actually two identical relays side by side: one for the fuel pump; the other for the headlights. I swap them over and the problem never reoccurs. I take off the pipe and contact a welding company, they say they can fix it and to wait for a price. I reconsider the possibility of riding to Bulgaria. It's all too rushed now, could I make tomorrow's ferry if I really wanted? Perhaps, but do I really want to? I'll go next month, take the KLR and take my time.

One of the recurring themes of my presentations is the need to slow the pace, reduce the stress, ride less, see more, it's not a race to the destination. Well, this is proof. Of what, I'm not sure. Hypocrisy?

I call Motocamp in Bulgaria where I was due to present, and tell them what's happened. They are OK about it. They are a refuge and provider for overland motorcyclists, they know only too well how plans are what we make before we hit the road.

I open some wine and spend too much time in the virtual world and not enough in the sun. The day passes and nothing positive happens.

It's more than the need to ride. It's knowing that, should I choose to, I can. I've spent summer days at home before, and I'm comfortable with that, at peace in the knowledge that in the garage with a turn of a key my freedom awaits. It's like being locked down during a beautiful spring, apparently for the survival of the planet, preventing the spread of a pandemic – your liberty to choose has been taken away. I need two wheels that I know will turn at will.

I have a confrontational and antagonistic Skype call with my daughter's mother. She's just had her partner's name tattooed on her wrist. In case she forgets it? It's trashy and I thought she had better judgement than that (not in choice of men – I like him, he's cool), but in the location and design of the tattoo. I knock the wine over and it spills onto the laptop. I thought I had better judgement that that. Pessimistically, I think it was over half full. I unplug the laptop, remove the battery and put it in the greenhouse. I'm not sure if it will germinate or dry out. I should probably do the latter.

I watch Motörhead at Glastonbury on TV. It isn't their finest hour. It's another example that feels like the performance was nothing more than resting on their reputation, and it pains me to say that. I've faithfully followed them for over thirty-five years and never seen a bad gig. That's why I'll have no hesitation in buying tickets for next year's tour.

The wine bottle is empty. European Breakdown never called back. The day, the book tour, the ferry booking – all wasted. I bloody hate waste.

Alcohol lies, not just inside my laptop but to my judgement. No matter how convinced I am that what I'm writing tonight is eloquent and articulate, it can be improved tomorrow. Thankfully, without internet access the world-weary web will not be subjected to the wine-inspired rant I scrawl. I'm motivated by wasted time, driven by anger: my bike is broken; my band played a bad gig; my daughter's mother is turning Chavanese, I really think so; all my thawed food had to be thrown out; Team Rock has gone off the air permanently; the welding company never called back; my laptop is marinating; and European Breakdown have fucked with my trip, my social life and my career and they didn't even return my call. My life's motto of 'everything happens for a reason' is getting stretched too thin to incorporate this clusterfuck of incidences.

Social media vengeance

Tuesday 30th June

Drink and hard drive, there was no excuse for my misjudgement but I seem to have got away with it and, as predicted, I can improve on what I wrote last night. I have nothing better to do: my ferry has just left.

I type out an open letter about my experience with European Breakdown, and with every hour that they don't return my call I'm vindicated in my fury. I walk away from the laptop and look at my cracked pipe. The welding company never called back with a price either. In fact, is my phone even receiving incoming calls? Because I'm waiting like an expectant father and life is passing me by.

The dustbin men collect my five bags of festering food without a fuss. Just as well really, I'm not in the mood to explain with remorse why I've exceeded my ration of refuge.

I strike with great vengeance, and publish my blog. I'm aware this sounds about as menacing as a slap with a mouse mat, but the internet is mightier than the sawn-off shotgun, and the ricochet builds to a volume that European Breakdown soon hear. I've never received a reaction like this to anything I have ever posted. It's midweek, the hottest day of the year so far, but everyone seems to be on Facebook today. Perhaps because they too are planning their summer motorcycle trips and my tales of breakdown abandonment resonate around the web.

My post gets shared and reshared. My website has never had so many hits. I have nowhere to go, no bike to ride and nothing better to do except watch what is happening to my post. I take occasional walks out into the sun; the day is getting hotter and the thread is getting stickier. The phone rings – oh, it's European Breakdown. They are looking into the details and will offer compensation.

An American traveller I met in Ireland who also rides a KLR has found a comment box on European Breakdown's website. He is telling them what is happening, who I am, reminding them of their inactions, and encouraging others, via his own page, to also comment on their site. This thing is exploding. A small person can have a very big voice if he chooses the right topic and forum. I am loving this response: as the world wakes up, has its lunch break or gets home from work, the reactions escalate. Website hits, shares, engagements and reach-numbers are going up like an electric meter reading when the freezer door is left open in the summer. I've even got five offers of different bikes to borrow so I can still get to Bulgaria, but it's too late for riding now. Insurance agents and breakdown companies will never know how it feels to be an individual in need within the international brotherhood of motorcyclists. It's phenomenal, it's humbling, it's spectacular. My day ends as I fall asleep to the paradoxical lullaby of MotoGP.

The heat is on

Today, we are told, is going to be hot. Super-hot. Mega-hot. Train tracks will warp, lakes will evaporate. For one day, the temperature will reach 30°C, and the predicted chaos will be debilitating and devastating. On the plus side, they've stopped talking about Glastonbury now. How I miss Team Rock.

I want to see the postman – I know there is a welder in the village and he'll know where I can find him. In the seven years I've owned this house I have succeeded in finding welders in Bulgaria, Kazakhstan and Mexico, but I've not had a need for one locally. It turns out he's a very short walk away. Looking at the two bits of exhaust, he says he'll do it today for £20, the price I paid for some bright Jewson waterproofs, not that he'll take them in exchange. Shame I didn't walk that way two days ago.

Doug at Motocamp has offered me a bike to ride if I fly to Bulgaria. Flights? Planes? Of course, I always forget about them in relation to destinations that aren't an ocean away. I look up prices, it's short notice and there are few availabilities. The best price is £200. Well, I suppose I could, but I'd need picking up in Sofia, and I don't want to be a burden on this, Motocamp's busiest weekend of the year. Apparently, there are buses. That public transport thing again, what a convenient and thoughtful service. I must remember that.

Yesterday Greece defaulted on its $1.6 billion debt to the International Monetary Fund. This has significant implications on a global and European scale, and on a personal level, changing pounds sterling to euros gives me the strongest exchange rate in eight years. I think some retail therapy is in order and, so that my rebuilt, yet-to-be-run-in, SORN but loved KLR doesn't feel left out, I buy it an aftermarket exhaust from Italy. And, now that I've broken the seal of apathy and I'm being proactive, I look again at properties for sale on Rightmove. Once again, I feel my thoughts, common sense and intuition clash with the overbearing pressure that I should stay on the housing ladder.

I recall distinctly going around a friend's house after school one day and staying for dinner. At maybe fifteen years of age, I was beginning to feel there was something wrong with the system. I attempted to articulate this at the dinner table by asking his parents why we should work from our teens to our seventies, with only a two-week holiday to look forward to once a year. Surely there was an alternative way. This was the beginning of the '80s in Thatcher's Britain, the prospects for a school leaver were grim – although, not to discriminate, grim prospects weren't reserved just for the young. There were no jobs, the vacancies that were advertised started with the words 'Wanted: Experienced …', but no one was prepared to train you. They didn't have to. The employers had their pick of two and a half million jobseekers to choose from. The point is, I saw my words strike a chord, and I always remember the time I first voiced my formulating theory that there had to be more to life.

European Breakdown call and catch me off guard with their offer of compensation: £200. The same price as a flight to Bulgaria. I accept it too quickly. I don't even haggle, despite my strong position. The satisfaction of getting recompense is shrouded in a shadow of irritation that I accepted it too willingly. They are off the hook now. I think they deserved to wriggle and squirm longer for their fishy practice.

The predicted heat is omnipresent, 30°C both inside and outside the house. I have no transport but some whiskey left over from the Irish show. It's with a lovely little buzz that my proactivity stops and I wait: for the exhaust to be fixed, for the other one to arrive, for the moving-out date to be announced, for time to pass and plans to come into action. It will all happen, I suppose, as the summer passes.

Smiling from Éire to air

Thursday 2nd July

It's a full moon but its gravitational pull isn't enough to get me out of bed. The laptop is within reach and the first thing I see is an email from Polly at Motocamp. She says their Horizons Unlimited event is going to be huge, and if that's not incentive enough there is a house for sale in her village. The sellers are very motivated, it almost reads like an estate agent's spiel. I've bought into it, though; I really want to go now. It's so warm outside that my frigid house is actually warm inside. The prospective owners turn up unexpectedly. Apparently, we exchange contracts tomorrow and completion will be in a week. They are certainly motivated buyers. I can't get rid of them. I have to smile when the wife remarks how cool it feels in the kitchen. *Wait until the winter*, I think, *if you leave the fridge door open your milk will freeze.*

So, I've got a week before I have to move out. It seems like the perfect excuse to go. I book a flight to Sofia for the day after tomorrow with the compensation from European Breakdown. I'm going to Bulgaria, after all. This, I suppose, is the reason that everything happened. I spend the rest of the morning waiting to pick up the repaired KTM pipe. It's a neat job and when I bolt it back on everything lines up perfectly. The bike fires up, there's no pop. There's no wine either so I ride to the Co-op for some ready-chilled white. I still think I'll sell the bike; I want something lower and slower, which won't leave me high and dry.

This morning, when I should have been writing, I was daydreaming about doing a presentation in Bulgaria, and now I'm going to be. I'd better get some material together. I finish the last of the whiskey from the last presentation. It seems like an appropriate way to start.

Rider after the storm

The radio tells me it's Friday. These anonymous days are not due to holiday hobbies. It's not been the break I expected, although this level of inactivity is some people's definition of a holiday.

After rush hour I take the KTM out. My mum's shed has slowly been filling as I've emptied my house. Actually, it's my shed. I built it, it's full of my stuff and I have the key. It just happens to be located in my mum's back garden.

Having had more than my fair share of leaving parties over the years, I've developed the talent of storing all my possessions in a small space, and developed an intrinsic system where I can locate and access all I need. Premature returns have had me living in garages while I've waited for tenants to leave, or sleeping in sheds while I've been between trips, surrounded by boxes and living out of just a few. Another constant is, I've almost always owned a van, so when I'm not a traveller, I'm a mover.

You can tell a lot about a person when you help them relocate. One girl labelled every box, not just with room location but weight and level of resilience – 'books' or 'glasses'. It makes for happy stacking and damage-free transportation. Unfortunately, more often than not the moving process is a chaotic multi-trip affair of dustbin liners and IKEA bags. Or maybe that's just a reflection of the company I keep. I once moved a trio of stone-heads from one rental property to another with a ten-ton tipper truck I was driving for the water board. It even had a grab on the back. Their lack of organisation made it very tempting to pull the hydraulic lever at their new house and let the array of yucca plants, fish tanks and wicker chairs tumble to the level of equality.

31

So I'm well practiced in the area of relocation. With stackable crates, no plants, no pets, no partner, it's an efficient system. Admittedly, paddock stands are a big pain in the arse, but overall my transient lifestyle has me boxing more than Bruno.

To prove this, in a shed crammed with a household of implements from tumble dryers to toasters, I'm able to put my hands on an exhaust pipe clamp, a bike cover, a padlock and chain, plus some books to replenish stocks. It's impressive, but as is often the case, the bigger the miracle the smaller the audience.

I keep forgetting it's Friday, but not that I'm flying to Bulgaria tomorrow to do a presentation and to look at a house to buy. That's pretty cool, if a little daunting. I fit fifteen books into my daypack and stuff some spare socks and underwear in the rear pocket of my bike jacket. Both the solicitor and estate agent call, congratulating me on the exchange of contracts. I never thought for a minute we wouldn't, they seem more pleased and surprised than I am. As a token of celebration, I take what is probably my last bath in this house, in this bathroom I built.

I have an early night, but a storm wakes me at 2 a.m. and I drink chai and see lightning – but not directly. I've lived in a bungalow surrounded by conifers for seven years on and off, and I've not seen the sun rise or set from here. The horizon is something beyond the housing estates and trunk roads. I have vertical tunnel vision to the little piece of sky above me, where the street lights drown out the stars. And, other than the Red Arrows flying over on their way to the Queen's Jubilee celebrations, everything else passes by as unnoticed as this week of warm summer days has.

I pack the bike in a humid night. I don't have to be quiet. The thunder rumbles away and takes the obnoxiousness out of my Akrapovič exhausts when I fire up the KTM at 5 a.m. and ride into a moist, misty dawn.

Back to the place I was before

The journey around the M25 and on to Gatwick is as enjoyable as the mundane can be. Even as a truck driver, a motorway weekend dawn had a more recreational feel. The speeding ravers were going home, the commuters had filled their cars with family and were driving for pleasure, and I was on overtime. Today I'm an orange streak and the bike is doing its best to win back my affections after it broke up on me. I park it for free under the ramp to Arrivals. In view of a security camera, and with a chain through the frame, wheel and helmet, I cover and photograph it. See ya when ya older.

The transition into the turbulent terminal is a vicious sensory overload. I bypass the bag drop to check in, do the zombie walk through the duty-free labyrinth, and then let myself be herded onto the plane. EasyJet seems slightly better than Ryanair, not that Ryanair sets the bar very high. I jam my bulging bag into the overhead bin, the contents of which will *not* be shifting around over the course of the flight. I get an unassigned window seat, rest my head against the cold curvature, and doze with my jacket over my head. My pleasant drifting thoughts are tinged with frustration when I see snowy mountains below. I could have been riding round them.

I'm back in Bulgaria. This airport is nothing more than a concrete terminal on the edge of a capital city, but there is a vibe here. It feels right. It's not just familiarity, it's a belonging. Something inside me opens up and radiates well-being when, in reality, I'm just standing outside an airport. Built ten years before the forty-five-year Soviet occupation, in the quarter-century since they left it hasn't moved with the times. They are building Terminal 2, the twinkling twin that will steal the attention.

33

Conveniently, Peach, who got me drunk on plum brandy when I was here two years ago, is dropping someone off, so he can take me to Motocamp. Inconveniently, his fan belt has just snapped. It only takes one call, he has connections, and the hardest part of the fix is trying to persuade the assistance to accept payment. This is how Eastern European breakdown operates. It's the way forward.

Istanbul may be where East officially meets West. That Turkish city and the continent-dividing Bosporus Sea is only 350 miles to the east. But for me, on a European level, East meets West here. Horses-and-carts run alongside German cars with tinted windows; the brutal but functional Soviet architecture stands next to the steel and glass of the multinationals. The Cyrillic alphabet looks like a reflection of the recognisable and is used on the essential. The Roman characters are reserved for advertising the types of things the bilingual might need, like German cars. Trabants and Ladas are still commonplace, there's more to the modernisation of the country than the vehicles, but from the passenger seat the cars are the most obvious comparison.

Sofia is only a city of 1.2 million in a country of 7 million people in a space of 111,000 square kilometres. This means England has sixteen per cent more land mass with 49 million more people. This is immediately evident beyond Sofia's ring road. Open space in a country with a declining population is hard for an Essex boy to get his head around. There are more houses than people. Imagine that! Empty abandoned houses in nearly every village. And in between those villages is pure nature: trees, rivers, rocks, hills, mountains, lakes, canyons, cliffs and views. All connected by atrocious roads, and the only thing worse than the roads is the fuckin' driving. Everyone overtakes everything all the time, regardless of blind corners, oncoming traffic, brows of hills, weather conditions or whether they are going to turn off immediately after the overtake. You don't see the indicator of the car that's just passed as it pulls in front, only the brake lights. It's expected, it's tolerated and it's what divides natives from immigrants. They drive like they are death-proof – which they clearly aren't, judging by the amount of roadside shrines and memorials. Perhaps that's why the country has a declining population. The most expensive road toll of all: the death toll.

Besides the natural beauty, many of the lay-bys have pretty vacant and available girls standing in heels and short skirts. I find this absolutely perplexing. It's so blatant, the elephant in the room. If I comment it shows acknowledgement; if I don't it suggests harboured thoughts. It doesn't provoke 'Cor, I'd give 'er one' exclamations, because you can, if you like, and apparently the price is very reasonable. Everyone seems to know the fee but no one's paid it. Perhaps there's a website. Not only is it a blatant display of sex for sale, but the cars that pull up don't do it sheepishly or discreetly. The rendezvous seems to have bragging rights – 'Look at me! I'm going to get laid for just fifteen euros!' It makes me reel with intrigue. I see no pimp or protection. Is there an honour among motorists? *Support our lay-by girls!* How does it feel for the girl to make a split-second judgement as a tinted window goes down and reveals her next prospective customer? Talk about blind date! Cilla Black would be traumatised. 'Now this question to customer number seventeen, where would you like to take your date in your lovely car?'

'Well, Cilla, first I was thinking of taking her up the ...'

Anyway, as I say, it occupies too many thoughts. Oh look, snow-capped mountains.

At Motocamp, I get a bigger welcome than I deserve. I'm the only one who didn't ride to this overland motorcycle meeting, other than the hosts. I see foreign faces I know, an Australian couple I rode round the coast of Ireland with a year ago. They haven't got very far; I was there last week. There are some expat Brits who have relocated, some of whom I've met before, and the now customary but still awkward (for me) people who know who I am. I still introduce myself as Graham, what else would I say? To assume is pretentious.

Sticking out from the gaggle of BMWs is a Yamaha R1 ridden by a Dutchman called Sjaak Lucassen. Another longhaired, left-handed Libran, but far more hardcore than me, he's ridden right around the world: up on the frozen polar sea, deeply immersed in Congo mud, and through China with his girlfriend on the back of his solo-seat bike but without the compulsory official chaperone. Perhaps it's because of our shared birth sign or that we let our freak flags fly – whatever it is, when his face isn't obscured by a beer can, it is as friendly as my own reflection, and I recognised that the first time we met. Meeting him again provokes the kind of spontaneous, heart-warming hug that encapsulates the essence of the long-distance motorcyclist, and would have made a great photo for the Horizons Unlimited website.

So, this is very much a comfort zone. Many of us have come from challenging countries, rides, roads and circumstances to be here. I myself have just braved the M25 only hours before, but there is no one-upmanship here, everyone is as laid-back as Pringle.

Sometimes, returning to a place you have such good memories of can be a massive anticlimax and disappointment. That is why I will never go back to Laos or Mongolia. My experiences there were so unique and perfect I could never recreate them and I don't want my recollections discoloured with the regret of returning. However, I knew with absolute certainty when I left this place two years ago that I would be back and it would be just the same. I am, and it is. There are little improvements – it's ever-evolving, but it's growing in character not commercialism. There are still no signs pointing out the bleeding obvious and controlling the common sense of consideration. The beer is still self-service on the honour system.

There are only five rooms and some shared bathrooms. It's got communal tables and shady corners, and if you don't want to participate or integrate then the balcony is a place for an iPod and observation. The hosts Ivo and Polly have unlimited levels of hospitality and helpfulness, and Doug – whom I'm meeting for the first time – is the silent partner only in a business sense.

I drink slowly and listen to tales from Brits who live here. Ironic really, when I'm at an event about travelling, the conversations I'm most interested in hearing are about stopping. When dinner is served, I seem to find myself eating alone. But that's OK, I'm going over my presentation in my head. And then it's showtime. I have a full house that I can't see because the lights are out, and then they're turned back on again because the projector has broken. It's a little annoying, but eventually it's replaced with a big-screen TV while I take a few trips to the toilet. It's the first time I've spoken to an audience for whom English is not their first language, but either their comprehension is remarkable or they are very polite, as they laugh in all the right places. Sjaak heckles and I bounce back. He can't throw me off track. Later he says he wanted to heckle more but felt it was rude. I wouldn't have minded, not from him; he's not interrupting, he's enriching. Despite an enthusiastic response, sales are slow.

Sitting with the Australians, it's very evident they are burned out. They've been on the road such a long time that they've seen too much of everything and not enough of the same. I can tell even if they can't, but I can't tell them that they need to go home. I'm not the only one at this table of perception. There's a younger lad, who's in the process of buying a house here. Bruce is not a biker, he's a musician and has clearly listened hard to what I had to say, and his comments are insightful and thoughtful. I like him immediately.

The guy I'll be sharing a room with introduces himself and says he snores but won't be coming 'home' until 5 a.m. I've been up for twenty-four hours and head to bed. So, I'm back in Bulgaria and it's so close if you fly. Planes could be my new mode of overland transport.

What you see is what you get

Sunday 5th July

Something about the beer means I'm not hung-over. Something about the time difference means it's 9 a.m. when I wake up. My room-mate never came home last night.

This must be the after-party. It's got that Sunday morning feel without the newspapers. We have our own travel section and funnies. I even sell a few books and a T-shirt. There is a presentation about a bike and journey tracker system. I only watch because I happen to be sitting comfortably in the presentation area. However, as the presenter describes the functions and abilities of this gadget, I see what an ingenious idea it is. It's the advert in the classifieds that most overlook. Sjaak has been using one for a while and when I speak to the designer, we come up with some inspired additions his website could provide. I was so sceptical at first, but this device has massive potential. I had said that I felt something open inside me when I arrived in Sofia. Turns out it was my mind.

I wander around the grounds barefoot and hand out my stickers as people leave. Everyone loves a sticker.

I suppose I should take a look at this house that's for sale. I've been told where it is, and that I saw it when I was here before. But that was a derelict nasty place with defecation in the corners, piles of discarded, flea-infested clothes, no glass in the window frames and rotten to the core. It was beyond consideration, beyond restoration and I'm confused as to why they are enthusing about the place. I walk to the neighbouring house where the Brit lives who will introduce me to the sellers.

It's just a short walk down the road from one end of the village to the other. With wide, wandering eyes, it's all uncharted territory on foot. Cows and goats are led down the street to graze, dogs bark, chained to rudimentary kennels, it's like a Mexican wave of growling that follows me. I make my way past old Russian trucks, overflowing dumpsters and a formidable municipality building which apparently contains a social club, shop, post office and a sanctuary for the part-time bureaucrats of the village. It's not neat and manicured, but it's not disreputable and uncared for. It's typically Bulgarian – it's functional, not let's-get-on-with-something-else.

Many of the houses have little benches outside where the residents simply sit. I noticed a lot of this when I rode through this country in 2013, and probably a lot of them noticed me too. Sitting outside your house is a ritual that's practised countrywide, and in Romania too. Staring is a national activity and I lose every time, in the blink of an eye. There are some vacant houses with broken windows and one where the roof has given up and fallen into the void of abandonment. It's a short walk through a tiny village which clearly has a posh end, and that's where I arrive.

It all begins to make sense. There are three houses: the one I'm at now, the abandoned one behind and the one that's for sale make up a triangle. They are all of a similar design, apparently built by three brothers around the end of the Second World War. With the typical Bulgarian construction of an oak-beam framework inlaid with soft red bricks and local stone and then rendered, the walls are two-foot thick, insulation against the penetrating winter cold and ferocious summer heat.

It's time for the viewing. We walk up six steps to the elevated platform the house sits on; a car is parked in a subterranean garage below. There is a giant pine tree at the entrance. It must be a hundred feet tall. The owners, however, are very short but welcoming. The man is a little ball of muscle, so I'm not about to point out I'm literally head and shoulders above him. Anyway, it's soon evident his wife wears the trousers. She takes me round the garden, nearly two acres of it with over a hundred beehives. It is tiered,

and the three terraces each have their individual characteristics. She doesn't speak a word of English and I don't
understand Bulgarian. I soon figure out 'perfect' is the
same in both languages and use the word repeatedly.
There is a sizable outbuilding on the middle level that
screams 'bike shed' (and, simultaneously, 'how ya gonna
get them up there?'). The lawn is neatly mowed and
strimmed, the roses are pruned, and I think I can feel her
pride. There are random pots, a tree-stump table with log
stalls around it, even a painted old wooden cart. The jux-
taposition against the natural beauty is the obligatory
plastic chairs. Conifers, Christmas trees, hazelnut trees
and, to top it off, a cherry tree.

Perhaps, I think as we walk into the house, they have
played their ace too soon. But no.

I hit my head as I'm shown into the utility room. Next
to the washing machine is a multigym – that would explain the muscles. I hit my head again as I leave, the
shower room has an equally low door frame, but I don't
have to stoop to enter the kitchen/diner/lounge. It's
pointed out that the house will come fully furnished.
Knives, forks, coffee cups, microwave, fridge-freezer, pots,
pans, couch, table and chairs, the lot.

The floors are beautifully tiled, the windows all UPVC
and double-glazed, and underneath each one is a double
radiator powered by a built-in log burner. The doors and
frames are thick solid wood. Up the tiled half-spiral stairs
is a blank canvas: the floors are concrete and the rooms are
empty spaces, but still the power, heating, windows and
doors are in place. And then, then they play their ace and
take me out onto the balcony, with its view of the Balkan
Mountains. Both the opposite side of the valley and the
multiple layers of the range to the west. It's the best view
in the village and they know it. Obscured only by their satellite dish and the exceedingly tall pine, which also pro-
vides some much-appreciated shade. And there's more

stairs. They lead me to the attic that some of us can stand up in. It's got a mud floor which is dry so the structure is sound and the roof tiles resistant to weather. A string of cowbells hangs from the joists. I love cowbells. I photograph it all and we sit down for coffee. There is only one question left. The price.

At this point I would like to thank the Greek government for its irresponsible and unsustainable spending, American capitalism for enabling this, and the Greek people for voting in a new government who had no intention of paying the debt, sending shock waves that have shaken the entire Eurozone. Because today, in my money, the price of this three-bedroom, fully furnished detached house, in a plot of nearly two acres with garage and outbuilding is … £27,000. Oh my God, you'd pay more for a beach hut on a scabby Essex shoreline. The word *perfect* comes to mind again. It's ready to live in, but am I ready to live in it? I can't just buy the first house I see. I've got to look at some others. I'm taken back to the garden, there are no holes to pick, no grasp for a haggle, and no time for a poker face. It's abso-fuckin-lutely brilliant. I want it. Take me away, now, before I spoil it all by saying something stupid like, 'Well, will you take £24,000 for it?'

Back at Motocamp everyone is keen to hear about it. I could just move in and live there, it needs nothing except personalising. It's hard to think about anything else. I text my mum, she replies: 'Is it a Ducati moment?' She gets it. There was once this 900 SuperSport, a model from the early '90s – it was redder than the reddest thing there ever was, and consequently the sexiest little motorbike you could have had in your shed. It would hold its position round corners with the loyalty of a Table Football figure. It stuck to the road like gunmetal magnets on steel while the engine sounded like panting stamina. Sometimes in life you see something you just have to have. The person who said money doesn't buy happiness didn't know where to shop. I'm too excited to sleep on the decision, homeless problem solved, no need for a camper van now.

It's a steal, it's a deal, in fact, I think I'll have it

Monday 6th July

6.30 a.m. So many thoughts going round my head. I've got to get my bikes here. My van. What else to bring? How do you live here? But, ultimately, there is no doubt in my mind. I want this house. I don't make big financial commitments easily, I generally do a lot of research, a lot of thinking, a lot of asking and eventually, when I have all the information I can gather, I have a few drinks and make the decision. Yet here, today, though my mind may be racing the decision is clear. I've deliberated harder over a choice of tyres.

I've got this ex. I call her my best ex, we're still good friends. Once, she met a man she liked and said to me, 'I'm fed up of being cautious and sensible, I'm just going to go for it, see what happens.' Ten years later, she's married with two kids and it turns out her wild whim was an excellent choice. I wonder where I'll be in ten years, but then I always have.

I go to the club house/ restaurant/ presentation area and make myself a cup of tea. I chat to another early riser and he buys a book. This is a good start to the week. The Australians come in. 'Just another day in the office,' they say. It's almost funny, but I can see they are so tired of travelling, they are getting nothing out of this at all. I check the internet for some other places for sale in the vicinity. My potential new neighbour picks me up and we head out to view some alternative villages and houses.

We drive past fields of towering sunflowers and the two years since I was last here fade as I see the familiar in roads, signs and buildings. As we drive, he tells me of feuds between immigrants in the village. It's inevitable, I suppose. Gossip, judgement and petty behaviour are an inescapable part of a small community. Soap operas need

44

a plot; the idle mind needs occupying. I suppose an expat community comprises early retirees who once had their own business but now mind others'. The houses we find have views and are unfinished but they scream isolation, not just solitude. I consider the hardships of getting a fridge, for example. I wouldn't know which shop to buy one in, how to speak the language to ask for it, I have no transport to collect it, can't give directions to have it delivered – the purchase would be a time-consuming process. Even if the house and the village where Motocamp is located is not for me, it's a good place to start. There is a lot to be learned and the expat population have the experience and knowledge I will need. We haven't seen much other than the beautiful countryside. It convinces me that the house I saw yesterday is being handed to me on a plate, and the time to look at alternatives is three years from now when I know the country, the culture, the climate and the language. All those little things that I take for granted in the country I grew up in will become a challenge here. 'Is this yoghurt or sour cream?' How can I explain I need PTFE tape? Buying this house will take a lot of hardships out of the transition.

Back at Motocamp I speak to Doug. He tells me to calm down, be a cool buyer. He earns a living from buying and selling, mainly old motorbikes and parts. He has a valid point. When I lived in the US, I used to do a lot of swap meets with my friend. He also made a living in the parts market and was a very shrewd businessman, despite being a total stoner. I remember one particular show. Having set up his booth, we were walking round the stands before the place opened to the public. He saw a bunch of old Harley solo saddles with sprung seat posts. They all had price tags on them. In a serene, almost dreamlike manner he gathered them up, waved over the seller and held out the full asking price in cash without a word. As we walked away with his new purchases, the only urgency in his actions was to remove the price tags. 'I'm not spending money,' he said to me, 'I'm making it.' He put them on his stand with a 400 per cent markup. I always recall that transaction – he knew their worth, and he didn't want any delay in the purchase with some pointless haggling. I feel like that with this house. To knock a few grand off would be pointless, insulting and futile. However, I don't like to ever pay the asking price of anything on principle.

Later, when Polly is available, we go back to the house and wake Mr. Muscle from his afternoon doze – not a good start. She translates for me; it seems the buying of a house is a very simple and fast process. There are no solicitors, surveys, or searches, unlike the UK where the system seems to have been manufactured and manipulated to make their services a compulsory expense of a house purchase. They confirm that the entire contents of the place are included in the selling price. There has to be a huge element of trust in this transaction, not least as I'm reliant on translators and have to sign forms I can't read. However, they now ask for a month before they will be ready to vacate. At last, an opening. I make my offer, through Polly – who squirms as she has to relay it – and we settle on £25,000. Now, that really is perfect. We have an agreement, and I'm not sure if I'm relieved or even more anxious that the sale will come to fruition.

Back to Motocamp and the Milkybars are on me. I've always wanted to say that – although most people opt for beer. Polly and Ivo seem more excited than I am. Everyone is genuinely pleased for me. I'm shell-shocked, not from buying a round but a house. I tell Polly I will wander down whenever I hear a bike so I can sell a book. I sense envy in the Aussies. It's not nasty at all, but they've just witnessed a wanderer buy a base. They can see I've made an excellent decision. They say I will become a fat alcoholic living here, but I tell them the house comes with a multigym so I won't get fat. They aren't sure if I'm joking or not. It's a tightrope, always has been, but I've maintained balance so far. I go to bed wondering only if I should think harder about this decision.

Deposit at the drop of a pin

Tuesday 7ᵗʰ July

Apart from opening a bank account today, I'd also like to try and get a ride in that doesn't involve stopping in a lay-by. Opening up the laptop, I find Amazon has not received the books I sent to restock my inventory. Annoyingly, I didn't insure the shipment as that pretty much takes away the meagre profit margin after the faceless, unaccountable multinational company takes its disproportionate fees.

Breakfast is a very social event – this is the international, face-to-face, accountable company that Motocamp creates – and I'm enjoying being social. I'm happy, I don't want to look at my charging laptop, I want to interact. It's most uncharacteristic. I realise my life was full of emptiness, and has been for a while. I just didn't see it as I wrote my words and sold my books. As always, travel brings perspective, and I can see the big picture from here. Really, something changed when I got off the plane, I swear it did.

There is excellent chemistry this morning. The wit is ferocious. With the mix of nationalities and a common interest, we are all very much on form. I think whether your tyres are resting, being changed, rolling through, punctured or tired and balding, this is a meeting of clans who are all at different stages on the same road.

It's decide we will take the car into town but nothing happens very quickly. There is only one thing that will get done today. I sit around and watch others not do what they intended to. I need some toys here, at least one bike, and a dirt bike would be useful too. The Australian is looking at his laptop, cursing and sighing. He says he's so behind in his blog and he's bored of writing it. It's all church this, ancient ruin that, hotel, drink, meal. I tell him if he's not inspired to write it, imagine how dull it will be to read. Skip to the present, tell your followers it was an insignificant

48

few weeks through Greece, they'll appreciate that. But he labours on under the commitment of continuity, missing the point and pointing out all he's missing.

Eventually we all pile into the car. In town I'm taken to an ATM. The Bulgarian currency is the lev and it's pegged to the euro. The ratio is about double – that's good enough when you're buying a beer. For bigger purchases, at 1.95 lev to 1 euro the difference is more significant. So, for example, if you buy a drink for 2 lev and think, *OK, that's 1 euro,* you are close enough. But buy a house for 20,000 lev and it's 10,234 euros. Simply halving it leaves you 234 beers out of pocket.

Anyway, I pound in my PIN and out comes a wad of cash. I do it two more times and that's the deposit sorted, although unfortunately it's all in tens. Opening an account is easy: I just show my passport. That's the wonderful thing about the European Union: twenty-seven countries we can all legally live and work in. It beats the below-the-radar existence I lived in the US, forever looking over my shoulder and covering up a paper trail.

I don't recall ever being so ecstatic in a supermarket. They have everything I can think of and a rough calculation makes it all affordable. A bottle of wine for 69p, two litres of beer for the same price. Lucky I have a multigym. I won't be getting fat.

Polly has made a contract and we go back to see the sellers. I give them the deposit and everyone seems happy. They say they will be taking the swing chair on the porch as it was a gift, also the cowbells.

'What? The cowbells?' I wanted the cowbells, I need more cowbells in my life.

Then, rather apologetically, another thing is mentioned. *Here we go,* I think, *now what's it gonna be?*

Turns out it's the religious icon above the mantelpiece.

'That's okay,' I tell Polly, 'I'll replace it with a photo of Charley Boorman.'

She doesn't translate. We all laugh, we all sign. I will be back in two weeks with the rest of the money. I've left bigger deposits for bikes. All I can do is trust and read body language as best I can.

There are some Germans in the village, a vet and a physiotherapist. They have inadvertently become a dog rescue centre. They have a KTM with a side car. It's an extravagant conversion, Öhlins suspension all round. It's good to hang out with some non-Brit immigrants. Still, the views don't seem to change – no one really has anything bad to say. They tell me my end of the village is Beverly Hills, here is Hippy Heights. Man, I am moving up in the world.

Back at Motocamp I say my goodnights and goodbyes. What a life-changing four days it's been. Now I'm going home for more goodbyes.

Last of the lasts

Wednesday 8th July

6.30 a.m. My phone isn't going to make it through the day and it's too late to charge it. I suppose I'm going to have to look around me.

I'm picked up and off to the airport before I can even scavenge for breakfast. It's a two-and-a-half-hour drive. The first half is single carriageway, then the smooth multi-lane highway to the capital, via four tunnels, some elevated valley crossings and a couple of mountain passes. The road winds through ever-changing scenery and many views have no trace of human impact. A fully charged phone could neither win my attention nor capture this countryside. There is a point towards the end of the journey where the road rounds a corner and below is the full panorama of Sofia. The highway blacktop draws the eye to the backdrop of a dormant volcano and often a dark toxic cloud hangs over the city, a trait of being one of Europe's highest capitals. Denver often wore a similar hovering halo of effluence despite its affluence. To my mind, due to its relatively small size, I think the pollution must be cleaner here. You can see the other side of the city from this approach. I've found Bulgarians don't like me pointing out how small their capital is, but in England we have more people in our capital than they have in their entire country. 'There, there, it's OK, you've got this lovely mountain … I mean volcano … yes … it's a volcano …' Well, actually it was formed by volcanic activity. Still, it's lovely to look at regardless of its status and origin.

There is a café close to the terminal that caters to international travellers in much the same way as North Korea caters to independent tourism. I get an omelette that may also have been formed by volcanic activity. Unfortunately, the burnt bits are craftily folded into the ingredients, causing everything to taste like scrapings from the bottom of a burnt pan.

I leave sunny Sofia's 30°C and land in Gatwick's cloudy 18°C. The KTM is obediently waiting and responds willingly to the press of the starter. It gets me back home on reserve in hard rain, although I barely notice the soaking. My thoughts are full of Bulgaria: logistics; vehicles; the possessions I must prioritise for resettlement; the tools needed for alteration; the improvements and the individualising. For the first time, I have a house with a room that will accommodate the corner couch I've always longed for – funny to think that for most of my life the thrill of corners was the lean angle, not the comfort aspect. My beautiful house on the hill.

There is absolutely no doubt in my mind that I am doing the right thing to leave this place. Bought seven years ago as a stepping stone, my house instantly became a millstone. The property market crash of 2008 was occurring while I was up to my ankles in plaster, plumbing and general remodelling. The quick turnaround, renovation, retreat-and-retire I had hoped for never happened. I've rented it out many times and ridden off, but I was never able to find a buyer who was unique enough to have the imagination my 'quirky' accommodation required. So basically, it's been seven years in limbo – which doesn't quite have the same ring to it as seven years in Tibet. There is no sorrow in leaving it or anything else behind. I doubt it will ever get a blue plaque to commemorate the three books I've penned there.

I book a ferry for next Friday – yes, for you, KTM. Let's try again. I'd leave sooner but I have a presentation booked for Thursday. I call the editor of an online magazine I write for to ask if he'll promote it a bit: my last hurrah. And then I eat my last dinner in the house. Fish & chips with white wine.

I speak to my uncle. Other than my mother, he is my only living blood in the country, and he disses Motocamp based on name alone and the community that has sprung up around it. He also has no interest in hearing about my presentation. He's a distant family member, and if he'd been my father as opposed to his brother, I'd be a very different person, and I'm not sure it'd be for the better. I'm annoyed after the call.

With my two-hour jet lag, I can't be bothered to do any packing. I'll be up early tomorrow and do it then. I have another last bath, the last of the wine flows, and I play my bath time playlist loud.

It must be ten years since I put that playlist together, back in the days of fitting kitchens, bathrooms and general hardships. My weeks then consisted of hard physical labour. Lying on a tile floor with my shoulder blades digging into an inflexible surface as I worked on my back, hands above my head plumbing in a kitchen tap. By the end of each week my body was bruised, cut, blistered and aching. On Friday nights, I would take three big bottles of San Miguel to the bathroom and soak away the stress and strains of my trade. I slowly dunked down and drank down into a state of half-conscious flotation. At the desired moment, I would sing out loud to the most powerful songs on the playlist. It was excellent, and it still is. I love that playlist and a drink in the bath. It's my decadence, and I deserve every moment of it.

There is no sentiment in my feelings. There was no moving-in party and they'll be no leaving party. Leaving my previous house was genuinely the end of an era – it was a non-stop party house for thirteen years. Situated on the main road out of town, everyone passed all the time and always stopped by. I still know of people who use the address as their password, that's how significant a place it was. I moved to this place ten minutes out of town as everyone settled into happy couples and started families. That's how you find time to write three books, when no one interrupts. No need for a writer's retreat. Instead, my social life retreated, and I wrote.

I think of how pleased the Aussie was for me when I said, 'I've got the place.' If his blog is as open, honest and emotional as his facial expression was, it will be compelling reading.

The to-do list now only has good things left to cross out: not many 'lasts' left; a lot of 'firsts' ahead. Will I get what's left in this house in the van and the KTM panniers? Do I even care? There's no need for compromise anymore. I'm just looking forward to my European relocation.

Goodbye mortgage, it's over

Thursday 9th July

It's not the early start I expected, but it's not a frantic one either. They say one of the most stressful things in life is moving house, and – being forever contrary – whatever 'they' say, I'm going to do the exact bloody opposite. So I have a shower, a chai, and check the internet before starting to load the van. The postman says goodbye and that I was his favourite customer, probably because I never got any mail.

I think I'll empty one room at a time, see the progress as I move through the house. I dismantle my bed. I've never liked it. The room was so small I had to sell my king-size bed and this was always a creaky compromise. How often on the road I'd hear 'I can't wait to get home and sleep in my own bed'. Not this home, not this bed. Perhaps that's been a contributing factor to my compulsive travelling.

The emptying of the kitchen overflows into the lounge and then the garage. The system is failing. I'm not sure it's all going to fit. I might need to do another trip. The washing machine is a reluctant traveller, and once in the van I can see I'll need a second load. The fridge confirms this. I don't even need this stuff anymore. I drive to my mum's, leave the van, and she drives me back. She's in a hurry as she has a lunch appointment. It's the most stressful part of my day. All of the items that litter the floor get thrown into boxes and rammed into her little Ford Focus, and she gets on her way. All I have to do now is clean. The vacuum cleaner is blocked and my tools are packed. That'll do. The place is empty, except for the big mirror, ladders and the outside table and chairs.

I go to the pub and sit in the sun by the fish pond with a beer and order a burger. I envy and admire the cleanliness of the water and contemplate their filtration system. When I bought my house, the purchase was based mainly on the oversize garage – however, there was an unexpected bonus of a pond of carp and goldfish. If I took my time and slowed my pace the koi would eat from my hand. It was a very calming activity, and surprisingly I became interested in fish-keeping. There was more to it than fish. Sometimes, I would get a courting duck and drake visit, or a hungry heron with its intimidating wingspan. The frogs would spawn and plants would flower and bring dragonflies. Pond life has diversity, and water treatment and plant balance became a constant challenge. So, as is often the case with a new awareness, I now ponder every one I see.

The phone keeps ringing. The cleaners want to get in. Cleaners? I've just bloody vacuumed and wiped the skirting boards – what an insult! Anyway, the money hasn't been transferred yet, and my solicitor says on no account give them access to the property. This is not my problem, not my stress. My solicitor assumes I'm in the house. I tell him I'm in the pub. 'As your solicitor, I advise you to order another beer' is my interpretation of his words. So it is with forced relaxation that I sip my second pint.

I get the call. The money has gone through. I put down my glass with calculated deliberate movements because the biggest transaction and transition of my life has begun. I put on my helmet and ride the half mile back to the house which is no longer mine. The tranquillity of the beer garden is supplanted by irritability: a voluptuous moving truck is blocking the road and has bought traffic to a standstill. There they all are – the buyers wanting the keys, and their kids antagonising the hovering cleaners (who give me dirty looks). It's not my stress. I will rise above the manic I've ridden into. The Exposed Cleavage Cleaning Company are anxious to get in so I give them the keys. The moving van is reversing very slowly down the driveway, mirrors pulled in, power lines propped up, scraping the fence on both sides. The hyper-obnoxious, unrestrained son exhibits speed-bump potential with his lack of discipline and self-preservation. I'm fed up with him already. His sister is OK. I show her how to feed the fish in the pond.

I put the last of the unmoved into my neighbours' garage. The drive is completely blocked. It's a skilful bit of driving to get a ten-ton removal truck down it, and to think of all those prospective buyers who said the driveway was too narrow for their 4X4s. Says it all really. I go out the back gate and glance behind me. Nothing. Like the ladders, I'm unmoved. Not a hint of emotion, sadness or regret. Glad to see the back of my seven-year mistake.

Now I have my own business to take care of. The 'Ride the Dream – Graham Field' T-shirts I ordered are ready to be picked up. I'd seriously underestimated the demand of my large fanbase and ran out of XXL's. Now I've got a dream ride, I take the KTM into town and park outside the solicitors.

'Hi, I'm here to collect my cheque.'

'Do you have some identification on you?' says the receptionist. God, I've been in here enough times.

'I've got my name on my T-shirt.'

With an unfeasibly large number written on a paying-in slip, I'm free. My life sentence, the twenty-five-year mortgage, is over. Unless I'm in a low denomination country, I generally deal in a maximum of four figures, and any increase can be very confusing. The cashier at the bank catches my mistake. I have the same feeling as when I'm buying condoms. I wonder if the cashier wonders what I'm going to blow it on. She's probably seen bigger. Just another day at the office.

I have a bike with a vacuum cleaner bungeed on the back, a kettle, tea cup and fifty T-shirts in the panniers, a healthy bank account, and I'm homeless. The day, the week, this year's obligations are all fulfilled. I'm absolutely spent. Maybe there was some stress in my day after all, because now it's over all that I was running on has run out. I do what any of us do when we have nowhere to go

– I go to my mum's. The exhaust for the KLR has arrived. More stuff. I'm feeling the burden of materialism more than the thrill of the purchase. I unload my mum's car. The shed is filling up. I'm dragging now, can't face the van. Where the hell are the washing machine, fridge and freezer going to go? Why do I even need them? I've got all I need in the house in Bulgaria, and I just want to go back there now. It's going to be a long week.

At least I'll get my washing done

The long week: Friday 10th – Thursday 16th July

I've never lived in my mum's house. Other than Christmas night on the couch, I'm not sure I've even seen the place in darkness.

I sleep on a narrow strip of floor between towers of stacked possessions. At 5.30 a.m. the anxiety of finding a space for the van's contents has me vacating the materialistic canyon.

I get online in the dining room. I need more space. I need *my* space. I relocate some furniture – the back room becomes a guest room, my storage room becomes an office/bedroom, and with the van unloaded it could also be a kitchen/utility room.

One more trip, the last move, back to my old place. No one is home. So, for the last time, I jump the gate and, for the first time, I'm trespassing. There's floating debris in the fish pond. It's only lacking a half-submerged supermarket trolley. Poor fish. I get my stuff from the neighbours. Their eldest says the kids are 'gobby'. Yeah, sorry, with seven years to find a buyer, I couldn't afford to be picky. I leave the situation with guilt and relief.

I may not have a home anymore but I still have my own little world, and that's where I'm happily residing whilst wandering round ASDA, until the checkout chatter brings me back to reality. What did he say? This isn't the usual customer-engagement conversation. I have to take out an earbud to receive compliments on the tasty treats I've laid on the conveyer belt. Crab paste, spiced chai, smoked cod, curry and naan – just because I'm homeless doesn't mean I'm scavenging for scraps.

The day consists of doing little jobs for my mum, stacking crates on white goods ceiling-high, and repeated trips to the shed looking for specifics while munching on a baguette.

The transition to transient and the taste of crab paste makes the ordeal as pleasurable as possible.

I find the copper exhaust gasket for the KLR and put on the new exhaust. The test ride takes me to the village I grew up in, where I progressed from Raleigh Choppers to riding choppers to rallies. The only thing that has changed here is the age. I take every corner knowing the lines like lyrics.

It's Friday night, the first weekend in four weeks that I'm not at a show. I spend it looking at the bikes in the garage, drinking beer and talking bollocks, a pastime from past times. Mum is clearly enjoying the company – perhaps more so, knowing there's a timer ticking.

* * *

The pressure is lighter now. I can sit at my dining table, which has also become a desk, as well as the packing and distribution centre for book sales.

I try to update my website but it won't load. Turns out Mother has unplugged the router. When I last lived at 'home', the virtual world existed only in my head, the one thing that couldn't be confiscated in the name of tantrum-inducing punishment. I try to make a sausage-and-egg sandwich, my Saturday morning treat. I was the one who fitted her induction hob but I have no idea how it works. I can't turn the bloody thing on. I'm getting very heated and the pan stays chilled. There is no brown sauce and I can't listen to Team Rock because the internet has gone off. Interesting how, back at 'home', the independent mortgage-paying man has become the co-dependent brat. So, if I can't listen to my rock music I may as well work on my bike. And, while I'm in regression, I text an ex. Thankfully, she doesn't reply.

I have a column deadline looming and nothing is coming. I just want to go to Bulgaria. I pad around barefoot on this sunny Saturday, feeling captive with my limitless options. Both my mother and I have become very used to living alone, so I take the KTM out, visit my friend Drob, the doctor, and prolong the stay into a dinner invitation. He says he will come and visit me in Bulgaria. I'm hearing this a lot, mostly from the people who stopped coming around when I moved ten minutes out of town.

What will I do if I have health problems? Typical bloody cautious outlook. I'll do the same as I would've when I was in Siberia or Brazil, I'll deal with it. Anyway, I've never spent a night in hospital in my entire life. It's a ridiculous thing to be concerned about – Bulgaria is in the European Union and I've got an EHIC card, so what's to worry about? *Turns out I was destined to lose my overnight hospital stay virginity, repeatedly.*

My main preoccupation is logistics. I need to keep my van here for a show in August, but equally I want to get my tools over. Painting seems to be my top priority, though. I can't call it home until I eliminate that insipid pink décor. I've lived in tofu-bland magnolia hell for seven years, daring not to personalise my house as prospective buyers are so conditioned by house-buying programmes. The colour-controlled can't see past the paint and need a blank canvas. Now is the time to rebel. I want strong dramatic colours, bloody-steak crimson and rich egg-yolk orange. No more rice-cake insipid; gimme a living colour chart with non-vegan variety.

* * *

I wake up with a topic in mind and draft my column, then wander around between garage and shed telling myself I'm contemplating but actually it's procrastinating. The new owners need me to sign something so they can get a landline. I take the KLR. I'm more used to the new exhaust now, it's seven pounds lighter than the stock one, and knowing that is the only difference I feel. This is the final upgrade. It had a 685cc conversion this spring so the oil-burning days are over. It's ready for the long-awaited ride to Iran, which is a less significant ride now I'm moving next-door-but-one. Just ride across Turkey and I'm

61

there. The tricky bit is getting in as an independent traveller. Still, now the bike is ready, I've just got to jump the bureaucratic hurdles like Steve McQueen - though without getting caught in the barbwire of red tape. And anyway, I want to enter the great country, not escape it.

Pulling into the driveway, something feels different. What's changed? They've cut down all the fruit trees, the fuckin' reprobates. That apple tree had to be fifty years old. The plum, pear and other apple trees all gone. Apparently, their little angels need somewhere to play football. So, the fields beyond the back gate weren't adequate then? The fish are also to be relocated to the pub up the road, as the new owners are worried their precious progeny will fall in the pond. I don't see a problem myself. Why did you want to move to the country when the first thing you've done is eliminate nature? Right, for that I'm not telling you about the hidden tap, the free flow, the mains side of the meter. You don't deserve unregistered water. I don't think I have any want or need to ever come back here. It never felt like home but, somehow, they have violated it.

My longing to leave has me packing the KTM panniers. This will almost definitely make Friday come sooner, even though I know everything's got to come out again. With alcohol-instigated inspiration, I start my review on the Continental tyres. My evaluations always end up like stories. I'd rather set the scene than describe the qualities of the product, and every time I try to cut the word count it gets longer. I should stick to books, but you don't get free gear that way.

Surfing through my mum's multiple channels, I find *Shed Of The Year*. Didn't even know there was such a thing but, now I do, I'm going to build mine to competition stan-dards. And once again, my head travels to Bulgaria while my body lies hopelessly dormant.

* * *

It's a grey morning, which is always good for writing. Today is thirty years since Live Aid; thirty years since I was at the Kent Custom Bike Show. A bit like Bob, I too have a bulging bank account and a need to distribute my wealth, but not to feed the world, only my selfish need for better interest. I hit the high street and soon discover it's not very easy opening a new account. My identification has my old address on it and, strictly speaking, I don't have a new one. If I register at Mum's, she loses her single occupancy council tax discount, and anyway, I'm leaving in three days. The scammers cause the rules to be made and with my honest income I can't cut through the formalities. My legitimate lifestyle has me living out of boxes but I don't fit into one. My option box is generally:

☑ Other

It's easier to open an account online than in the flesh. And there I was, thinking that the banks were the lifeblood that kept the high street alive. Apparently, it's the British Heart Foundation charity store and the 99p shop that pound a defibrillating shock onto the dying centre of town. If you have bigger denominations, or first-hand desires, shoppers and investors go to the internet. The parking's easier too.

It occurs to me this has been a year of waiting. For spring and for my third book to come out, then for the reviews to be published. For the house sale to go through, for the bike shows to come around and now for the move to Bulgaria. Once there, I'll be waiting for August so I can take the van, my tools and materials to really start work on the house. I need to appreciate the moment more. If I don't live in it, I can't recall it, and if I can't recall it, I can't write about it. However, the day has run out of moments worth living in, the evening is dull, the house is dull, and TV is bloody awful. I've never watched *Coronation Street*, but – like *Star Wars*, which I've also not seen – I can't help but know some characters. Anyway, today is Darth Vader's funeral … no, Deirdre's, it's Deirdre's. I always get them muddled up. A significant episode nonetheless.

* * *

Another grey morning. The column gets sculptured and is gaining form. I manage to find my premium bond holders' number but not my password, so I can't buy any more. Distributing my wealth is a difficulty I don't expect to get any sympathy for. It is most definitely a First World problem. *REV'IT* contact me to say my report about using their gear in Central America is now on their website. They have done a really good job. It's refreshing to work with a company who actually do what they say they are going to, without being reminded and without me having to correct their mistakes. It's good for both of us: I take their product into the field and give it a thorough test in a variety of extremes; and it helps us both to get our names out there. Makes me think I'm a little bit of a cult. Someone else I think is a bit of a cult is an American who writes for *Rider's Digest*. I wouldn't have known of him if it wasn't for his contradictions. He slates everything he reads. You don't have to delve far into his back catalogue of reviews to see his hypocrisy, and it takes all credibility from his words. Anyway, apparently with predictability, he's just slagged off my second book *Eureka*. I don't need to read what he's written, but I can't stop thinking about it now and that makes me angry that I'm wasting my thoughts on him. If anyone regularly reads his reviews, they'll see his pattern of pessimism and make up their own minds. They say there is no such thing as bad publicity, but on this low platform I've clawed my way up to, I think there is, and this cult has kicked away a supporting column.

I was given a very clever watch as a present for being Drob's best man. Among its many features is an altimeter. I like my stats and for the ride to Bulgaria I want to know how high as well as how far. So I buy a new battery for it and then take it down the beach to calibrate it. Kneeling down by the lapping tide, I press buttons until the watch says I'm at sea-level. There must be other factors that determine how high I really am, because as I walk back I seem to have submerged, but that's probably just the mood I'm in. I didn't realise it had a function that measures that too.

* * *

It's another wet morning but not because I'm under water. Well, I am, but it's rain. I look at my list. Annoyingly, once again things I don't want to do have appeared on it. I have to get my passport notarised, because I don't want to send it off and be without it. By getting it notarised, I can send off the notification and that will suffice. The first place I call wants £40, the next £80 and the third £325! Is half of the solicitor training about how to acquire the ability to quote such disproportionate figures and make them sound perfectly justified without a hint of guilt? Anyway, who's the idiot? I can get a duplicate for £75, so their fee for this service is somewhat out of touch.

I take the KTM into town armed with more documentation in an attempt to open a savings account. The bank confirms my identification, but I can't open an account because of fraud and money-laundering regulations. My identification does not confirm my address.

'I know,' I say. 'I sold my address.'

'You are not on the electoral role.'

'I know, I elected not to be.'

'Well, you need to be registered at an address.'

'If I had an address, I wouldn't have the money.' Perhaps I should spend it on a fraudulent identification so I can do illegally what I'm trying to do honestly.

I kill some time in the newsagents to see which bike mags have reviewed my book. I look in five and buy one. It's not necessarily a bad thing that they don't synchronise their reviews. It keeps the sales graph steadier – the Prozac sales technique: shallower troughs and lower peaks. A pair of motorcycle gloves I'd advertised on eBay sold last night. It's good timing. I get them sent off. She should have them by the weekend.

I see my hairdresser for the last time. He'd read the book I gave him for Christmas and gives me a bunch of free products, telling me he can't sell them as they've passed their expiration date. Hmm, we complement each other then, is that why I'm getting them? He works his magic and my hair looks fabulous, too fabulous really for the Dulux shop. I'd better wait for my helmet to take the glam out of my usual limp, rocker locks.

The afternoon is spent looking for things and not getting the service I'm waiting for. The club I'm doing tomorrow's presentation for still haven't mentioned it on their website so I can't link to it on mine. The printers doing my flyers haven't been back in touch, nor has the bank with an alternative option for opening an account. Today the euro dropped to another low against the pound and my Bulgarian house is £300 cheaper.

During a prolonged stay in the US, I worked with an interior painter. He'd been doing this work for thirty years and was a very chilled, experienced and talented man. We can all paint a wall, but I learned some excellent tips from his trade. When I came back home, the house was looking like the long-term rental accommodation it was. Full of my imported American optimism, I was ecstatic to find the prestigious professional paint brushes I'd used in the US were available in the UK. I repainted the whole place. Why not? You change the sheets after a guest leaves, I was freshening up the walls after the tenants vacated. My new skill became my new living and I've painted many houses with those brushes, meticulously cleaning them with water from the dark side of the meter. I've looked after them and they will probably last me the rest of my life. But I can't find them. I go back to my old house. There is one place they might be, but they're not.

I go to meet my best ex. We have a halfway pub we meet in three or four times a year. She wears contact lenses and across the table gives me a lesson and a few disposable ones to practice with. So that's how it's done, I see. I continue to exercise my willpower – this is my third consecutive alcohol-free day.

I ride the KLR home with closing-time, summer-night thrill. Like trying to open a savings account, I'm once again righteously on the acceptable side of the law – well, my blood-alcohol levels are, if not my speed. The new exhaust seems even happier in the cool air, or maybe that's because it's the only sound around. We are both ready for something big. The waiting is over, things will begin to happen tomorrow.

* * *

I just want to make some final adjustments to my presentation while they are in my mind, but the laptop decides it wants to update. *Please don't shut down or turn off.* I watch the installation ticking my life away before finding another pursuit. In the bathroom mirror, I put in the contact lens effortlessly. I still can't see – it's not my prescription – but I've got the technique down. It's time to load the KTM panniers with books and, while I'm doing so, I discover my paint brushes were sitting at the bottom the whole time.

It's time to go. The printer calls, he has printed so I pick up flyers and posters for Motocamp. Having slept on it, I feel my hair is suitably subdued for the Dulux shop. It's a convoluted journey to tonight's venue but I've got all day. Back to the opticians to pick up the contact lenses but they still won't give them to me – under pressure in this environment, I can't even get one in. I take the prescription and will order some in Bulgaria. Regulations seem less stringent there.

It's very easy to develop a 'fuck this country' attitude now I know I'm leaving. It's a defence mechanism. I did it when I lived in the US and switched it around when I was forced to leave. I've seen the traits in many long-term absentees.

Either to prevent homesickness or to assure themselves the choices they made were right, they hold a simmering disdain for the place they used to call home. It has annoyed me to see expats slag off England in their adopted country to natives who have never been there. It's the only time that patriotism rumbles inside me. Regardless of circumstance, it will always be home and – like ya mum's – it's a place you will end up when there is nowhere else to go.

Riding down the A12 again, I think about how this is certainly a road I won't miss. The commute to the capital has never been a glamorous journey. I stop by my uncle's. He dotes over his sausage dog like a neurotic mother. He has bought Marks and Spencer's quiche for my visit. It's only slightly less stimulating than the conversation.

Off to the presentation, I have a couple of beers in my panniers to loosen up in the village hall car park as I await the throng of avid adventure-book buyers to arrive. A Bulgarian turns up. He shows me where he lives when he's not working in the UK. It's not so far from me. He writes his number on my paint pot and invites me for Christmas. Well, that's a good start. I get an adequate response from my audience and post-presentation sales make it worth my while. Everyone hurries home as lightning flashes and I'm the last bike to leave. It's a warm enough night to ride with just a T-shirt under my jacket until midnight, until once again the monotony of the A12 makes me mindful of the chill and has me reaching for another layer.

Back in the garage I count my sales money against the books left in the panniers. They never, ever tally. Tomorrow is here at last. I'll grab some sleep before I restart the day.

Fields of barley or something

Friday 17ᵗʰ July

Waking up the same day I went to bed, it's like working nights again, but today has been anticipated like retirement. I'm up at 5 a.m. to load the panniers. This is a ritual that should take weeks of preparation and planning. I don't have that luxury, only luxuries: piles of them, based on priority. Thankfully, the panniers swallow them up. Speakers and subwoofer, camera and gifted haircare products, hairbrush, paintbrush and roller, a Motörhead poster, some clothes, my diary and laptop. This is not a packing list, this is the last-minute stuff from the old house, the only things I can think of to make my new house a home.

How different the mindset, ride and packing procedure are today compared to when I rode to the Balkans two years ago. That was an adventure, that was a book. This is just a new page in my life … well, it's a book now, but … actually, I suppose once the day is recorded in my diary it becomes a book … I don't know where I'm going with this. I'm going, I'm leaving to catch a ferry to Holland from Harwich. It's sunny and last night's lightning was a display without rain.

The ferry is late to leave. There is a lot to load, mainly redirected freight due to problems at the Channel Tunnel. The Middle East exodus has created a refugee crisis. When they reach land's end, the northern French coastline, the levels of desperation have brought about the hysteria of 'get to the UK, or die trying'. It's caused disruption to haulage companies and individual drivers regardless of where their sympathies lie. It's a clash of realities, and it could be any one of us. First, we establish our survival and, once that's sorted, we work on enhancements. It's life, we all have one. Only the quality varies.

While we sit in port, I can see from the ferry lounge a

69

house I'd really wanted. Its garden goes down to the River Stour (which divides Essex and Suffolk) and it even has its own mooring. The house is only accessible by a footpath or down half a mile of dirt road and, when I saw it, was in a state of disrepair. It was inherited by a millionaire, apparently, who wanted nothing to do with it but wanted lots for it. I looked at it many times but it was out of my range, I couldn't afford to bring out its potential. It was my dream house – well, the location, at least. But I've got a new dream now, a realistic one. As I wait to ride towards it, I'm not nervous at all, just excited. It's a poignant moment though. The house I'm looking at across the river was a place of hope and occupied many of my thoughts. When I had to acknowledge that it was simply beyond my means, although I didn't realise it at the time, that was a turning point. I couldn't afford a hovel in my desired setting and I wouldn't compromise. I deserve better and I'll go wherever I have to to find it. Girls, bikes and location: every one was better than the last. It's time to move forward again.

Speaking of which, I text the girl I call my second-best ex (but not to her face – well, only once, and I got such an endearing slap I had to reconsider her position.) She lives in Germany on the Dutch border. Surprisingly, I don't get an instant reply.

I succumb to the full English breakfast temptation and work on the laptop until the Wi-Fi slows and my battery dies. I suppose I should think about investing in some European plugs. I struggle with a book that I really want to like but just can't get to grips with – as soon as the subject matter finds a flow the story switches to a different topic and loses all momentum and continuity.

We dock late and, with no time to put my phone on charge, I'm waved down the unloading ramp. It's OK, I've written the key towns and turn-offs on a piece of paper and put it in the tank bag. With a roaming signal I've got a response from the ex I texted. She's not home, she's in

Holland. 'So am I', I write, but again I don't get a reply. It's Friday night rush hour round Rotterdam but the traffic is calm and considerate. Within three hours I'm in Germany and speed limits are irrelevant. I sit at my comfortable cruising speed of 80mph – well, I thought it was 80mph, but my phone says it's actually 74mph. For all this time I've been less illegal that I thought I was. I'm not sure how I feel about that.

It's the perfect summer evening and I want to ride as much of it as I can. The sun sets in my mirrors and I grab glances over my shoulder to see it without reflection. Sunsets, hopefully, will start to make a regular appearance in my life again soon. I'd love to ride right through Germany, right through the night. I don't know where I will stop or stay tonight and the liberation of that feeling keeps me going into the summer darkness. West of Kassel I pass a windfarm standing in a field of golden swaying wheat. Stopping in a parking lay-by, I walk into the field and find a little path. Without hesitation I run back to the bike, and ride up the curb, past the picnic tables between the hedge and down a track that weaves between the giant turbines. The track ends and looks out over fields and a village below in the valley. I kill the ignition and am engulfed by darkness and silence. This is perfect. I roll out my sleeping bag and lay on top of it. A rabbit comes by, either blind, brave or maybe just friendly. The blades turn, the wheat bends and I look down at the quiet sparkling village. The nomad in me loves this.

I get some emergency sleep and no deluxe extras. When it's time for a wee I touch something that isn't me, a slug is inside my waistband. It wakes me more than I'd like. Still, it was a free night, a place to pass the dark hours. There is light in the sky now, but not enough to write my diary by. That will have to wait, I've got a new day to ride into.

Ride free, sleep rough

Saturday 18th July

I roll up a slightly damp sleeping bag and put on a cool sweatshirt. I got away with a wild camp. I make my get-away into a misty morning with dewy mirrors and a screen of moisture. Back to the parking area, I contemplate a toilet stop but just ride out. No dinner to speak of last night, no drink this morning; I just ride and slowly the day lightens up. I was aware last night that the sound of traffic never stopped. As I join the permanent flow it remains constant but light. It was a 3 a.m. start according to my body clock – that's about eight hours sleep in the last forty-eight. After a few hours my delusional thoughts alert me to the need for more sleep. This is the only accurate deduction I can make from my reflections of misperception. I pull over and doze with my head on the tank bag. It's not enough so I lay on a bench and an hour passes. Air escaping from a truck's suspension wakes me from my Nick Sanders dream, it's not my tyres, wheels of confusion, making me crazy.

I don't need to make this an endurance ride but I'm enjoying this aspect of it. It's not my usual style at all, and it's exciting to push the limits of my stamina. Knowing there is no prize to win or deadline to make, I'm just playing at being hardcore. I can stop whenever I want. There hasn't been much of anything across the landscape and when a service area and the double yellow curves of an internationally recognised restaurant appear, it seems like an opportunity to fill the tank and empty the discomfort. Full tank, full tummy, empty bladder, fully charged. The momentary delight of no reason to want. Everything is at desirable levels.

I also buy a European road atlas for €10 because I like to know where I am in relation to everything else. As a truck driver, the purchase of a map was a much calculated and anticipated action. In particular, back in the early '90s I needed a new London A to Z but the Docklands area was under development. Predicting when to make the jump and purchase an updated tool for my trade was like deliberating upon the right time to change a currency. Paradoxically, the euro having lost so much value recently makes the atlas little more than an impulse buy at the cash register. In fact, with my newfound wealth I'm not even looking at prices that much. This, on the one hand, takes the stress out of the lifelong 'am I paying too much' conundrum, but equally it takes the challenge out of finding the best deal. Which just shows that a frugal mindset can't be changed by money, the loss of poverty is replaced with missing the thrill of a good deal.

As soon as I get going everyone else stops. The traffic is backed up, and the Saturday morning pleasure drivers are wandering around the autobahn stretching their legs. They are without consideration or awareness of a moving vehicle. In this case a big orange Austrian-made motorcycle ridden by a sleep-deprived, relocating Brit who has the filtering abilities of a garden shed due to his excessively wide panniers. For their benefit, said Brit doesn't even know if it's legal to ride down the middle of stationary traffic, and consequently is exhibiting extreme caution. This, combined with his obtrusive Akrapovič exhaust note, means no knees are knobbled by protrusions, wing mirrors removed by misjudgement and, if words of hostility or disapproval are spoken, they are not heard.

With the affronted and motionless behind me, I'm faced with the open mouth of a closed tunnel. It has the appearance of a facility that shuts at night, and the man who opens it has overslept. So, with the bike on its centre stand I get out my diary and try to catch up on the journey so far. However, before I've got very far, Herr Schlafen has risen and raised the barrier. My creativity is hastily stashed, and so begins the onslaught of all those outraged Audi drivers making up for downtime as I ride at a speed faster than any British law allows.

As I head east and see signs for Leipzig and Dresden, the sun shines. Nothing feels foreign and loneliness isn't even a consideration. Again, this is a world away from how I felt on these roads two years ago.

I've got friends in the Czech Republic who enter my thoughts as I cross the border, but this is a destination-driven journey, not a social jolly. Another stop to rehydrate my body and tank. It might be 11 a.m. I manage to zero my trip gauge as I try to change the time, so that little statistic is gone forever, but I know I'm 570 feet above sea level.

Prague has a ring road that requires constant attention not to deviate from. When I do, there is stationary traffic in the other direction. I hope I don't have to double back through that lot. A sign for Brno says I don't, I'm on the right road. This feels fabulous. I stop for a slice of pizza and a coke and have my motorway snack in the shade of a parked truck. The stench of rancid piss radiates up from the asphalt. As a trucker for seventeen years, I did my part to contribute to this truck stop aroma, but it's still a nasty environment and a heavy downpour doesn't do much to dissolve it.

I change to cooler clothes and queue for a vignette only to find bikes are exempt. I suppose I'm pleased. Into Slovakia and I think I need a vignette here, but I'll be out the other side in an hour and I'm not stopping. Bratislava is a capital that, even from the motorway, coaxes out the camera. The city that Ryanair would take me to when I wanted to fly cheaply to Vienna. I've been here on many occasions at scheduled antisocial times. My second-worse ex lived in Vienna and I'd come over for long-distance relationship city-break pastimes, which mainly consisted of sex, hugs and sushi rolls. I glance at the castle and bridges as I cross the Danube. 'See you in Romania,' I say under my visor.

In Hungary I definitely seem to need a vignette. There are a lot of signs emphasising this. While I'm stopped, I get out my new atlas, look at the big picture, and decide at Győr I'll get off the motorway. I have a want for some slower evening roads. It's still 33°C, I'm feeling the fatigue I've generated now, and I may possibly have a cold coming too. The back-road bonus: I stop at a village shop and stock up on some healthy food – a perfectly ripe avocado, cheese, tomatoes and bread, the staple of the road warrior.

One more fuel stop and then with the kind of timing a solo traveller would wish to share, a sign for a campsite appears. I pull in. It's deserted. Closed. With the stealth and instantaneous reaction of a lone biker, I ride past the gate. There are multiple gatherings of caravans and mobile homes, empty playgrounds and locked toilet blocks. It just looks so available, but is abandoned. Fuck it, I'm staying anyway. I strategically park in a way that could be seen as out of sight if no one notices me, or looking for a site if someone does. Some people come, a Dutch couple, they open up their caravan and confirm the place is closed. I ask if it's OK to stay and don't get a straight answer. I make a spectacular sandwich, and decide to put up my tent. It instantly turns into a sweat tank. I turn it round to face the evening breeze. It doesn't help. I lie on top of my sleeping bag and get my second night's free sleep. Wild camping in a campground, it's naughty-lite.

Home is a two-day ride away

Sunday 19th July

At 5 a.m. I see pink clouds through the open flap of the tent. I'm late, I'd prefer to be riding into that sky than looking out at it. Still, I slept soundly despite the gunshot crow scarer in the neighbouring field. With the regularity of a chiming clock, it soon lost its irritating qualities – to me, at least, if not the crows. It's peaceful now, only the chirpy buzzing of this Hungarian Sunday morning. I pack with such efficiency I can't imagine anyone's help could make the process move any faster. I brush my teeth as I roll my mattress and talk into my voice recorder – *listening back to this now as I write – I have absolutely no idea what I was trying to express*. I know a girl who can not only speak while brushing her teeth but can also sound just like Sean Connery. I just sound like I'm choking on whipped cream from a nitrous-filled aerosol.

In an act of reckless bravado, I'd let the KTM charge my phone as I slept. This morning I have the satisfaction of full charge and the bonus of the bike coming to life like a wake-up call. I definitely have a cold; I can feel its unmistakable onset in my throat. Conversely, the sun this morning has a haze about it which says it's going to be an unmercifully hot day.

Leaving the motorway last night was exactly the right thing to do, but this morning, with progress paramount in my mind, it's a little frustrating to be zigzagging through the countryside. I don't think I'm adding mileage to the journey – I have chosen to miss the Budapest ring road – but I am increasing the time the trip will take.

At Baja I cross the Danube – *so we meet again*. We are both taking indirect routes to the border. I have to admit this river has chosen some very picturesque places to flow through, or perhaps it paints the picture as it passes. I wonder if I could do that.

76

Same name, same heat, and same clothes as when I was riding in Mexico four months ago. The similarities end there though. I won't be getting fragrances of fajita drifting under my visor. However, now I'm back in travel mode the distance between the journeys has disappeared. There is a continuity, this could be the same road, further down the journey of escapism, on a quest for contentment.

An awful family-owned haulage company I once worked for wouldn't give me the unpaid leave I wanted, so I left anyway. Six months later, I applied for the vacancy I'd created and was re-employed. Riding back into the yard and parking my bike by the Portakabin felt like my African sabbatical had never happened. I had that dreadful feeling that I'd been recaptured to continue my sentence. What I'm experiencing now is the exact opposite of that. I've got the ratio the right way around at last.

I pass a field of burning stubble. Flames lap against the road. The bright orange KTM in a flaming field, burning up the parched soil under a smoke-filled sky, would make a fantastic photo. However, I don't stop – instead, I spend the next hour wishing I had.

I head east towards Romania as the sun goes behind clouds, it looks like rain. I won't believe it, this morning's greasy humidity has barely worn off. The sky won't lie, it's only for me to misinterpret and the truth will reveal itself as I ride into it. The laptop-and-desk days seem so far away already. My Wi-Fi withdrawal is at manageable levels, liberation fills the void.

I do feel a bit of a hypocrite: the preacher who extolled the benefits of a slower pace is really enjoying this fast and direct style of riding. The only slow thing about this trip is my growing confidence in the KTM. I'm thinking of breakfast but the motorway is new. I take the service slip road to nowhere. On the concrete plains of potential, porta-potties are the only conveniences.

The rain falls mainly on the Romanian side of the border. The praise of my *REV'IT* suit may have been a little premature. Standing under a motorway bridge putting in special waterproof layers is a tedious process. To be fair it's worth the effort and I stay dry, the only cost is time. The motorway is incomplete and the road turns to truck-choked single carriageway. Overtaking is pointless as the procession is endless. It's only the rear-end view that varies and the filth that is thrown up distorts the differences.

This is a new personal record: 285 miles and five-and-a-half hours riding before I break my fast which, by now, is brunch. At a roadside restaurant with rooms, every need is satisfied with ease and I'm back on the road again absolutely loving this pace. Hazy Sunday afternoon sun shines through the spray to reveal a mountainous horizon and that never fails to induce a thrill. Perhaps these are the ones I saw last week from the Ryanair window seat. The rain becomes a memory. The only drops are stains on the screen.

It's 35°C and I'm wondering if my pannier contents were stolen while I stopped, the bike feels so light and responsive. A wiggly road up a mountainside happily corresponds with a break in the traffic. The bike flicks round the bends and the Continentals hold the road with reverence, but still I misjudge the lines like I'm partying with rock stars.

I meet up with the Danube again. The land on the far shore is Serbia and at this point the river has flowed into its most stunning setting so far. Navigation is as simple as following the road that follows the river that divides countries. It has cliff-cutting, gorge-forming, dam-making, lake-creating and turbine-generating variety and grandeur.

At 3 p.m. the temperature tops out at 39°C. The benches of pensioners are back. Old men with big bellies and no distinguishing features sit in the shade, younger men pour out of the bars, working on growing their stomachs. But they always wave – well, not always. Some of them wave, I've definitely had some waves, I can categorically state that I've not been totally blanked. God, I'm hot … I think I'm delirious … flash a passport, over the bridge, goodbye Danube, hello Bulgaria, time for some serious helmet whooping … I'm hot beyond hot, I want a shower more than I want a beer … the roads are bad, the traffic scarce, and I'm so forgiving anyway … in love with it all … long may it last.

I pass a truck stop. The resting drivers are soaking the steaming concrete with a high-volume hosepipe. I missed the fire photo shoot but I'm stopping for this. I pull up in front of them, euphoric for making it here, demented from the heat. I point at the hose and open my jacket. 'Yeah? Are you sure?' is the expression I'm getting. I confirm I am. Underestimating the amount they have had to drink and the unexpected break from the boredom I'm providing, the flow is directed at me. For a second it's shocking, for the next three it's refreshing, then it's soaking and soon relentless. 'Enough!' I roar away, thumb in the air, leaving them wracked with laughter. I think I wanted that. I'm definitely cooler now and, simultaneously, perhaps a little stupider too.

The home straight. Got to keep my speed down. I stop for some food at the same place I visited last week with Peach on the way from the airport. Shadows are stretching, the temperature falling, the smell of pines drifts down from the mountain highs as I cross a valley. The scenery is engulfing and I will stay under its spell watching every day, every season, every sunrise and set.

I think another beginning is occurring. I pull up at Motocamp. I'm home.

An eleven-hour riding day, 635 miles, the KTM performed faultlessly. It may be too tall and too heavy, but it certainly made Europe smaller. Ivo opens up the gates for me, more in disbelief than with a welcome.

'You did it in forty-eight hours?' says Ivo.

'Well, from the ferry, yes.'

Polly has just ridden in on her bike too.

'You rode in forty-degree heat?' she says.

'It wasn't all that hot,' I say. Perhaps playing at being hardcore wasn't a game, maybe I really am. Polly, Peach and a part time Brit in the village, Raymond, have just returned from an annual Red-Bull-sponsored motorcycle event in Romania. Apparently, Raymond had an accident on route.

By pure coincidence, Mr. Muscle, the man I'm buying the house off, just happens to be at Motocamp. Any doubts he had of how serious I was have left with my arrival. I shake his hand and want to speak with him via Polly but Raymond won't stop talking at me. *Shut up, I want to know what's happening with the house sale.* Apparently, most of the beehives have been transported but there is no exact moving date yet. We have an appointment with the notary at 9 a.m. on Tuesday. I could have taken a day longer to do the trip, but how much fun would that have been? I don't want to make a habit out of this high-speed commute, but equally it was an exhilarating journey.

They are all going out to eat. I can join them but prefer to have the much-needed and long-awaited shower. Among other statistics of personal records broken in this journey is one of personal hygiene. Two nights wild camping means I've worn the same underwear since I left. That's nothing to brag about and I'm not. In fact, I'm seriously considering how relevant it is to the story, but it will certainly enhance the power of the shower experience. So, the bike is unloaded and given a kiss of redemption, mother has been texted – 'Made it to my destination' – and now the indulgence in the delayed gratification of a long hot shower followed by long cold beers.

As well as clean undies I've also been deprived of people. There are some here. Different bikes, different nationalities, different journeys, different destinations, different observations and ways of expressing them. Yet there is a variety of similarities too – some abrasive, some opposing, some uninteresting, some intriguing, some with wisdom, some full of questions, some full of themselves. I instantly warm to a German who says that after he'd ridden through Georgia his 'soul was full' and so he's heading back home to his wife. What a beautiful, simplistic philosophy to travel by.

I too am full. I go to my room. I briefly hear the chatter, but deep sleep soon takes awareness away. The journey was for a reason and I've reached it. I wonder where I'll go from here.

A dry run

I used to enjoy writing poetry, just for myself. No one will ever see it. I once submitted some to a local society and their sanctimonious feedback was based on subject matter rather that the merit of the work. It never saw the light of day again. It was cathartic to put my strongest feelings and emotions into verse. The point is, most of what I wrote was melancholy, inspired by too much time on my hands when my relationship, bike or spirit was broken. When I was riding high, there were better things to do than trying to make the good times rhyme.

Conversely, keeping a daily diary has been a strict, but very rewarding, self-imposed ritual for over half my life. Time is always found to write; it is top priority and, like anything that is done daily for over a quarter of a century, you inevitably get better at it. The journey down here was all-consuming – in time, importance, intensity and endurance. In such exceptional circumstances, the diary gets neglected, and that's why I have a voice recorder. Occasionally, on the road or in the bottle, when I'm unable or incapable of putting my thoughts, feelings or mood onto paper, they are stored temporarily in an audio format. This morning life is on pause until the transferring process from recorder, to recalling, to written word, is completed. That may sound a little bit obsessive, but there's more. The other thing that gives me great satisfaction is working out some trip statistics. So, first with a head torch and then with a streak of sunlight through the window, I look at my European Atlas, Google maps, fuel receipts, and now I know that from my Mum's house to here is 1,623 miles, and that I got 48mpg from my bike. The percentage of wear on the Continental tyres based on the temperature of the asphalt and lean angles was … no, that's it. I just wanted a few facts, I'm not making a graph to offset time, cost and carbon footprint against my flight here last week.

I hear chatter and laughter downstairs. It's a good sound. With all the information available to me, I sum up my trip here: it was bloody brilliant. It's time for breakfast. Breakfast is a very social affair. I'm social too. The Romania trip that Polly and two others have returned from is the main topic, I quietly recount mine. Some fellow authors from Northern Ireland who I know from the show scene are heading this way. Having done the Americas, they are now heading overland to Australia. They'll be here at the weekend.

My life seems to have fallen into one of those non-stop modes. It's good for my confidence and well-being. Without much consideration, I sit in the shady VIP area. It's only exclusive by name, there is no list and anyone can get in. However, choosing to sit here is very significant to me. I feel comfortable in a communal area, secure in my consciousness. I cast my mind back six weeks. I was getting counselling for my deep dark thoughts which had reached menacing depths. Imagine getting a call from Ted Simon to ask if you are coming to meet him at a show – pretty cool, eh? Now imagine being so distraught, in a turmoil of despair, that you look at the name of the caller and cancel it. I sat on the floor listening to Antony and the Johnsons, knowing there was an empty seat with my name on it next to a living inspiration. A few days later, I called for help. I could paint a picture of empty bottles, screwed-up wraps and overflowing ashtrays, the drug and alcohol induced delirium of a debauched lifestyle. But that wasn't the case. The house was clean, the washing up done, the fridge stocked. This was a chemical imbalance that occurs from time to time. Though it is mostly manageable and passing, this particular storm of negativity got stuck in my valley of despair and engulfed me. The clouds have long since dispersed, but the memory remains like one of winter. So, sitting here, I'm gathering virtual fuel to burn away the cold isolation when it inevitably returns.

You don't have to be a recognised name to be an inspiration. I'm joined by someone I've seen a few times but, until now, we've not spoken much. Martin is an older, very English gentleman, tall and slim. He's ridden from the UK on his annual pilgrimage, and he spends several summer weeks here using Motocamp as a base. He is full of wit, charm, and appropriate anecdotes. Now in his seventies, he gives me hope that my riding days have at least another quarter-century to go. He sits swatting flies, which evokes shell-shocked reactions in some. Like a barking dog or screaming kid, if you happen to like the source of the sound then it's not annoying. The German looks at his phone and another Brit, a quieter type, who considers more than he converses, tells of a rift between my neighbour-to-be and Raymond. Apparently, they butted heads last night at dinner. I'm even more glad I opted for the shower now.

An Irish couple arrives. The father of the girl had a house here in the village and was tragically killed in a motorcycle accident last year. She is here with her husband to sell his property to Peach. Not a fan of motorbikes to begin with, now that she's lost her Dad to one, this environment is a difficult one. That, combined with the duty of selling on his home, means she's probably had more pleasurable 'holidays'. They all have to go to Sevlievo, our nearest place of civilisation and facilities, to start the process of the sale. This is exactly what I will be doing tomorrow, so I tag along to get a head start on the procedure.

The notary tells me what documents I will need to bring tomorrow. The money I sent is sitting in my Bulgarian bank account. That in itself is reassuring, more so when I see the rate at which the conversion was done. Notice is given to make a large cash withdrawal. I just nod, smile and sign forms I can't read. Well, that seems as good a reason as any to indulge in lunchtime weekday drinking.

I sit at an outside table in a pedestrian area with Peach. We are approached by a well-built, well-dressed man who speaks English so well I'm not sure of his nationality. My introduction almost demanded, Peach is very cagy, contagiously so, and I'm wary as small talk is bypassed directly to interrogation. I rarely trust a suit, to dress to impress is to disguise what lies beneath the threads. He has the smarm of an estate agent, the assertion of authority and the menace of mafia. After he leaves, I'm told that Jim is a Bulgarian, married to Tammy, a Brit. The pair of them live in our village and they preach God as they do the devil's work.

Back at Motocamp the socialising is never ending. I meet Phil who welded up my KLR exhaust when I was here in 2013. Raymond was causing a rift last night and is now annoying me. He has no self-awareness and seems over-assertive but without depth. Annoyingly, I find myself seated by him when the pizza arrives. He's clearly not over his divorce and his divulgence of the details is a topping I didn't order.

I go to my room and find time to check my laptop. I've received natural feedback for the pair of gloves I sold. Not because of the quality but because the buyer had to wait too long for me to rate the transaction. For fuck's sake, I was selling them because I was moving, I sent them immediately I received payment, then hit the road. I explain this to the buyer. Fourteen years on eBay – I was using the site while the rest of the country were still browsing Exchange and Mart – with impeccable feedback, and now I have a malicious scar on my unblemished reputation. I hope she soon gets to test the impact qualities of those gloves. I compose my feedback response with the poetic licence I failed to obtain.

Money talks, mine says goodbye

Tuesday 21st July

I'm woken by impatient pacing outside my room. The soulful German has realised I'm a writer of the books in the restaurant and is keen to purchase one. That's a good way to start the day, I think I'll buy a house. My needy website is demanding my attention and before it's satisfied Mr. Muscle is outside with his wife. I have a quick shower and shave the sides of my face; I've decided to grow a goatee due to a lack of shaving cream.

Attending weddings, funerals or dealing with US immigration are all occasions worthy of wearing a shirt (to disguise what lies beneath). This is my third house purchase, which makes it rarer than the above events, but I think it's a shirt day. I have half a cup of tea and, with Polly, the four of us are off in the seller's Mercedes. It's not a super-posh, sleek status symbol of a vehicle, it's just faded blue and functional. The morning is already very hot. We drive the ten minutes to Sevlievo, first to the bank. Again, I sign forms I can't read. My bank card has still not arrived, not that it would help with its 400-lev withdrawal limit. I transfer 40,000 and draw out 30,000 in cash. I watch the cashier on the other side of the glass count the money and band it into wads of 2,000. She passes it under the screen to me. I'm wearing shorts and a shirt; the pile has to be a foot high.

'Err … have you got a bag?'

She sighs, thinks, looks around her kiosk, and then takes her lunch out of a blue plastic bag and passes it to me. To me it's bleeding obvious what an immigrant walking out of a bank with a plastic bag of oblong bulges is trying to hide. Thankfully, the car is parked outside. Feeling somewhere between a robber and a dealer, I get in the back seat of the car and we drive off. I take a photo of the bundle on my lap. I have total trust in Polly, which is just as well as I am one hundred per cent reliant on her. This could all go very bad very quickly, but it's not a huge concern. Probably because I'm not familiar with the Bulgaria currency yet, I'm not holding this stash in reverence. It's just coloured paper with numbers on, it has no value to me. If they were red fifty-pound notes I'd be rolling up windows, locking doors and checking out every vehicle and pedestrian in sight. But with a breeze blowing through the car I'm throwing caution to the wind. No one else seems tense, I'm not about to initiate a nervous vibe. Actually, there is a little agitation. I'm asked for the money and I hand it over the headrest to Mrs. Muscle in the passenger seat.

Next, we go to the notary and are ushered into an office where the four of us sit at a large table facing each other. It's not awkward but there isn't much to say either. The bag of money has disappeared as has the notary. There is a cup of perfectly sharpened pencils on the table. They are asking to be taken – well, that's what they're asking me. They clearly aren't communicating this to the Bulgarians in the room. I mention to Polly that this would never happen in the UK, someone would nick them. It's not a risk here, or at least it wasn't until the Brit arrived.

Two smartly dressed people enter the room, exchange pleasantries, shake hands and sit down. I'm glad I'm wearing my shirt now. Multiple printed documents are passed around the table and we all sign them and pass them on. It's a bit like a game of consequences. *Graham* met *Polly* in the *notary's office*, he said to her, *what happened to the bag of money?* she said to him, *trust me I've done it before*, the newspapers said *another immigrant buys property in Bulgaria*, the world said *I bet he won't bother to learn the language* and the consequences were *Graham now owns a house he bought for 70,000 but has signed under oath that he paid 40,000.*

That would explain the bag of money. The smartly dressed go to make copies, we all shake hands again and

I blatantly put a pencil in my shirt pocket. If I could speak the language, I would say, 'I know about the blue plastic bag.' Instead, I have to hope that's how the sellers interpreted the look I gave them.

Well, that was fun, what shall we do now? We go and get a coffee. The notary calls – shit, they counted the pencils. I have to go back and pay 700 lev for their fee and the court fee. I will receive the papers in two days. I'm assuming this is for the house and not the theft. Still, it's a bit of a blow.

So often on the road in a poorer country it is almost a rite of passage to be overcharged. Some people will fight the principle as their limited travel time ticks away. The alternative is to convert the difference into your home currency and brush it off like having to pay for an extra hour when you were three minutes late leaving the multi-storey car park. I've not had a survey, no search, no solicitor's fees and no slimy estate agent with his sale-percentage-based tariff to pay off. This is the only fee beyond the sale price, so as I hand over the equivalent of £250 and let it go like a helium balloon – that's still less than the gain I made in the exchange rate. I should have pencilled in some additional fees anyway. I could have been signing anything, I joke it could have been a lease or rental agreement, one day I'll come home to find an eviction notice stuck to my door and it will be too late to call a solicitor then.

On the way back to the village we drive past an obligatory hooker in a lay-by. It's Mr. Muscle who makes a comment. Apparently, as a hunter he was once staked out in view of a lay-by. In the hour he waited for his prey she had ten customers. At thirty lev a pop that's more than a notary earns. That's got to leave a bad taste.

Likewise, ours was a fast transaction and I'm back at Motocamp before breakfast is over. I don't have much to show for my morning. No papers, no key, nowhere to live, if it wasn't for the pencil the morning would seem pointless.

Back to work, I finish off my column and email if off to the editor. It's not my preferred way of writing, but deadlines loom and this one crept up on me as I sped down here. I've sold two books via my website and Charley Boorman has liked my Facebook status. I clock off for the day.

Raymond had taken his van back to Romania to pick up his crashed motorcycle from his accident last week. He's outside Motocamp now and needs a hand to unload it. As I get in the van, what I'm seeing is not a collision-damaged bike but a wreck that was ridden. What he had wasn't an accident, it was an fuckin' inevitability. I feel sorry for the Romanian tractor driver now. Even his paperwork is faked. I don't want to dirty my hands in this messy situation.

I've actually got some leisure time. I take off my panniers and ride up a mountain pass to the effigy of a flying saucer, an abandoned communist headquarters called Buzludzha. Remarking on the difference in the bike's characteristics with the panniers off is tantamount to the increased dexterity when a cast is removed from a limb, so I won't mention it. I've been here before but it's a sight worth repeating and, even if it wasn't, the ride up the pass is thrilling. All this on my doorstep. In Essex I'd have to ride for hours to find a mountain pass, and there's certainly no space for a flying saucer.

I expect infinite challenges await me as I move to this new country with a Cyrillic alphabet I can't read, Slavic language I don't speak and all the things I don't know about. I seek solace in the talents I do have. Driving on the right is second nature to me and I have an excellent sense of direction due to my truck-driver instincts. However, I get completely lost as I ride back into Sevlievo. All I want is a supermarket. There are three of them in town and I'm not seeing a single familiar landmark. It's ridiculous. By pure chance, I find a Billa, my least favourite of the three but good enough for the basic supplies I need. I'm not keeping track of my spending at all, my mind seems to be constantly on other things, flitting from topic to topic and focusing on nothing. My eyes aren't doing much better – I left my glasses behind and the foreign labels are a blur of indistinction.

The evening's conversation in the VIP area, instigated by the quiet and considering Brit, is the imminent clash in a small community of the strong personalities he feels many of us have. I hadn't given it a thought. Strong they may be, but there is no obvious alpha male or one-upmanship. There are the inevitable abrasive types, and drink-induced honesty, that will cause an eruption. Alcohol is the remedy to decorum and tolerance, necessitating truth where once was diplomacy. I generally manage to hold my drink and leave with it if I sense that occurring. Now would seem like that time. Before I go to my room, Martin gives me $20 for a book sale in my absence. What a great day, perhaps I should buy another house.

The village becomes my world

Wednesday 22nd July

I'm awake early and expect I'll be the first one in the restaurant but Polly, Ivo and Martin are already there. All this talking first thing, so very different to my quiet Essex existence. If the radio wasn't on, the only break in the silence was the fridge clicking on and off. I can do it, this talking as soon as I wake, but it's not my normal. My last lodger or live-in girlfriend was nearly ten years ago. Since then, there has been no permanency to the overnight inhabitant, regardless of which room they slept in. Breakfast was reflective of dreams and contemplative of the day to come and never in the distracting company of the computer. I don't eat by the light of the screen any more than I post my food on my feed. Or, at least, that was the case at the time. I've since discovered people 'like' food photos and 'likes' sell books and book sales put food on my table and the circle continues.

So awake and instantly social is not my default setting, but I am enjoying this interaction. It's like going out on stage. Suddenly, there is a need to perform to some degree, be aware, listen, comprehend, respond – this is live, I have to be alert. Why is Martin hovering over me? This is causing me unnecessary anxiety. When asked, it transpires he has designs on my yoghurt pot and he's anticipating whether I am going to leave it on the table when it's empty, throw it out or do I have uses for it too? 'You can have it, please, just sit down.' And, now the ambiguity of the yoghurt pot's future has been resolved, I can relax back into the morning. I'm living in the moment, stressing about nothing and patiently waiting for a moving-in date.

Back at the office, or at least online, I have to okay an advert for my latest book and message my IT man to make some changes to my website. Once I'm finished with virtual work, I check over the KTM. The chain needs adjusting. Martin has crafted his hovering technique but as a former KTM owner he has some useful knowledge. Between us and with the help of my phone it takes thirty seconds to find out how to change the speedo setting from miles to kilometres and another ten seconds to do it. I could have done that when I rolled off the ferry in Holland.

I walk to my new house, just to look from the outside really, and see my neighbour's granddaughter, who's staying for the summer. She seems bored, so we look for the kittens that were born in the woodshed. We only see the mother – Tabby Cat, she has imaginatively been named (to describe her would be pedantic and contradictory). I'd love a cute little kitten for my new house, a streetwise, independent one, who just came over now and again to sleep on my lap while I watched a movie – so, basically, the same qualities I look for in a girlfriend.

All the bee hives have been moved now. Apparently, a big truck comes in the night, as they can't be moved until after 10 p.m. when all the bees have come home. If a bee was particularly diligent and doing some overtime, she would return to find himself hiveless. There are quite a few enraged and destitute workers fuming and buzzing about. As you would, if your only reward for tireless toil was to have lost your house, family and friends. It's not unlike the story many a truck driver tells – lose ya honey while making the money. Still, homeless bees notwithstanding, it looks like the place will be vacated soon. Until then, like the bees I have nowhere to go, so I walk slowly back through the village.

I've got an email from a magazine I've worked with before; they have invited me to join them on their stand at the nine-day Motorcycle Live show in Birmingham this December. I'm really honoured and chuffed. This will be my fourth consecutive year at the show and, apart from the book sales generated and prestige of just being present, the interaction and flyers distributed keep sales ticking over into January. Regardless of that, it's actually really good fun. I'm part of a team who works for the magazine and we have a turnover of guest authors too. We all stay in the same house, cook, eat, work and live together. It's absolutely exhausting, but for the entirety of the show we are a family, and the company is exhilarating and stimulating. Much like Motocamp, it's non-stop socialising, and when it's over and the others go back to their families, my solitary existence loses some of its appeal. I come out of the show bubble and discover what everyone else knows: it's Christmas time. For me, it's bloody miserable. Time to ride somewhere. In the past, I've booked a cheap flight to the US, got my KLR out the goat shed and ridden to Mexico. It's become a bit of a habit.

At Motocamp they are setting up a big blow-up swimming pool. As is often the case here, there are too many chiefs involved in the job. There isn't a lot of stimulation and when anyone attempts to do anything it creates a crowd. I've seen people doing simple maintenance on their bike, they inadvertently gather an audience of beer drinkers all offering advice and pointing with their feet. It's not a good environment for concentration and quiet mechanical meditation.

The usual suspects appear, the pool fills and my wine bottle empties. I listen hard to stories swapped between other immigrants. There's a lot to learn and this will be my primary school. It's an outside lesson today, sitting on the grass in the evening sunlight chatting with a variety of nationalities, warmth, wine, laughter and an overriding feeling of serenity. It's a festival, a bike rally, a barbecue; it's a holiday but it's permanent. This is my life now.

After every completed task as a kitchen- and bathroom-fitter, I'd load the van up and drive off thinking, 'I seriously undercharged on that job'. I used to joke that what my bank account lacked I made up for in karma credits. I was right and they are paying out in full now.

Living the dream and not writing fiction

Thursday 23ʳᵈ July

Recognition for your art is a strange phenomenon. Initially, of course, with my first book I wanted to get the word out. Every waking thought – and the ones that woke me – were all about book promotion. I worked it hard: magazine articles, shows, presentations, social media, I was driven on my solo quest and I progressed. However, unlike the journeys I wrote about, I wasn't exactly sure where I wanted to go. Much like the appearance on the TV game show, it became a turning point in a lifetime of motorcycle obsession and compulsive foreign travel. My motivation to be on the show was not fame or fortune, I just thought I'd be good at it. It wasn't *Mastermind* or even *Who Wants to be a Millionaire?* There was only one question and I already knew what it was: *Deal or No Deal?* It turned out my fellow contestants were not of the same mindset, that's why some would cry if they didn't win big. The obscene ecstasy of pure greed and tears of despair as hope slipped away.

Equally, with the book I just wanted it to get the audience I thought it deserved. I was proud of it, people liked it. Of course, we all dream of making an income doing what we love. However, on more than one occasion I saw the advantage of a Salman Rushdie promotion technique. Not the pissing off an entire religion bit, but the keeping a low profile and letting your written words do the talking. That, however, was not an option, and with the illusion that is so easy to create on social media I became a known name in selective small circles. The trick is, not to find yourself in a circle so small that you disappear up your own arse.

People treat you differently when they think you are successful, and perhaps in my case that was basically because they'd had a tantalising forbidden insight into my diaries. They feel they know me intimately and I don't even know their name, which is an uneven platform to start a conversation from. Three books and five years into this 'motorcycle travel author' persona, I have to admit I've reaped a few benefits when the beams of the limelight shone on me. Other times I felt like a rabbit in that mortifying light and wished I could have been beamed up out of it.

The single biggest shock is the impact the words I've written have had on the lives of a few people. This morning I got an email that left my fingers shaking on the keypad unable to reply.

A lady in the US had the job of clearing her ex-husband's (and father of her two sons) apartment after his death. She came across a copy of my book and something made her put it aside. Thirty days after his death, she felt an urge to pick it up. Inside, she found an inscription from the friend who'd given it to him and, in her words, the book gave her 'hours of pleasure and bought her a little closer to a man she feels very conflicted about'. Well, fuck me. Little did I know as I conceived the title while riding across the barren Mongolian steppe, and then googling '*In Search of Greener Grass*' to see if anyone else had used the title, that it would, on the other side of the world and five years later, have this effect upon a complete stranger. With a letter like this, I have to suppose that perhaps I have done something worthy, and the book has got the recognition I so desperately wanted for it.

Meanwhile, back in the real world, Ivo has contacted the internet people and they will come today to connect my new house. Apparently, this is unheard of. People have waited months to get connected – it must be because I'm a famous author. He instructs me I will be going to town later this morning with him.

We collect the papers from the notary. The courthouse has approved them and now I have to go to the municipality and register for tax. I also get a Bulgaria SIM card and take a copy of the house deeds to a translator who will … well, translate, so I can see exactly what I've bought, which will be useful, I suppose. We then have to rush back to the village as the internet people are at the house installing. I haven't even bought a router yet. Bloody hell, this relaxed Bulgarian way of life seems a bit full on. I'm riding a wave of luck and productivity, how much longer will this last?

When we arrive, the internet is all installed and working, the company have loaned me a router and Mr. Muscle has left a very long extension cable for it to be plugged into. He would like it back though, it was only so they could test the system.

Peach looks under the sink at the plumbing situation and pisses off Mr. Muscle who misunderstands and thinks his workmanship is in question. He has removed the car battery for the heating system. There is a box called a UPS – which is nothing to do with express parcel delivery; it's an Uninterrupted Power Supply. When, in winter, a snowstorm brings about an inevitable electricity cut, the car battery will kick in and drive the heating pump. It will distribute the water to the radiators while the fire in the log burner dies down, thereby averting the potential pressure-cooker bomb that would occur as the trapped water sits in the heating compartment of the log burner boiling to the point of rapture. So, I need to get a battery then, but this being mid-July it's not as urgent as a router. Mr. Muscle says they will be leaving on Sunday … or Tuesday … and I'm welcome to come and mow the lawn if I want. Well, how very generous of him.

Back at Motocamp it's pointed out to me that Mr. and Mrs. Muscle are now living in my house rent-free. The others seem to be more agitated about this than I am, I hadn't actually looked at it from that angle. However, it is *my house* and that is the most important thing. I own it, I've bought it, there are no more possible bureaucratic hiccups, it's done, signed, stamped and registered and there really is nothing else worth worrying about. The conversation turns to solar panels. I don't think as a single occupant, for me, it's worth the expense. Raymond is a bloody fun-sponge, he takes over any conversation and can kill the mood like the putting on of a condom. Anyway, he leaves tomorrow for another continent where he's got a two-year work contract.

Life being what it's become, I grab a beer and get in the pool to drink it. The water is uncomfortably cold and has shrinkage qualities and, anyway, the Irish girl is sunbathing in a bikini so I get out and chat with her while her husband buys a copy of my book. Honestly, I'm not making this shit up, it's my diary. I'm just having a bloody brilliant time right now. And to crown it off, a curry arrives. The lady from the next village is a phenomenal cook and, hailing from Southall, her curry-making ability is inherent. I tried one when I passed through two years ago. Today, as then, I didn't even know a curry was being delivered. I invite her to my house-warming party, both professionally and socially, as it would be ideal if she could bring some onion bhajis and samosas. She says she'll message me on Facebook, I tell her my name, she says she knows it.

My tummy isn't the only thing I need to keep an eye on: the multigym isn't going to decrease the size of my head. I need to keep this thing under control. I think I'll go and mow my lawn tomorrow, keep myself grounded.

A pat on the back

I thought Raymond was leaving at 7.30, yet I hear the taxi at 6.30. I wave from my window, but he's looking at his phone, so I send him a message.

At breakfast I discover that today is market day in Sevlievo, apparently every Friday is. I'm beginning to realise that the word 'apparently' is how I start most of my sentences lately. This is because my new life has become a constant of being told what I was previously unaware of. Every conversation, be it about event, location, obligation, tradition, weather, all comes to me via someone else and first-hand interpretation is rare and frequently wrong. I don't know anything, I only echo what I hear.

However, my reading of body language is definitely improving. As my requests are relayed via my interpreter, I look hard at the recipient's reactions to anticipate the response.

Anyway, it's decided that we will all jump in the Irish couple's rental car and head to the market. I love the spontaneity of this as much as the company and occasion. I always feel so alive when my unattached and capricious lifestyle can be utilised to its full. No permission to be asked, no plans to be postponed, just a simple *yes* and the day takes a direction previously unknown, as my lawn lies unmown. It may only be a trip to the market, but it represents proof that every decision I have made in life to get me to this point was right for me. It also shows that when you are feeling good about yourself, and your surroundings, positivity reflects off everything.

Not that it lasts for long. Having still not quite grasped the value of anything other than wine and houses, I'm blatantly ripped off when I purchase a T-shirt. I'm not a fan of the western style of shopping: high streets, malls or retail parks I find equally horrendous, they are all so sterile and there is not an inkling as to the origin of the product or what was involved in creating it. But I've wandered round markets from Armenia to Zanzibar, they are a condensed insight into a locality. Foods, clothing, implements and accessories for transport, farming and the kitchen tell a story of native needs and production. I've seen wallpaper being a hot export product from Ukraine to Moldova, transported on foot ferries across dividing rivers by crumpled babushkas; I've felt the thrill of knitted garments in a misty morning mountainside bazaar in the Yunnan Province of China. Here, among the many telltale commodities on sale are two framed pencil portraits, one of Hitler, the other of Stalin. I'm tempted to buy them just because they are so outrageously unique. There is also a disproportionate amount of angle grinder safety guards. They represent another insight into a country where you are still free to make unhealthy safety miscalculations.

There is a flaw in my reading of body language. There is a misleading action that all Bulgarians have: a 'no' shake of the head as they say 'da', the word for yes. Sometimes, they just shake their answer without a word. This initially brings about a brief feeling that my request is denied. However, my disappointment is fleeting, as in fact that negative shake is an affirmative response and things are going ahead as hoped. I don't think I will ever, no matter how hard I try, be able to speak the language and simultaneously shake 'no' when I mean 'yes'. Equally, when I'm being begged for money or to buy some shitty fake or stolen phone, I instinctively shake no, giving the hawker hope that he's got a potential sale.

When I walk into the bank I'm patted on the back and given my bank card and PIN. In thirty-five years, HSBC never gave me a pat on the back. Perhaps a little physical contact would bridge the divide between struggling manual worker and absolute banker, more effectively than all the clever advertising campaigns do, and give a personal touch to a faceless financial institution, assuming health and safety allows it.

The Irish couple have to leave for home soon, their time here is running out fast. Paradoxically, I want to leave Motocamp soon to move into my new home and the days are dragging. Ultimately, time is moving at one pace, in one place, and to prove it our hunger has become synchronised. We manage to order something that will satisfy and call it lunch.

I'm not quite sure what this is. It's not really retirement; it's not work; it's not moving. It's just waiting. It's not a holiday either – I live here now. But it is still foreign, and therefore everything is new. I decide to go for a ride, it will inevitably help me figure out my current circumstance.

The KTM feels like it's running really well this afternoon, so quick and smooth, until I remember I've changed the speedo to read in kilometres and I'm actually not going that fast. I take the familiar route up the pass because I still can't believe how close I live to a proper mountain. Then I remember I'm supposed to be an adventure biker and find another route to take. I'm rewarded with seventeen kilometres of smooth, twisting, empty road that winds up the other side of the mountain. God, I love this country. How much longer will this feeling of love and luck last for? I survey the wind farm and monuments on the surrounding peaks. The land is deserted, the breeze warm, the sky is clear and there is no chatter or traffic. I consider my chosen direction, it seems to have been the right choice, but where will it go from here? On any climb there are false peaks before the actual summit. With every step forward, every milestone, every accomplishment as a writer, I always wonder if I'm on the edge of glory or the peak of my success. It's downhill all the way as I ride back to the tiny village I will call home, the word for which in Bulgarian is 'dom', spelt 'дом'. When I rode through Russia I always wondered what that shape which represents a 'd' in the

Cyrillic alphabet was, I used to refer to it as the letter that looked like a little house, and what do ya know, now I'm going to live in that Cyrillic character.

So 'bez dom' ('bez' means 'without'), I return to Moto-camp. The bike and tyres have performed faultlessly. I drink two pints of water in quick succession. It's not some-thing I'm used to taking out with me but I'd better start. I open my bottle of wine – it's all right, it's good, it's good enough. A bottle of drinkable wine for 69p. This is temp-tation to the point of torment. How am I going to resist it? The drinking goes viral, the stories flow and as we all tell lies the laughter gets louder. Kebabs are consumed and the levels of relaxation and hilarity reach new heights. Martin and I decide we will go and mow my lawn tomorrow … almost definitely.

Meeting Denis

Saturday 25th July

Martin is definitely the hovering type. It's not annoying, I see it as a kind of enthusiastic impatience. This morning he has made me coffee. He's keen to go and mow. So, with just a banana inside me, we take the KTM and ride to my end of the village. It's not exactly a long ride, but the bike is a source of fuel for the mower.

I describe my location to people who ask but have not the slightest clue about the geography of Bulgaria that I live halfway between the capital and the coast. That's a simultaneously accurate and vague explanation. The coast is the Black Sea, which shares a shoreline with Turkey, Georgia, Russia, Ukraine, Moldova and Romania. It's practically an inland sea, the only way in and out is via the Bosporus which flows through Istanbul and divides the continents of Asia and Europe. It was this passage that Jason and the Argonauts managed to squeeze through without getting crushed on their quest for the golden fleece.

The only fear of getting crushed now is on the crowded Black Sea beaches of Varna. Varna is the coastal town that the main road will take me to if I do a right instead of a left to Sofia. It occurs to me that on the north side of the road at least, mine is the last house in the village. I am the furthest east, and consequently the closest to Varna. I will therefore call my house 'Near Varna'. Occasionally, I come up with an idea so inspired that I give my brain the rest of the day off, and lawn mowing is the perfect brain-dead pastime.

Thankfully, no one is home, so between us Martin and I figure out how to start the mower. With no further need to hover, he takes off up and down the garden and won't share or let me play.

So, I stack the pallets that the beehives were on and move the stones the pallets were on. I'm sweating already, mainly I just wander around the grounds in continued disbelief of what I've bought and the view I have. The outbuilding is oozing with bike shed potential. The back wall is stone and built into the rear terrace, the front is open. It's divided into thirds: wood storage at one end, a bench and rusty metal on the other, and the middle section is housed in netting, presumably for some bee-keeping activities. I won't be keeping it like this. Being further up the garden than the house, it has the best view of all. I contemplate the ultimate shed, in location, landscape, construction and outlook. There aren't many daydreams better than the planning of a bike shed. I remember I have internet now and get online on my phone. Every day the house becomes tantalisingly closer to becoming my home. The abandoned house behind is obscured by the growth of neglect. It's practicably inaccessible, the roof is missing tiles, the windows - glass, and it has a ghost-house romance to it. Polly said it will fall down soon. I'm not sure. They are sturdy structures, but the weight of snow and the rot of damp will, I suppose, level everything in time.

The mower throttle-cable breaks and we bodge it running at full revs and Martin runs after it. He does the whole lawn except the bit with wild chicory and daisies. We decide to keep that as a meadow, the *bez dom* bees will appreciate it. Feeling more like the groundsman than the landlord, there is little else I can do except leave when the job is complete.

Motocamp is quiet and I decide to take the KTM out again, this time in the direction of Varna, but I'm not as near as I thought and turn off discovering back roads and hidden villages. There may well be better views available than the one I have but, overall, where I am is the perfect place to start. I'm slowly figuring out the lay of the land and how to get from one place to another. I even find my supermarket of choice and buy another bottle of two-lev wine. Well, why not? It's Saturday.

Back at Motocamp Martin suggests going to meet Denis. It sounds good to me. Denis is one of only two people who have been banned from Motocamp. I'm not going to judge him before I've even met him. We walk down a path of potholes and barely sealed road – all uncharted territory for me. In fact, I've seen little of my tiny village. I'm yet to deviate off the through road.

We press a door bell that doesn't ring and go through a gate that won't close properly, shouting our arrival as we walk around the outside of the house. Apparently, he's a bit deaf and doesn't like to be surprised. I'm intrigued. Who is this man, barred, and living as a recluse in a broken-down house?

The only entrance to the place is around the back. There is a fabricated lean-to over the steps to the door. In this outside-but-undercover area, sitting on a chair wearing only boxer shorts and with his feet on the table, is the man. An oscillating fan is blowing up his shorts. He is grey, in his mid-sixties, stubble on both head and chin, reading a book as some blues music plays from his laptop.

'Ooo, fookin' 'ell, I did nee 'ear ya comin'.'

Oh, he's Scottish then.

'Let me poot sum fookin' clothes on.'

And that is my first impression of Denis.

He is not what I was expecting. He's smart – not in dress, obviously, but in intellect – well read with an extensive vocabulary, hospitable, humble, thoughtful, sensitive, informed and opinionated, but humorous and very relaxed … well, he is once he's dressed.

It seems we've met before at a bike show in the UK, where I'd been sitting next to Ted Simon in an author's tent.

'Fookin' Ted Simon, stook oop coont, wouldn't even talk ta mi so I boot a boock off the fookin' 'ippy sat next to 'im.'

I would be that 'fookin' 'ippy'. I'm laughing already.

"Fookin' good boock, en' all,' he adds, not that he has to.

And so, the conversation starts and my Scottish impression ends, I'm not Irvine Welsh I can't write in Scottish. The three of us drink beer, listen to blues and find there is more common ground than I'd want to mow. I get the tour, see the expansive library, there are shelves of books in every room. I cast my eyes across the spines: we have a shared reverence for Dan Walsh as a writer and Ian Dury as a musician. He has no hot water and an outside toilet. He had new windows put in the kitchen but they won't open as they hit the countertop. Terrible judgement, but he doesn't seem too bothered by it, or anything at all.

In his shed are two Honda Transalps, both incomplete. 'You meet the nicest people on a Honda,' he quips. He's ridden one of them to Egypt – there is a photo on the wall of his bike in front of the pyramids. The shelves are lined with empty five-litre wine boxes, the fronts cut out and used as tool and spare part storage.

He says not to listen to what they say about him at Motocamp, it was a misunderstanding. What little I heard didn't make any sense to me anyway. It's just he said-she said bollocks. He moved someone's beer and they took umbrage, but, with his strong accent and poor hearing, to me this screams miscommunication. I think I've just met my new favourite immigrant. I cannot believe how perfect everything is: instant house, view, social life, scenery and roads to explore, and it's all so affordable. This can't go on. I bet I'll fuck it all up.

Back to Motocamp and the good times haven't finished with me yet. The leprechauns have arrived: the Northern Irish couple Maggie and Norman Magowan, who are fellow authors. I walk around the corner and bump into Maggie.

'This is surreal' she says. How very succinct. That just about sums up my day, my week, my new life.

And so the Motocamp ritual continues, meeting, drinking, talking, laughing, learning. Being the weekend, some Bulgarian bikers have swung by. One of them remembers me from 2013.

'So, you are going to become a permanent resident then?' he asks.

'Well, I'll give it a year and see how it goes.'

'Only a year?'

'I haven't even moved into my house yet; you wouldn't propose on the first date, would you? I want to see what it's like to live here and if I like it I'll stay until the desire in me changes.'

He seems satisfied with this response; I didn't actually know that was what I was thinking until I said it, but it seems to make sense now I've voiced it. I'm the first to go to bed, I'm exhausted. I've not given a thought to the UK and what I left behind. The day has been non-stop company since the mowing. There's been no time to feel forlorn.

Korma comedian

It's an early start but Martin is always ahead of me. As we eat, this morning's conversation is about bubble cars – specifically, the BMW Isetta. My father had one long before I was around and he rolled it on the A12. Due to its design it kept on rolling, and he broke a collar bone. How many times did I hear the story growing up? Every time we passed the point it happened, or saw a bubble car, or spoke of accidents or broken bones. The ten-year anniversary of his death is approaching and it's playing on my mind a lot. It will be followed by my fiftieth, and I'm not sure how socially I want to acknowledge that milestone I never expected to see.

Still, no time for that now. We are off to get Denis and then the three of us are going to a car boot sale. My village is on the edge of a three-town triangulation. Veliko Tarnovo is the biggest and, as we pass through it, DIY, electronic and furniture stores are pointed out to me like architectural triumphs. I am not sure I have the capacity to retain all I'm being told.

We arrive at a narrow country lane with cars parked on the verge both sides. The stall holders and customers are about eighty per cent Brits, which is not an environment I really came to Bulgaria to be in. However, where there are British immigrants, the immigrants to Britain have followed. There is an Indian supermarket, they not only sell curry paste and naan but HP sauce and Marmite too. Shiva bless the enterprising Indians. Other Brits have stands of ready-made curries in foil containers, and the on-site restaurant offers sausage-and-egg sandwiches and bacon butties. I wasn't home sick, I didn't need a Brit fix, but I know where to come if I do.

One British stall has a motorcycle padlock amongst the piles of classic car boot paraphernalia. It looks as if he forgot to clean out his van before he drove it here; he certainly bought his white-van-man attitude with him. I ask the price.

'It'd be eighty quid in England.'

Yes mate, I think, *my house would be a million quid in England, but we're not in fuckin' England.*

As a token gesture, I buy a bacon sandwich, but this is not the kind of community I want to be a part of. I see a blue LDV van exactly the same as mine which I used to take my merchandise to shows and sleep in. The owner sells books out of it, that's a coincidence. Keeping the (British) book and food theme, I buy a Marks & Spencer curry cookbook, knowing it will be nothing more than a kitchen ornament. Denis turns out to be a right charmer – he seems to know a lot of women and has a lovely manner with them, not creepy or smarmy but definitely uninhibited and available. I call Motocamp to see who wants curry and buy four takeaways.

Back in the village I visit another British immigrant who's buying a house here. The place is run-down. Just considering the work it requires is tiring. With every place I visit I'm realising how lucky I am to have found the completed package. I can do the work on any one of these houses, but I just don't want to. And neither, it appears, do the new owners.

Back at Motocamp I talk to Maggie and Norman, they say how pleased they are to have stumbled across this place. We talk about the unexpected bonuses of travel – that was the topic of my last column and they have some insights I wish I'd mentioned. This place is going to be a great source of information and inspiration when it comes to writing projects. So, I can add that to the list of things that have fallen into my lap.

I'm obviously not going to be getting the keys for the house today so I decide to ride north to a town called Lovech.

I see two other cars the whole way there, bloody Sunday drivers. The town is ugly high-rises, but I'm just out looking. The mountains are to the south and that's the direction my future rides will take me. Back at camp a German girl has arrived and is banging furiously at the laptop. It turns out she writes five-star reviews for stuff she has never seen and earns a living on the road by doing this. This makes me absolutely livid – apart from being generally misleading, it's completely unethical. You're not going to get good road karma doing that. She defends herself by saying, well, somebody has to. Do they? Who? And why? I'm so proud of the genuine reviews I've got for my books, even the one-star ones are real and probably of help to some people. When I need to research a product I know nothing about, I rely on the reviews to inform me. Her contribution is to deliberately misinform, solely to line her own pockets. She is without principle.

Luckily Maggie is a yoga instructor and we have a group session. It's just what I need to stop my self-righteous ranting and relax. She's a very good instructor too, not that I have much to compare her to (and there's no point in reading any reviews – apparently, they are manufactured and fictitious). The paradox for me is her Northern Irish accent. I can't help it, I grew up in the '80s when 'the troubles' were rife and frequently on the news. With the BBC's agenda-driven reviews, I grew to perceive the Northern Irish accent as the voice of violence. I know better now, of course, but, like the smell of a dentist's waiting room, the first sense evoked is fear before I can calm and control my senses to a more logical response. So listening to relaxing mantras in that intonation is like hearing a dentist drill from the waiting room.

A Turk has arrived. He's friendly but I can see he is struggling with the various accents and fast English chatter. I divide up the curry onto five plates, give Maggie hers for the yoga lesson, Peach his for looking at my

110

plumbing and Martin his for mowing my lawn. I can't just charge the Turk, he already feels excluded, so I say this is for all the chai I was given when I rode through Turkey. We eat and laugh and the German taps her keyboard vigorously, spreading lies around the internet to finance her travels around the world for a first-hand truer picture. It's very hard for me to keep my mouth shut sometimes, but I'm silenced by good korma.

Riding without reason

I see Maggie and Polly doing yoga, so I go and stretch the morning out with them. This is actually pretty good, a slow transition into the new day. The problem today is there will be no transition. It looks like I'm still not going to get the keys and I've been here a week now. There is nothing unusual about this: everyone stays longer than they intended to, some for several months, some buy a house. I've got a house and I can see it from here, but it's still so far away. I'm tired of socialising, need some quiet time now, some personal space. The best I can do is escape back into sleep. I'm getting despondent and the apathy is affecting everything. I don't have any inspiration to try and write. There is only one solution. The situation has been raised to orange; it's time to take the bike out.

I find a dam and ride round the reservoir it creates. Damn, there are some large bodies in the villages. The inhabitants resemble their houses and I think they have the same life expectancy. However, this is perhaps a prolonged moment in time. When the old men and babushkas pass on, the next generation won't be replicating their iron curtain facial features and dark dress code. It's as if the buildings and residents are all listed, left in a life that hasn't quite passed. There are very few kids and youths – it seems that the young migrate to the towns for work and to start families. Only the gypsy population stay put and raise their children.

I'm riding for all the wrong reasons, it's killing time rather than spending it. I don't have to and I'm not sure I want to have a tour imposed by no alternatives. It's not the '80s London dispatch rider do-or-die, to avoid the dole-queue deadlines type of riding, but the pleasure is taken from the pastime when I'm just passing time, riding through a past time.

Back at Motocamp the undercover parking space is occupied by the Turk's BMW. It's not that there is any ownership, but it looks like rain and now the KTM is stuck outside. It symbolises our homeless situation, up the road is a garage it could shelter in and neither of us are where we want to be.

The other Brit, Les, whose place I looked at yesterday, officially purchased it today. So, my new-kid-in-town status was short-lived and I've not spent a night in my house yet. I hope this isn't an indication of a new wave of British homing migrants. There are just enough. I want to be a minority in a Bulgarian village, not part of an expanding expat one. For some reason, Les' taxes were higher than mine. He probably didn't use the plastic-bag-full-of-cash technique.

Apparently, Mrs. Muscle is cleaning my house and that's what's taking all the time. I wonder what polish she's using. I think I would rather live in the dust they left behind because the shine is wearing off the longer I hold on. It was only two weeks ago that I was keeping the cleaners waiting outside my old house while I sank my second pint. I console myself knowing that, when I get the keys, the boredom will be over. I can plug in my laptop and speakers, play a suitable first song as I decide where to hang my Motörhead poster, and that's me moved in. It's not a neglected shrine to dead granny and the lifetime of possessions she left behind.

I play nicely with the German girl; we will just have to beg to differ on how she chooses to earn her travel money. Her tapping keyboard is a source of irritation though. Polly and Ivo have bought me a 'Bulgarian for Beginners' book. I clearly haven't reached that level yet. Until I understand the alphabet, and learn the sounds the letters make, I won't know how to pronounce the word I'm reading. So knowing what it means won't help at this point.

113

With Raymond's departure, the regulars return. My neighbour comes over with his granddaughter. I don't feel like drinking, but I do. Anyway, there are free beers to celebrate the latest village resident. I help Polly and Maggie make the food. Well, when I say help, I sit on a stool and talk bollocks while they cut, slice and chop. Maggie compliments me on my yoga, they say I need to find a shiny girl for my shiny house. I say that whenever I share my life it generally becomes half as good, but it doesn't get the laugh I was expecting, perhaps they had someone shiny in mind. What have those girls been discussing?

Thunder rumbles and the rain starts. My bike sits in the wet. It just seems sadder than it should.

An Englishman who is staying elsewhere drops by. He says he is writing for *RiDE* magazine and riding to Georgia to do an article for them. That's interesting, I did exactly that two years ago. I don't say anything. He seems very excited about his assignment; he's even got business cards with his website and quest printed on them.

I've had enough of drinking, listening and talking. I go off to my room and find I have some missed calls, but I can't face them. A girl has contacted me on Messenger, she has seen my pictures of Buzludzha on Facebook and asks if she can share them. How very refreshing to be asked, and I tell her so. 'Yes, of course you can share them. It's my local flying saucer now.' She seems quite pretty. This waiting is just getting to be a drag now. There's relaxation, then there is just annoying inactivity.

Get in, get out

About six weeks ago I was at a travellers' show doing that thing I call work. Sitting next to me in the author's tent was Ted Simon. His life was also going through a period of transition. Just split from his partner, he was leaving his California home to return to his beloved France. His plan was to renovate a house and have a writer's retreat room. He'd get the company of creative types while providing a service.

There was an organisation called 'The Ted Simon Foundation'. It encouraged mostly solo travellers by promising them a platform to promote their medium of how they saw the world, be it film, photos, the written word, song, mime or embroidery (although I think it was mainly the written word). It was supposedly going to be a source of true first-hand accounts to contrast and compete with the media agenda-driven hate-machine. I was accepted, or recruited, into the frame. In theory, it sounded fabulous, a place of truth and integrity for those who had the capacity to acknowledge there are two sides to every country, race and religion. Those of us who told our stories in an accurate and compelling manner would get our world view out to a wider audience. It seemed like everyone would be a winner. There was no downside, the countries of ill repute would be seen in a positive light, and the world will live as one. However, in practice the theory failed, the volunteers elected to advise were too busy struggling with their own ventures, and when the launch hype faded it left a void best avoided. Most of us came to discover, 'ask not what the foundation can do for you but what you can do for the foundation'. That's kind of cynical, but several of us were disappointed with the failure of the enterprise of promise. It wasn't long before a prime instigator of the project had created another 'ambiguous' scheme, the sole intention of which seemed to be to profit from people who travelled. It's been tried in many forms and is generally an unethical journey.

To be fair, I don't think Ted lent much more than his name to the foundation, and the people who borrowed it left it unattended. However, it being his name on the packet, his new location was something he could control, and offering a creative space in the south of France was possibly the best thing to come out of the whole endeavour.

So, there I was, a kitchen- and bathroom-fitter about to become homeless, and he was about to purchase a place that needed attention. We discussed the possibility of me driving my little blue van down to France with all my tools and living rent-free as I renovated. It wasn't exactly the creativity the foundation had in mind at its onset, but for me it still involved travel and new experiences, so for a while I considered it.

In the month or so since Ted and I had spoken of the no-madic handyman idea, my life moved in an easterly direction. The one thing we all had in common as travellers was our transiency. I mean, if we weren't – transient, that is – we wouldn't have been eligible to be part of the movement in the first place. So, this morning I get an email from Ted asking if I am still interested in that plan. Having just re-located and seeing exactly what renovation can involve, it's no longer an option on many levels. It's always an hon-our to get an email from Ted. Not just for his two-wheeled inspiration, but also because his emails are naturally sculpted, eloquent and a pleasure to read. I can never reply instantly as such a correspondence demands a considered reply which I have to write in Word and cultivate until I have a ripe and worthy response. This morning, however, I withdraw my offer too hastily, with possibly too little em-pathy for his position and too much enthusiasm for my own good fortune.

Yoga is becoming a part of the Motocamp morning ritual and Martin joins in today as well. I particularly like the laying-on-your-back-looking-at-the-sky bit. I'm not sure what that position is called, but it heightens senses and releases tension. Plus, it's always a beautiful clear sky which, from this position, can be given the time and appreciation it deserves. From Jägermeister to yoga master – I'm still flat on my back, but with the opposing attributes of my mouth shut and my eyes open.

A German rider is going to a Tuesday market in a town I've not been to before. I'm told I will find my mower's replacement cable there and I can follow him. I've met him before: he's a total womaniser, and I never really click with such types. They seem to see every male as competition and every female as a conquest. It appears to be a full-time occupation to compete and consume and I've never been very competitive. I give as much effort as I feel the achievement is worth, and if someone wants it more and tries harder, they are welcome to it. I'll find something equal to my endeavours.

Anyway, we have to swing by my house to get the cable end, Mrs. Muscle knocks on the window as I leave the shed. She has finished the cleaning; they are ready to leave. This is the moment. I call Polly and she comes with Peach. I'm shown around the place again, she's very proud of how spotless it is. The German is stressing as he's meeting a girl at the market, or was that a meat market? I don't care, I've been waiting all week for this, it's a significant moment in my life and I won't be rushed by his need to get laid. Anyway, it's only a nipple I need for the mower cable and I can probably do it without his help. How hard can it be?

Photos are taken and hands shaken. Mrs. Muscle sobs and I give her a hug. I've never wanted Bulgarian words as much as I do now. I'd cry too. Although unfinished, the completed work is of such a high standard it says to me they hadn't planned to leave. It doesn't look like renovation for resale, it's more a personal touch that can't be held. The story I was told was they want to be nearer grandkids and ailing parents. Relocating to a high-rise in a city to the south, from this tranquil paradise? Sob all you like, I'd be inconsolable.

This is a moment that I would like to have sole focus on, but I've got a horny German sitting on a rumbling Husqvarna, and my tummy is grumbling too. OK, we'll go. So, blowing a kiss over my shoulder, I ride my bike away from the house I've just been given the keys to and locked behind me.

It turns out to be a long way to the market town and I don't even want to go there now. I'm on reserve and I really need a toilet. Conveniently, I have my very own for the first time in two weeks. Inconveniently, I'm riding away from it. As soon as we get to the market, the German heads off. I thought he was stopping here, but he was only showing me the way. I'm uncomfortable and it's hot and crowded. I could be sitting on the cool and clean porcelain in my own bathroom now. I find a cable that I hastily decide will work. Then I'm tapped on the shoulder, it's the musician lad who was at my presentation. His sale has gone through too and he'll be moving to the village this week. Man, the place is filling up. He's looking for a machete and haggles in Bulgarian. I'm impressed. Then, in a café, he knows the waiter. He's far more established than I am.

I'm back on the bike and get lost looking for fuel. I just want to ride home, it's so hot and this could be done under such calmer circumstances, but my manic mindset can't be calmed or composed. I leave my jacket at my house and go to Motocamp where I put on my panniers. There's no point in loading precisely, I'll just make two trips. The Georgia-bound Brit is questioning me about his crusade. I'm sweating and trying to pack, can't this wait? Then he says he wants to come and see my place. I don't even like him that much, I don't want him to be my first visitor. Actually, I don't want any visitors. I want to savour the moment in my own company. It's not like I've got a moving van coming and need help unloading it.

I ride back to my place without a lid on and then do a second trip in shorts and sandals. Right, I'm moved out of Motocamp and that bill has stopped ticking. Everything is just slung on the floor in the hallway. My neighbor is off to the supermarket, do I want to come? Ooo, in a big air-conditioned car to get a house full of supplies? Yes please, perfect timing. On the one hand, I'd like the time to browse alone, but on the other hand shopping without pannier limitations means I can load my trolley to my tummy's content and my liver's displeasure. My neighbours are waiting in the car once I've finally left the checkout. I've spent a lot of money, but it wasn't the champagne that pushed up the bill.

I'm trying to prioritise and get the chilled food in the fridge, before deciding what cupboards will be allotted to which products. Then the bloody Georgian-bound Brit shows up. Oh fuck off. He says he doesn't like the colour of the walls. *Oh fuck off.* Then he asks if I'm going to open the champagne now. OH FUCK OFF! I can't help but wonder how insightful an article can be written by someone this unaware, this tactless, oblivious and insensitive. But then I would think that, based on his invasive, insulting and uninvited company.

Then Martin comes. I offer nothing. I just want them to leave. The first song I play in my new house is 'Wish you were here', because I can't concentrate and lack inspiration. And I don't, I wish they weren't here. Well, I've got a lifetime to find appropriate songs for the moments to come.

At 6 p.m. I try to slow the pace; I have a chilled bottle of bubbly and a place to chill out. I take a chair and sit on the south-facing Balkan-viewing balcony. The last of the lasts have been replaced by a long-awaited first.

This is my sunset; this is my space. This is where I will heal my hurts and watch the sun dip behind a different peak as the seasons change. I won't be looking in rear-view mirrors, I won't be peering between high-density housing, I won't be stopping for a photo to look at later. In real time, in my time, with enough time, I can finally see the sky signify the changes that define the thing I raced against to get here, and waited to pass once I was: time. All futile wishes for the speed of its passage to conform to my desires stop here. I have time to be pulled like a tide, to view the waxing and waning of dawn and dusk skies. No alarms, no overtime, no deadlines, just a desire to peacefully watch and listen, heightened senses, less stresses.

However, the mind has a lifetime of momentum and slows like a supertanker – it can drift but can't stop. The biggest intrusion into this scene is the satellite dish bolted on the wall. There's no TV but the intrusive obligations of communications continue. The dish is coming down tomorrow.

I Skype my Mum and my childhood friend and riding buddy in the US. 'I'm retired now,' I say. 'Beat you.'

But am I? What's retirement? Sitting in a chair listening to a clock tick or passing what's left of your life with the most pleasurable pursuits you can think of and afford? The latter I've been practising for a very long time and, as if to prove it, the bottle empties. I crane my head to see the sun's last appearance on my opening night, and plan my house in my head. I need a westerly facing balcony.

The girl who asked to share my photo has been back in touch. She says she has a house here in Bulgaria too, and that she has to read my books now, does she? There are a lot of emoticons in her messages.

Habit takes me to Motocamp. There are a lot of drunks there, so I sit by the pool with my more familiar drinkers. Then I walk back, unlock the door, and lock it behind me. The house has a smell, not good or bad, just distinctive. It's my home. They even made up a bed for me. The house is so hot I lay on top of the covers. It's not a very comfortable bed, but it's clean and fresh. Will I live and die here?

I'm really happy. Two years ago this location was mid-adventure, now it's the end of the road. This is where all future journeys will begin and end. I have emigrated and relocated. I have chosen to live in a country I know little about other than I like what I see and how it makes me feel. And right now, it feels exhilarating. I've committed to something beyond my understanding, call it a gut instinct, a gamble, a desperate foothold on a property ladder I recklessly stepped off. All I know is that in the heat of both the moment and this stifling airless night, excitement and anticipation are at such levels that invited sleep is unable to honour, or perhaps just can't find, my new Bulgarian bedroom.

Gypsies, fans and fly swatters

Wednesday 29th July

Engulfed by the inescapable heat of the night, I lie in the unfamiliarity of my recent choices. The window is wide open in an optimistic belief that only someone from a more northerly climate could hold: the belief that the darkness outside must be cooler than this room which is radiating heat like sunburn. However, the only thing this village night has that the room doesn't is disturbances. Over the stagnant air is a chorus of invading and seemingly inexhaustible barking.

I bloody hate dogs, and have for most my life. It's not a popular view but it's mine and it comes backed up with multiple examples as to why.

As a teen, doing a weekend paper round, they were the bane of my life, with their unpredictable and aggressive behaviour protecting their owners from milk delivery and from having the experience of receiving a pristine, readable paper hovering in the letter box.

As a cyclist in India and China, their growling and panting would pull me from my thoughts as rabid fangs bounded towards my blood-pumped calves. I'd have to use every last ounce of energy to simultaneously out-accelerate their hostility and reach for my high-frequency dog deterrent.

As a night worker, I was relentlessly woken from my inadequate daylight-hours sleep by their inconsiderate high-decibel and pointless noise.

As a pedestrian, I've often been subject to the inevitable misjudgement of stepping in their stinking shit. Does any other animal have such rancid-smelling excrement?

As a handyman, having dear little Rover jump up at me as I was struggling with paint cans and tools always left me infuriated.

As a writer, I can't count the times their annoying, persistent noise pollution has distracted me from a stream of irretrievable inspired prose.

And now as an immigrant, relocated for a peaceful life, listening to the sounds of nature, the crickets, nightingales, owls and jackals on the hill side, the distant bleat from the sheep farm, the wandering cowbells and bamboo wind chimes, the flutter of leaves on the walnut tree with its enticing promise of a breeze – all those fleeting and soothing nocturnal sounds are obliterated by the audible onslaught of barking fuckin' dogs. They have been a major contributing factor to my moving on, from Asian beachside guest houses and more permanent residences. And here tonight their worldwide irritation is audible agony to my ears.

I am, though, in a philosophical frame of mind, and know that this phenomenon is as inescapable as the heat in this room. I have to find a way to deal with it. Lying on my bed, I create a mental file and in it I put my universal disdain for canines. All that has been, is occurring and that's to come. They mean nothing to me; they are beyond my control and beneath my contempt. All irritations that are dog related are discarded into the file. I visualise the file closing, and deposit it in a dark place with memories I never want to encounter again. That will be that, I will share the blissful oblivion that the unaffected seem to enjoy, the sound will be no more noticeable than my beating heart. And it works; they were here in this village before me, I have to come to terms with it and tonight I do.

I can now focus on the other annoyances. Like being in a hot-air balloon, living at the highest point and at the end of the valley, all sounds drift up to meet me. A bat flies through the window, I feel the breath of its wings, my only fear is that it gets tangled in my hair. I'm naked and vulnerable.

The other intruder is the distorted blaring of chalga music, a native folk music that, to my untrained ears, is fast and screechy. It winds me up like a spiral staircase.

I'm not necessarily against it, but I'm against the inconsiderate and drunken way it is being played. The instigator is playing thirty-second blasts at night-shattering volume, which in itself is offensive. It stops, presumably while he looks for the track he wants; the brief hope that the bombardment is over lasts as long as it takes the inebriated imbecile to press play again; and then it's back. My awareness of this continues until 4 a.m.

What the fuck have I moved to? This is dreadful, the tranquillity of the mornings – the days, the sunsets, the lifestyle, the idle village lanes – all disappears after dark. Well, it will be getting light soon, and that's enough to get me out of bed.

It's much cooler downstairs. July's relentless sun loses some potency as it penetrates two feet of thickness. Inappropriately dressed, I spontaneously climb the ridge behind my house, and down towards the lake. I'm not exactly sure where the sun will rise, and although I can see the eastern horizon it's not a full panorama and I could miss its sky-piercing ascent, so I'm anticipating with agitation rather than calmly contemplating. I'm way too early and the lightening sky has more patience than I do, standing with my camera poised. I can see I've not slowed my pace to the rhythm of this land yet.

Back at home I boil water in a pot to make chai. I'm sure there was a kettle in this kitchen when I viewed the place. I walk through the village to Motocamp. One of the gypsy workers is on the roof of a house. We met briefly at my neighbour's, he does a lot of work for them. He used to live and work in Spain and we discovered we could converse a little in Spanish. So – as I walk through this Bulgarian village hearing '*Buenos días!*' shouted from a rooftop and replying the same – all feels rather surreal. These are the first words I've spoken this morning and, for a moment, I have to remind myself just where I am.

* * *

The term 'gypsy' is going to come up a lot and I think I need to step out of my sequential obsession to define *my* interpretation of the word. This is not to calm the minds of the easily offended, nor do I intend it to disturb them further with my generalisations.

Before I even got to Bulgaria, I was warned of the gypsy population. If you travel by land from Western Europe, their presence becomes significantly more noticeable once in Romania and then continues into Bulgaria. The Romani people originated from northern India and, physically, they have a darker complexion and black hair. The men are mostly rugged and the girls often pretty. It's taken me a while to define their differences, as native Bulgarians too have idiosyncratic physical traits.

When an English-speaking Bulgarian asks where I live in their country, the second question is invariably: 'Many gypsies there?' *Gypsy* is the term I hear, so that is the term I will use.

By lifestyle, Romani appear to live hand to mouth. Here in a country with more houses than people there is no homelessness. But the level they choose to live at seems needlessly hard. Windows seldom have glass in them. Wood is gathered when the temperature drops, food found when hunger strikes. There seems to be no provision for the inevitable. To my very limited insight, they appear to have a 'live-for-the-moment' mentality. This is equally evident with the local individual rip-off merchants, be it petty theft or an underhanded overcharge for a pre-arranged job. It's a small village, a tight community and it seems so short-sighted to 'shit on your doorstep'.

Most villages have a gypsy population. We do. They may be a smaller minority than the British immigrants, but they, in my mind, belong here more than I do. They speak the language (although Bulgarians will criticise their literacy), their kids go to school locally, and they are established, not travellers. (It's ironic how the immigrants in this village *are* travellers – they found Motocamp as they came through on their motorcycle trips and ended up staying.) It did not take long before the village gypsy kids knew my name and said hello, and that welcome broke down any prejudices before I'd even formed an opinion.

Coming from the UK – where immigration is a topic everyone has an opinion on, from established Asian communities to the more recent influx of Eastern European workers – it's quite humbling to put myself in a position where I am the immigrant. What rights do I have to complain, criticise or try to change anything? I can't even speak the language, don't know the history, the traditions, the climate. All I did was come with wealth from a country with a GDP forty-one times higher than here. The way I see it, the barking dogs, drunken gypsies and anyone but the two latest Brits who arrived after me, have more rights than I do. The point is, until I get an understanding I can't judge, and if I don't like something the only thing I can change is my own reactions to it.

Just like every country I've entered, be it overland on a motorcycle or dropped in from the sky for a holiday, the first night is best spent observing from a balcony. I've done it from Iraq to Vietnam. Watch, communicate, integrate, understand, and then your criticism may have some validity.

However, my judgement is heavily swayed by what appears to be a national disdain many Bulgarians hold for their gypsy population; they are very much treated as second-class citizens. Having been a truck driver in the '80s and '90s, I know how this feels to a degree. 'No drivers: toilet for staff only', 'Restaurant for employees only', 'Drivers use side door' – these signs were as much a part of my life as 'Roadworks ahead'. And nothing breeds resentment like segregation. I could go on much longer on this topic. But for now what I see is what you get. I've been told who to mistrust in the village. From the religious bigots

126

to local gossips and gypsies, I will base my judgement on my experience as I continue to learn.

Immigrants, expats, part-timers, gypsies and refugees. These are collective terms I will continue to use, not to offend but to define. This is an expansive subject, like Soviet occupation and Ottoman invasion. And, from this point on, I will deal with it as it affects my daily life here.

* * *

I'm just in time for yoga. I nearly fall asleep during the relaxation exercise. We are all summoned together by Polly. Les, Bruce and I will all be getting registered with the utility companies today. How would I have managed all this if I'd decided to buy in another village? Since the purchase, I've been registering, receiving and applying for things I didn't even know about. Motocamp have been the instigators, collaborators, co-ordinators. They're the craft that has carried me through the transition to residency, and I'll continue to go with their bureaucratic flow.

It's so hot and my tummy is still not happy. In the supermarket I buy a kettle, fan and fly swatter. I also get one of those foam strips that kids use as buoyancy aids in swimming pools. I will cut it up and stick it on my low door frames. Headbanging is inevitable, but the pounding needn't be as painful. The shopping trip seems to cater for my immediate needs. Back home I assemble the fan, turn it on me and lie on the couch. This is the benefit of moving into a ready-made home, neither Bruce or Les have running water, let alone bathrooms. A 5,000-euro house, why wouldn't you? Sounds like a bargain and it is, but I paid a higher price and it got me Near Varna.

Somehow, it's 5.30 p.m. – are the days shorter here? I put the new cable on the mower. It sort of works. It's better than it was but it's far from perfect. So, I've fixed it in the style of Bulgarian tradition, functional not fastidious.

I've got a reply from Ted, three little words: 'So it goes'. Oh, I should have taken time to compose a more empathetic reply. But then he could have too. I'm sorry I let him down, but equally I'm annoyed at the guilt implication in all he hasn't said. He's pissing on my paradise.

I'm just about to make a sandwich when Maggie, Norman and Martin come round. I'm not used to having visitors. We all sit on the balcony and I supply them with beer and wine but stick to water until my tummy settles down. They are all in awe of the place I've bought. I'm beginning to have to play it down, it's getting embarrassing. They have bought me an incense holder as a house-warming present. I'd prefer something house cooling, the fan alone is not enough.

I'm not used to being host, I love it but I'm out of practice. Spontaneous visits took the social from my life when I left the main road out of town. They stay for the sunset and leave me to have a sandwich under an orange dusk sky.

I've been warned who not to trust or talk to, but I'm the new kid in town and I will make my own judgements based on my personal interactions. Some gypsies trot up the lane in a horse-drawn cart. Why wouldn't I wave from my balcony of decadence? I mean I can't just blank them, can I? I'm the hot gossip, the new resident, I don't want to make a bad impression, and impressions are all I can make without the language. So everyone will be given a wave and a smile until I feel they deserve more or less.

The days seem so short, they pass so quickly; I can't see myself getting much done until I bring my van and tools here. There is no real rush, a *mañana* mentality will be an adequate pace to work at. Anything rash in this heat would conflict with the lifestyle choice. I think I'll sleep on it. *Buenas noches.*

The hot Lada

Thursday 30th July

I don't really sleep properly so I don't wake up properly and when I do it turns out I should have done it earlier.

I make a cup of chai and write my diary: this morning ritual replaced the bedtime writing when I started working nightshifts. Exhausted and hitting the sheets between 4 a.m. and 8 a.m. was not the time to rush an account of the day. Far better to do it with a cup of chai the following morning, because for most night workers the mornings are the leisurely part of the day. The only thing you do after work is go to bed. Some night workers change their whole life around. At London's Borough Market, where I'd deliver fruit and veg, there was a pub that would open from 6–8 a.m. for the end-of-shift workers. I may have finished my deliveries but not my shift – as a professional driver, drinking after work meant drinking alone and delaying bedtime. There was a time a pallet of tomatoes went over on a speed bump and I had to repack and restack 500 kilos of squashed unpaid overtime. When I got home, frustrated and late that morning, I had a big Bloody Mary before I went to bloody bed thinking about bloody tomatoes and bloody speedbumps. The only round red thing this morning is a blood-red sunrise. It can warn all it wants, I'm not heeding the bleeding sky.

I'm late for yoga and join in halfway through. Now that I'm no longer a resident in Motocamp, my finger is off the pulse and my mind won't relax like it has in the past.

Bruce has bought himself a Lada. Typical London lad, he's only ever caught the tube. So, looking for transport, he applied the same technique, and for the price of an oyster card top-up he got what he thought was a gem. It's clean, I'll give him that. Basic too, to the point of archaic. I promise to look at it – he's got some problems with the

129

cooling system – and tell him I'll drive it to town for him as he's not confident in its abilities.

By the time we reach Sevlievo, the heat is relentless. I look under the thin tin bonnet of his car. The engine radiates heat upwards and a raised bonnet does nothing to disperse it, heat is coming off the tarmac, the buildings and of course that sun. We need to replace some radiator hoses. It's an arduous job in these conditions. Another thing that appears to be as inescapable as the heat is Kaufland, it has a gravitational pull and going to the supermarket seems to be a daily duty. Today I buy more two-lev wine and discover they sell tortilla chips too – not those shitty Doritos imposters which no Mexican would waste salsa on, but true corn chips. This country really does have the best of everywhere I've ever been. It may just be a Mexican chip but it saves me a Mexican trip to get my little food fix.

Everyone is gagging for the pool. I say I'll come, but after a shower I doze on the couch and can't face the 40°C temperature outside. I need a ceiling fan. I book a passage on the ferry to bring my van over, it's less than three weeks away. Then I look at YouTube videos on workouts specifically designed for my multigym. But I won't work out in this heat; I can sweat on the couch and lose weight.

The temperature doesn't really go down with the sun but I go out anyway. The pool at Motocamp has a pull. The place has local-pub leanings, where the day's events are discussed. Thunder rumbles down the valley. Peach says the music last night came from the house next to the one he's staying in. They had some work, earned some money and spent the income on rakia. He expects both will run out soon. And, if they don't, the illegal activities can be stopped with a number of increasingly drastic measures. Rakia is probably the third most discussed topic in the village after internet speed and firewood – that is, the price, dryness, and whether the quantity delivered matches the amount ordered and paid for. The occurrence with which these matters are spoken of increases as the winter approaches, as internet, alcohol and heat are what get you through the dark days. Rakia, I'm learning, is a social tightrope. It's made by distilling wild and locally grown plums, grapes and pears, either individually or blended. Everyone is very proud of their home-made brew. Recipes are handed down, and family secrets of the refining process make for a need of extreme diplomacy when sampling the product that is proudly handed to you. It's an acquired taste that I'm yet to acquire, perhaps being a full-blown alcoholic might accelerate the process. Possibly like ecstasy and dance music, rakia gives you a greater appreciation of chalga. I, however, am a whisky and Motörhead, red wine and Pink Floyd, kind of man. I have to learn though – firstly, how not to wince when the gut-rot goes down my throat; secondly, how to make a complimentary comment on it; and finally, the real trick is how to avoid having my glass refilled and getting pulled into a conversation about how this one is better than the rakia the old boy down the road makes.

Bruce tells about his days on tour as a musician, strange how his outrageous drunken antics are a source of intrigue and hilarity but the inebriated gypsies and their sound system are unacceptable.

It's another disturbed sleep. Tonight's culprits are thunder, a blue moon and the homeless bees who have taken up residence in my attic. So it would appear I no longer live alone.

Blue moon

It's still raining. I message with Polly: this morning's yoga is cancelled but the evening session will be staged at mine, after which we'll watch the blue moonrise. OK cool, first she arranges my house and now my social calendar. I'll make some guacamole. I've got an apologetic email from Ted saying the withdrawal of my offer corresponded with some other rotten news. He was feeling a little blue and wasn't able to switch fast enough, and to *Bluger* (sic) off with his blessing. So my hero turns out to be human and makes mistakes too. We're friends again now. I decide it's time for an announcement via Facebook to let anyone who is interested know I have officially moved to Bulgaria.

That's the virtual world dealt with, now back to the real one. In the UK I would ride in defiance of the rain (and because it was significantly cheaper than running my van). I only have the KTM here but riding in the rain is not done through necessity. I think I'm feeling so sunny inside that it can't get me down. I live within a triangle of three towns and take the bike up out of the clouds to Gabrovo. It's probably my favourite of the three – set in the Balkan foothills, the housing is staggered up the hillside. The centre has a pedestrian area, not of glass and chain stores, but the architecture and atmosphere of the old town. A river and orthodox churches, small parks and a spacious and relaxed feeling to it. The oppressive heat is left at the lower altitudes too.

Today, with more time and the right documents, I fulfil the application criteria for my residency card. I only make one mistake, I say I'm married … to myself, easily done. It will be ready in half an hour. Luckily for me and my lack of imagination there is a Kaufland here too, so I do my daily ritual. It's a complete mirror to my local one, same design but the alcohol is the first thing you encounter; not something you see if you have space in your trolley and money in your pocket as you approach the checkout. Anyway, I'm only here for avocados, so I can deal with the reversal of arrangements.

My temporary Bulgarian identification card is ready. I have my photo taken for my permanent card which I can pick up in a month. The girl even asks if I like it, she'll take another if not. It's rarer than a blue moon occurrence for me to see an acceptable photo of myself, and she captures my approval first shot.

I think I'll ride more. I go over the Shipka pass and head west until a better-maintained pass takes me back to my side of the mountain range. The obligatory monument at the top draws me off-road towards it. I could just keep on going, these mountain tracks seem infinite, it's very tempting. The problem is, when I bought this 950 Adventure S, I instantly got short-arse empathy, and without pannier compression my feet are barely tiptoes on the ground. It doesn't inspire the confidence to ride solo beyond my limits, and there's a lot of plastic that can break too. It was never purchased for off-road purpose; I have smaller and lighter bikes for such terrain.

I wind my way back to Sevlievo and stop at my local Kaufland – but I can justify it, I don't actually go in. There is a yummy little snack grill outside. It's not the quality of the food so much as the ease of the ordering. The pointing technique works very well. Friday has rolled around again, so the place is busy with market-day traffic.

This is the behaviour of the newly relocated, I think. I had two places to go to this morning, but the novelty of new roads wherever I go means I go wherever I want. Hours of indirection on my way there and on the way back too. There is no pressure in time, in petrol prices, or congested roads. I just can't get over all the ways there are to cross the mountains. It's not the ideal tactic to transport avocados, but sometimes it's about the journey not the guacamole.

My god, that Facebook post is popular. Plenty of congratulations and well-wishers. A reoccurring theme is what a 'brave thing I've done'. This move has provoked many thoughts, but being brave was never a motivator nor a deterrent. Brave was living a hand-to-mouth existence on an author's income in the UK, the variety in my diet was determined by what products were in the reduced section due to a rapidly expiring sell-by date. Brave was dealing with the high-density population and the pollution it brings. Brave was missing another sunset or season in presumptuous anticipation that I'd get another chance in the future. Moving here is not a brave move, it's a no-brainer. In Colchester I was surrounded by people who complained about what Britain's oldest recorded town had become and enthused about how things used to be. Here I don't have a past to compare, only a moment to live in, and I'm loving every one of them.

I make guacamole and listen to a BBC music radio station to try and generate a Friday feeling, but I find the hourly punctuation of news seems deliberately designed to debilitate, sending subliminal messages of apathy, hopelessness, and doom. It's really noticeable with the perspective of distance. That's brave, to live in a land where you're told there is no hope in a manner that you don't hear but only feel. I go back to my iTunes, something I've been doing a lot since I've been here. I'd got conditioned to having someone else decide my playlists. In my new-found freedom, I think I'll decide what music I will listen to – if it made it into my library, I must have liked it at some point. I came here to leave the UK behind, not to hear it being transmitted into my new world.

I go mow a bit of my meadow, the shady part. I think it will be the most suitable yoga location. That rain and the cloud cover it brought have made the air fresher and cooler. With a glass of wine, I wait for the yoga class to arrive.

Bruce's car has broken down and he's staying in another village. So the class consists of Polly, Ivo, Martin and me. Maggie will be conducting the lesson and Norman will be filming it. They have decided that 'yoga for bikers' is a gap in the market and will put it on their website. However, because of this, Maggie is not as relaxed as usual. Neither am I, as I have host duties. Martin gets cramp, stands up and walks out of shot, and then everything stops while he's persuaded to re-join. It would be funny if not for the filming. Instead, there is an air of frustration. No one is in the right mindset and it's only later that we see the comedy of errors, and the failure of filming. The bendy biker's video will never have a chance to go viral. That's probably for the best. The wine and beer relax like an asana – we grow louder than a mantra and nobody cares. The company becomes more comedic and rowdier than chalga. Peach turns up when he considers the exercises to be safely over and he can go straight to the refreshments. I absolutely love having friends round, we don't even see the moon come up. There are clouds to the east but after the sun sets, in the darkening sky, is a display of lightning that we watch until it brings the rain. The party moves inside, then further away from Varna. I'm left in peace and empty bottles. Will it always be like this? This is exactly what I came for, a new life, and there appears to be nothing lacking. Perhaps direction. It's hard to find direction when you don't want to go anywhere.

What a lovely hangover

Saturday 1st August

First day of August, first Saturday in the house and first hangover (in August, on a Saturday, in the house). Yes, it's definitely a hangover – I trip over the traits, wine bottles on the floor remind me it rained, the ones outside cast damp shadows. Indisputable evidence that the diagnosis is accurate and this feeling justified.

I am left with the legacy. The question is what to do with it. Yoga is absolutely out of the question, in fact most things are. I lay on the couch unable to face chai or food. I summon all my reserves and manage to find Team Rock's internet broadcast. The over-exertion pushes me back to paralysis. A summer morning turns into afternoon and I drift in and out of sleep and varying degrees of consciousness, triggered by reception and forty years of impressionable music.

My only communication is with Bruce the musician. I say I'll take a look at his car but he won't accept my offer. I genuinely want to, to consider something other than my wretchedness.

At 2 p.m. I force myself to eat some scrambled egg, my default hangover food. It's too little too late. However, it's not all wasted time. My pathetic pace generates a new awareness of my surroundings, the attention to detail that I previously failed to appreciate. The standard of workmanship is very high, particularly the tiling, from the uniform mosaic in the entrance hall into the functional design on the kitchen/hangover room floor, it reaches its pinnacle of forethought and proficiency as it winds up the stairs. I really have moved into a modest palace of craftsmanship. His plumbing, however, says afterthought rather than pipe dream.

I go out to the shed, enclosing it in my head, picturing the interior design. The framework is there, it's just for me to build the walls. It's going to be very satisfying work, but for now I'm just assessing and deciding. Anyway, it's really hot out here, too hot for physical pursuits and, besides, I have no tools.

At 4 p.m., out of options, Bruce accepts my offer. I jump on the KTM and go and find him, a ride that leads me to some hairpins I've not leaned round before.

I instinctively think the problem with Bruce's car is electrical and, sure enough, there is no spark. The wiring under the bonnet is atrocious, it's as if it has a secondary safety system, all the electrics seem to have been doubled up. My obnoxious bike has alerted the dormant to my presence; it's stimulated the village into some kind of life, an afterlife maybe. With zombie progress, the previously preoccupied advance. A fat, flesh-eating Belgian has assigned himself as my heavy-handed helper. He starts to yank at fuel lines like he's pulling cholesterol-filled arteries from a deadbeat. 'Leave it, the problem is electrical, not fuel,' I say, and he takes off the air filter. I can't work like this.

I detect a dodgy connection and we get ignition. I'm tempted to get the Belgian to hold the end of an HT lead but I doubt he has conducting qualities. Without his earthly presence, we still have a spark. Bruce turns the key and the car fires up. Blast off. Who's da man? Fuck the Belgian. This focus has dispersed my hangover. Bruce is euphoric and I'm inaudibly chuffed.

Back home I finish off the wine and the hangover, and continue to avoid the multigym. My Facebook post announcing my move here continues to get comments and likes. Two girls are conspicuous by their lack of acknowledgement: one who I lived in hope would like me as much as the other one hoped I'd like her. Maybe we can all move forward now.

I wander over the hill to watch the moon rise but it doesn't, so I pad around the garden barefoot. Then from the balcony I witness the ascent, acknowledge my own descent, and head back to the bed I crawled out of twelve hours ago. That was definitely one of the best hangovers I've had for a long time.

Dust and ruins

Sunday 2nd August

I'm still not sleeping that well, mainly due to excitement. As soon as I open my eyes – in fact, before I open them – I hear the crickets, jackals and no traffic. It creates an irresistible urge to go outside into the summer morning and be part of it.

I contact a friend in Sofia. He gave me tyres when I was here two years ago and took me on a demonstration in the capital. I want to organise my house-warming party around his schedule. It's looking like it's going to be this Friday.

Yesterday, being more functional than I was, Ivo bought me the recommended router so the internet company can take their loan one back. I wander down to Motocamp to pick it up. Again, I exchange pleasantries in Spanish with the gypsy on the roof. I don't think he lives up there, I'm pretty sure he's working, it's just hard to see exactly what he's done, is doing and has left to do.

No one is around at Motocamp. Now that I don't live there, I'm always at a bit of a loss when I walk through the gate. I can't see who, if anyone, lurks in the shadows of the undercover communal tables. I'm certainly not going to wander the balcony to see what rooms are occupied. To go up into the restaurant feels intrusive, as does wandering round the back by the pool. So I go up the stairs to the apartment where Polly and Ivo live. I'm invited in for coffee. I should have bought a bone for the dog, Harley. It's a dark space with low ceilings and a massive TV. I haven't quite figured out the layout yet, I'm not sure how many bedrooms there are. They tell me today they are all going to the Red Bull Trans-Balkan Off-Road Trial Bike Prologue for Positioning (well, that rolls right off the tongue). They are all going in Peach's car but there is no more room.

That's okay, I say, I'll ride, which is exactly what Polly was hoping I'd say because now she will ride too.

So I hurry back home, put on my bike gear and join the entourage. As well as the usual crowd there are the part-timers whose house Peach stays in. Harriet and Sid spend all their annual leave here, slowly restoring their house between leisure pursuits of copious consumption. The problem is, I'm beginning to learn, there is always a reason to drink here, and very few reasons not to. Motocamp by nature is a haven for the passing through, generally there have been some long riding days to get here. So ensues an easily justified prolonged relaxation period, and the day of the week is irrelevant. Often, the hour of day is too.

I follow Polly as she takes a back-road route to Gabrovo and then up the Shipka pass. It's a gentle ride and I'm getting to know the road a little now. At this slower pace, I take in more scenery, which is mostly pines with patches of aspen. On a hairpin I can see further down the mountain range, but that's when I most need to look where I'm going.

I'm still reeling from the excitement of this new country and the levels only raise when I remind myself that this is not a holiday, it's my life. As is often the case when I experience such exhilaration, I do wonder if it will all end and how.

My mate was killed on his bike ten years ago, while many of us were conspiring to arrange a surprise fiftieth birthday party. There was still a party at the venue in his name, the surprise being, it was his wake. I'm now at the age he was then, and over the past decade I haven't put on a helmet without thoughts of him entering my head. It keeps me rational and reminds me of my mortality. I've left it too late, and life is too precious to 'live fast, die young and leave a good-looking corpse'. A current option is to 'live at cruising speed, die middle-aged and leave a useful corpse'. I won't live in a bubble or a bottle but I'm aware that balance is the key if you live to ride. His death for me was a game changer and a new page in my life. I wish he could know that.

140

Just as we are about to reach the summit, Polly decides to overtake the car we've been following up the pass, only to stop at the top for a coffee while we wait for the others. She's an international girl, well travelled and well acquainted with travellers worldwide, but she's got that Bulgarian characteristic, she's just got to overtake, regardless of her next intended manoeuvre.

At the top of the pass is the Shipka monument, a memorial to those who fell in the Shipka battle, a conflict which played a significant part in liberating Bulgaria from Ottoman rule. Buzludzha, the flying saucer, can also be seen from here: an imposing structure from communist times deliberately placed on a higher peak to belittle the victory the Shipka monument represents. In the quarter of a century since the Bulgarian Communist Party was abolished, the former headquarters have been vandalised with justified anger and left in a state of ruin, decorated with fierce graffiti. Above the entrance was written 'Forget your past', to which someone added a poignant 'Never' prefix. I often wonder if the Bulgarian mission statement might be 'Just get past', because overtaking seems to be a national obsession.

It was pointed out to me by a Romanian that, during the forty-five years of communist rule in Bulgaria, there were inevitable shortages. If anyone was going anywhere, it was whispered they knew something was available somewhere. Hence, the inborn need to get there first, even if you don't know where 'there' is or even what is 'there' when you get there. I'm sure their driving habits can't be summed up any easier than the Brits' drinking habits abroad, but it's a theory worth considering.

As we wait for the four wheels to catch us up, I ask Polly if it's this much fun all the time. She says yes, in the summer it is. The spontaneity, the enthusiasm, the lack of financial restriction and the fact that no one has kid commitments. Life just seems to be about having a good time all the time. I can get behind that.

The event is free, hot and dusty. There is no security or rules, just some tape marking the track. It's utter chaos. Bikes speed up hills and round obstacles. However, when they get to the felled tree and truck tyres across the track, there is a bottleneck of incapability. The able and frustrated go up the bank and then fall on the stranded. They are fearless, I'll give them that. Impatient too, but this is a time trial. I'd rather be a spectator than a competitor. Free of charge and with no expectations, or even knowledge of the event until this morning, it's worth the ride. I don't really know what the hell is going on but I'm glad I came. We leave before it's over, but the dust has already settled – at least, there is a token layer on my bike.

A fast blast to Buzludzha doesn't remove the dust but it's fun trying. The road ascends the mountain with the predictability of rising smoke, and in low gears with high revs the bike picks up like a womble and grips like petrified faith to a religious icon. We all meet at a viewing lay-by where Ivo takes photos. How many times have you been here? How many photos of this place have you got? It is the kind of structure that pulls the camera from the pocket. Like bikes, spring, cats and sunsets, some things in life you can't photograph enough.

Back home I'm just composing an official invitation to announce my house-warming party when I hear a knock at the door. Keith introduces himself; he's lived here about a year and a half, he tells me we've met before at a show, he bought *Eureka* and, based on what he read, he decided Bulgaria sounded so good he sold up in Spain and came here to live. Bloody hell, I know of a few people who have gone off on journeys based on my books, but to actually relocate, that's quite an impression my words must have made. He seems all right. We drink a beer and I invite him to my party.

Another Bulgarian day has passed so fast. Maybe that's why they all overtake: the days are short, so much to do, you've got to beat the clock. I see Motocamp have put the day's events on Facebook. My neighbour sarcastically comments, 'Thanks for the invite', and, although I don't realise it at the time, that is my first insight into the darker side of the village.

Keeping the illusion alive

Monday 3rd August

Cut-off jeans, T-shirt and a palm tree and I'm on holiday. Leisure and warmth. A barefoot existence. But here I have upped my game and wear only a sarong. I learned how to tie one properly in India and I could probably use a hula hoop without it coming off – certainly the hoop would drop before the sarong, as I've never learned how to keep the ring up.

I don't think my little village is ready for a man in a sarong, so it's limited to the house and early morning garden wandering. It's been the bane of my life, being the leader of a look, taunted and then copied and no one remembers who was doing it first. That will not be the case in this little Bulgarian village. I'll be taunted for sure, but copied? I don't think so. My sarong, like my Wi-Fi signal, will stay within my boundaries.

The low sun shines on the hills. Birdsong and fragrances that drift through the open window still have foreign, exotic qualities. Foreign it may be, but it's Monday and I should do some work. Not driving a forty-foot truck through the night to swap trailers at a Bristol market, or levelling a floor for a shower tray, but opening up the computer to meet the demands of the day. Strange how that foreign feeling fades from the light of the laptop; location becomes irrelevant and the chores remain the same.

I remember speaking to a Swiss girl on a Thai island. She had a little hut where she baked her breads and traded with the tourists. She said she hadn't been to the beach in weeks. It was a tiny island, you could travel its length in half an hour. She travelled from her landlocked country to here but had recreated barriers that stopped her getting to the ocean's edge. I've always remembered that: hobby, desire, obsession, dictator. Making a living can take all the

144

fun out of the thing that once was your reason to live. To some extent, that happened when I was a bike courier in London. But more recently I've seen it in the adventure-bike world, be it in magazines, in accessory fabrication, in retail, in guest houses or in the written word. So often the planetary traveller returns inspired, thinking they've found a medium they can make into a paying lifestyle. Then, somewhere in the production process, bikes gather dust and sometimes have to be sold to finance the needed growth or bridge the shortfall in cash flow. Riding the dream can lead to a road of redundant ideas and a direction of desperation. As I have said, when bikes are your life, balance is a vital ingredient.

So I'm wearing the sarong of illusion, looking beyond the screen to the hill of enticement, with the sounds of the exotic coming through the window. However, my near view is only the worldly web, and it detains me from all that's beyond.

I have a boot review to rework. As ever, my report gets preoccupied with the country and terrain I was riding through while wearing them, as opposed to actually describing the quality of the product. For a footwear review, I've done quite a good job at promoting Guatemala.

Then I have to write a biography for a site that is promoting my products. Writing in the third person means modesty can be eliminated and my description becomes very enticing, the lifestyle more encouraging. It sounds so good I'm intrigued as to who this person is, it certainly doesn't sound like me, maybe I should read his books. Now, if it can just have that effect on everyone else.

There is a well-known motorcycle travel writer, probably the hardest working on the circuit. He helped my career enormously when I started. He still does, we Skype regularly, mostly to moan about all the things we dislike in our dream existence that no one else would understand. Today, he asks how I will earn a living now I've relocated.

I don't think I have to but I don't say that. And, anyway, I still have book sales, even though face-to-face promotion will be logistically more difficult now.

Based on expenditure, interest and exchange rates, I have enough money to last me the rest of my life, as long as I die at seventy. That seems like a perfectly good retirement plan to me. I'm not being fatalistic, but I want to live now and, if there is a later, I'll pay the price then. So often at shows I'm approached by people who tell me, 'When I retire, I'm going to do what you did.' *How*? I think, *I'm not even fifty and it bloody hurts when I fall, drop, pick up, sleep rough.* What makes these people think that with no provision, no exercise, overweight and unhealthy, they will be able to do it when they are in their mid-sixties? It may be a dream ride, but you have to be realistic about it. So based on the fact it's only going to get harder to do the things I most enjoy, I'll do them now and make sure the last cheque bounces.

Anyway, with the other author-of-more-greatness-than-I, it's decided we will share a hotel room at the NEC nine-day Motorcycle Live show this December. I'll miss the family atmosphere and communal living that was the magazine we worked with, but relationships have ceased and the house we all converged in has been sold. On the plus side, staying in a hotel will save us the commute, although actually I loved everything about those cold, frosty morning drives to the show we used to do from the shared house. It was a school bus for big kids, farting and giggling on our way to work. We would gossip about the other stallholders and the Lycra-clad girls whose job it was to obscure the new model bikes with distracting curvature. But the show is work, and without a commute we can spend more time networking (I hate that bloody word). It's an environment of opportunity and connections and that's how you move up the ladder. With social networking, creating a hysteria of hype as the event approaches, it can feed off its own momentum and promotion and that's how you turn some lifestyle books into a cult. I don't like the game, it conflicts with my integrity, but without an agent or publicist this is my only option.

However, when I should be booking flights and hotels for December, I actually see that David Gilmour is playing London in September and book a ticket for that, because it's not all work. Dates clash and overlap, so does that mean I'll be flying to the UK four times in five months or will I stay there for four weeks?

My friend, who I stay with in the US, slowly moved further south of Denver with every visit. His last move was into the Rocky Mountain foothills and, although you could see downtown Denver and its smog cloud from his elevated position, it took an hour to get there. When they first made the transition to the country, they would get home from work and, still in a city mindset, they would commute back in the evening to socialise or go to a restaurant. It took them some time to make the break and succumb to the slower, tranquil pace that their location allowed. I think it may take me a while to grasp the fact that traveling 1,600 miles to go to a concert is not the same as a ninety-minute bike ride into the capital. Much as I dislike the A12, flying over eight countries back to the UK is not so much a commute as a carbon footprint catastrophe – but it is David Gilmour, so no justification is needed.

OK, that's work done. I decide to stack all the pallets that the beehives were on up against the west side of the house. Then I precariously balance a plastic chair on top. I climb up and confirm that this is the best possible view from the house. I need a big hole in the side of the wall, and a glass door to a sunset balcony. It doesn't have to be big, just enough room for a chair and a bottle of wine.

I go and visit Denis; he has the company of the Spanish-speaking gypsy but doesn't seem that keen. The gypsy is drunk and has never visited before. He's strategically picked Denis as, being able to speak some Spanish, there's a potential for conversation (albeit one-sided), alcohol and to tout for work. Denis is visibly relieved when he leaves. There is a slight internal conflict as Denis has been banned from Motocamp, and I've been warned not to trust the roof-inhabiting local. However, I'm going to make my own judgements and invite everyone to my party. Whenever I've hosted a party, there is the inevitable conundrum of 'he used to date her and now she is with that guy' and all the other internal politics of any group. I can't cater for people's conflicts, so I invite everyone. Everyone knows everyone is invited and it's for them to play nicely or stay away. I've never had a fight break out or experienced theft at any of my gatherings. So I think I'm quite a good judge of character. I don't know anyone here very well, but a house-warming party seems like the right place to begin.

The evening consists of me watching an online adventure bike show. It's not very good but I am on it (perhaps that's why). Also, the new issue of the digital magazine I write for is out too. So that's the fame game played. It's been a busy day at the office. I haven't even had a drink today. I wonder if I will tomorrow.

DIY - Don't Improve Yet

Tuesday 4ᵗʰ August

Damn you, dawn, and your pastel shades, enticement to my tired eyes. I've just reached a point in life where I can stay in bed until lunchtime and I'm up before the sun. It's my choice though, and choice, I suppose, is what brought me here in the first place. Anyway, I generally do my best work in the morning. Based on that, I rewrite all I did yesterday and send off the boot review to a magazine. While I'm at it, I promote one of my own books on social media and instantly sell a copy. So that's today's living earned.

I don't have to do this full-time anymore, but my fickle followers are bombarded with so much stimulation on their news feeds that if I don't keep plugging away I'll be sucked down the drain of obscurity. Someone is always ready to fill my position if I neglect to keep my presence prominent. However, there is a space that has far more appeal than a virtual void. As soon as I get my tools here I'm going to be creating the bike shed of my dreams. I don't need a man cave, never have – living alone, my entire house has always been an uncompromising shrine to rock music, travel and bikes. But a workshop and insulated bike shelter has its own individuality and evolving identity. Once again, I go out to the shed to wander and wonder, which leads me to the KTM and a spontaneous research ride to the big DIY store.

As a handyman, the irritation of B&Q ineptitude regularly wasted an unpaid part of my working week. So I'm a harsh judge with high standards when it comes to such retailers. Stock, choice, quality, display, accessibility, customer service and, of course, price. This place rates adequately, based mostly on affordability. I have decking and hardwood floors on my mind; I leave with double-sided sticky tape and fasten the temperature gauge back on the KTM. I couldn't have got a balcony in the top box anyway.

I've been learning the Bulgarian Cyrillic alphabet. Once I can sound out a word, I'll be able to read again, even if I don't know what I'm saying. In the supermarket I try to pronounce the brand of the milk I buy; I splutter like water in fuel and nothing intelligible comes out.

Left in the sun, the temperature gauge reads 57°C, which kicks in a homing instinct: live to ride; ride to lie on the couch next to the fan and exchange hot air for a cool breeze. I feel guilty for being so unproductive. I'm back in the limbo where so much of this year has been spent. Time to attempt the multigym, so I watch a YouTube video and try to work out how to work out. It doesn't last long but the guilt is gone. I suppose I'm a little bit bored. This won't last, it's just a matter of establishing what to do with my days. I've spent enough time alone when I lived in the UK so I'm perfectly able to occupy myself. I'm just a bit overwhelmed by choice, paralysed by possibilities.

I see Motörhead are playing in London in January, supported by two other bands from my past. I manage to get a standing ticket. It's not cheap and I've been spending a lot lately. However, I've faithfully followed Pink Floyd and Motörhead all my life and I can't not go to this gig just for the sake of money. One day there will only be tribute bands, and that's not a rainy day worth saving for. I'm living while the sun shines. Anyway, I can probably tie that date in with the London Motorcycle Show. See, justified. Never had a problem with that, ever.

If I had a strimmer, I could do some work on the lawn. In fact, just about everything I look at could be altered, improved, personalised or maintained if only I had my van and tools here. Which means I'm not really living here – it's still a holiday until I can perform domestic duties. Based on that assessment, I walk to Motocamp. I see some faces I know but feel like a bit of an intruder. I'd intended to do the rounds, visit some more immigrants and invite them to my party, but I find myself walking home. Inactivity breeds apathy. I sit outside on my tower of pallets and watch the sunset, imagining being on a balcony, as I look at a meadow I can't mow and the skeleton Dutch barn with bike shed potential. Everything will get done, because everything always does, and then what will I have to consider?

Stone cold cynical

Wednesday 5ᵗʰ August

Today's task is to try and get a distributor to take on my books. There are two in the UK, one of whom already deals with one of my titles. Presenting yourself to these giants of dispensing is a lesson within itself. I find a thread on a forum and contact the administrator, as invited, to get some first-hand up-to-date information based on my own personal criteria. It's not long before it becomes obvious that this is another pay-to-be-published scam. It's a minefield out there of people preying on authors. They'll offer everything from first-page representation on a Google search to broadsheet literary reviews and publicity agents. Infinite lies and scams have been conceived by the devious to rob the hopeful, honest artist of what little income they manage to generate from their product.

The rule of thumb is, if they don't reply they are genuine, and too busy dealing with the better known and more marketable to bother with you. If they do reply they want a fee for their empty promises. This particular guy wants a sixty per cent discount off the cover price which, combined with postage and printing costs, leaves me at a loss, for both words and money. Fuck you very much, but if you bothered to even read the blurb on the back cover you would see the subject matter is solo international overland travel. An exploit rife with rip-offs, corruption, inflated fees, fictitious tariffs and bribe taxes at every border and in every city. I'm not immune to them, but I'm more worldly wise than your average chick-lit romance novelist. You can't take me for a ride, I've been on many. You are going to have to be more creative in your extortion if you want my earnings in exchange for your bullshit promises of Waterstones prime bookshelf positioning.

These agents of assurances in the publishing industry are up there with baldness cures and dating sites. They tell the despairing what they want to hear, and in hope and desperation the innocent throw their money into an abyss of betrayal. It's the blight of capitalism, the scourge of a free market. The people with the least integrity take from the people with the most, but are no more honourable for it.

And with that, the energy mustered for today's attempt at global recognition and world domination is depleted.

I again pick up a bad travel book I'm struggling to get through. I just can't believe it got published in its incomplete and unedited format. I fret at the unfairness of the business, and fear that this shite dilutes a market already flooded with bad blogs turned into butchered books. The only good thing about this scenario is that mine climb the rankings as more dross is published. There are some inspiring, mesmerising, compelling travel books out there, they whisk the reader away with a spell cast of eloquent, imagination-reeling prose. The words of the awe-inspiring story teller making the reader feel more like a participant than an observer. Finding those books, like discovering an empty road, gets all the harder with more traffic, riders, and writers. The race around the planet on a motorcycle is leaving a paperback trail of banal and fictitious travel accounts that fall at the starting block and entrap the writers with potential.

Bitter and twisted, I go hang a cowbell I found from the giant pine. This action may be symbolic or significant, but I'm no more going to pay for that action to be analysed any more than I am going to pay for a book to be reviewed by a high-profile blogger.

I wander to Motocamp and, other than the German girl banging out her fake reviews, the little social circle of diversity clears my head and fuels a more positive mind frame. Apparently, the Aussies of uninspired blogging and tired touring doubled back in Turkey to sell their bikes in

Germany and go home. I'm both happy they realised the answer to their problem and sad they have addressed the issue in such a terminal way. Selling the bikes seems a bit drastic, I think the journey could have been continued at some point. However, they realised that resting in transit was not going to cure their road weariness. Only a system reboot at the starting point will reignite their wanderlust.

On the other side of the coin, I get an update on a man who has been doing the show circuit over the last few years, soliciting people to pay for his round-the-world adventure. The departure date had been repeatedly postponed, but this week he finally left, and then returned after two days saying he can't sustain it. I wonder what his patrons think of that?

There is a clever invention for such scenarios, a concept that involves doing laborious and menial tasks in exchange for food, accommodation or financial reward to put fuel in your tank. It's a simple solution and has had global success in allowing people to maintain an existence. It's internationally known as 'work', and has been proved to do just that. It can be a reliable source to make the simplest of human needs become an available reality. It could also be seen, when performed in conjunction with a transient lifestyle, as true adventure.

Regardless of the reasons for the failure, it's another slice of credibility taken out of the branding of adventure motorcycling. High profile preparation followed by a total lack of commitment to proceed with the dream he sold to his subscribers. I should have gone with my instincts and bet my money he wouldn't go instead of donating to his cause. His Facebook feed is full of words of condolence and encouragement, but I refrain from commenting ... until now.

Of course, there is absolutely no link at all between my cynical disposition and this being my third consecutive alcohol-free day. Neither is it a 'I'm no longer able to be part of the party nor do I want to be' defence mechanism.

It could, though, be a growing sadness of disillusionment caused by the realisation about this scene that I was accepted into. I initially had so much belief due to the refreshing zest for life I found at the shows in the form of traders, informers, researchers and planners. But the veneer has cracked and through the fracture I've seen the light, and it's illuminated a layer of fraud that both disappoints and repulses me. The answer is to do what I did that brought me to this point in the first place. Get on my bike and ride.

After dinner, lidless and in sandals, I take the KTM to Motocamp for the first official Bulgarian lesson. We learn more sounds that the shapes they call letters make and write down a few choice words as the rain comes down on my exposed bike. To my ears and eyes there is no logic to the language. I'd find it easier replacing the electrical system of a Ducati from a Latin wiring diagram in braille than mastering the Bulgarian language, but my love for this location is my motivation that will keep me persevering until death or departure. It's an insult to the natives not to.

Polly will help me with my party preparations tomorrow. She seems willing. I'm still trying to find the balance between friendship and favour, offering and obligated. What's genuinely given and what's reluctantly granted. It's a boundary I want to discover before it is breached.

Human contact – the cure for contempt

Thursday 6th August

A routine seems to be establishing itself. It was always waiting, ready to fit into a few days that don't deviate in time and location. This morning an article has to be formatted. Which basically means copying and pasting from my blog and trying to cut it down into the requested word count without losing the way or the point. Typically, with every edit it gets longer. Overland motorcycling is travel without boundaries. Trying to write an account of it within such rigid restrictions is contra to the countries I'm trying to write about. However, if I don't make the cut the editor will and, without sentimentality, my submission will be slashed to fit the page, the flow stemmed, the point lost. And having my name attached to their butchered edit does me more harm than good. So I cut the ingredients and try to keep the taste for travel enticing.

Another part of my morning seems to have become a search for which bands are currently rocking the planet. Mötley Crüe are on their farewell tour. The closest they are getting to Bulgaria is Milan in Italy. I look at ticket, flight and hotel prices and it's quite affordable. This could be the perfect thank you gift to Ivo and Polly for all they have done in relocating me to this home sweet home – the same home where Polly was supposed to be at 11 a.m., but it's Ivo who turns up at 12.30. Weights rise and fall in the multigym as I pass the time.

In Kaufland we shop for party supplies. My trolley is full before we even get to the alcohol section. So we get another trolley and fill that with wine, beer and ice. I'm getting some indecipherable looks shot at me in the check-out line. Despite my increasing ability to decipher body language, I still can't translate what it is. It's not making me feel comfortable and it might be based on excess, unhealthy practices or the stereotypical drinking habits of the British immigrant. Ivo says something to the cashier and she snorts a condescending affirmation. Still, the till receipt is so long I don't need to buy toilet paper. The bill once converted is £80, or the cost of employing a local semi-skilled labourer for five days. *C'est la vie.*

In the same room at the multigym is a very large chest freezer. It's empty and, while I was pumping iron, I didn't turn it on, so there is pressure to get back before the ice melts and let the chilling begin.

Despite yesterday's toxic disaffection for what the adventure bike scene has become, it has connected me with some good people and today there is a touching and humbling reality. A couple who conscientiously run a shop that specialises in supplying accessories to the would-be adventure biker, and whom I've worked with on many occasions, had a third partner in the business, their dog. She featured in their rubbish adverts and was always present in their great shop, and I see that today she died. It's not a total shock. I had dog-sat for them when I was writing my last book – staying in their house keeping an eye on her as she was torn between asserting herself over her domain and resting her ailing, unco-operative body with a humiliating compliance. I'm not a dog person, but I'm not a heartless bastard either, and I feel sad for my friends and for the loss of one of the more credible creatures in the adventure scene.

Denis turns up and takes a seat before being asked, but this idiosyncratic obliviousness only endears me to him. He'll piss in your garden too; he sees it as being more polite than asking to use your bathroom. Despite his individuality, he does have some typically Scottish traits, an eye for a bargain or something for nothing. He's downloaded a free upgrade to Windows 10 and now he's got no sound. He's bought his antiquated laptop with him; can I change it back? I'm no IT geek but I do know the system restore trick and I manage to reinstate Windows 7. I've gone up in his estimation, and he can continue his plight to change the opinions of the virtual world with his keyboard-warrior tendencies. He's opinionated, he's astute but not too intense and, in some respects, he reminds me of myself. I like him a lot. I've just given him 7 out of 10 but I think I'll upgrade that.

This charitable mood is in no way related to the fact that I break from my dry spell and have a beer with him.

With more regularity than a book sale, another author turns up at Motocamp. I suppose my wave of negativity that came in yesterday's tsunami is retreating, and the tide has taken away the deadwood, leaving some treasure in its wake.

Dom is an informed man of integrity and honour. A teacher of history and politics, he may spend too much of his time agonising over social injustices and unsustainable planetary practices, but he is active in making a difference. He did volunteer work as he rode his bike from Alaska to Panama and on through Africa. As with so many of these people, our paths have crossed repeatedly since we stopped riding and attended the travel shows. Although we've often chatted, we've never really talked, and tonight I discover much more than I got from his book. Among his many efforts to save the planet he has chosen to be a vegetarian, and I'm embarrassed now that, on my party invitation, I said: *There will be a BBQ and beer and wine, probably juice too but no tofu so if you're a vegetarian eat first.* I went on to say: *At my new home 'Near-Varna'. Kicking off at 7ish, come as you are. C U Zen*

Since Dom is the Bulgarian word for home as well as the name of my planet-saving friend, it seems appropriate that he should be at my party to celebrate making my house a *dom*.

Tonight is curry night at Motocamp. There is a huge English contingency and a token sheikh too. He just happens to be passing through on his bike, having left Singapore earlier this year. I invite him to my party tomorrow. Peach has some bad news: the taxi-share to the airport next week is off and now it will cost me 150 lev. Ouch. There has to be an alternative. I try to eat slowly but still stuff myself and the curry saps my energy, taking away my drinking capacity before I've had a chance to pitch the Italian concert idea. So my delivery lacks the encouragement I wanted to enrich it with. I'll leave it with them, and the leftover curry too, which I help put in the fridge. Tomorrow the leftovers will come to my party.

House-warming party held today

Friday 7ᵗʰ August

While I'm online there is a power cut. It doesn't last long but, when it returns, I can't get online. It doesn't matter though, I've got better things to do. I make a 175-song party playlist from my iTunes library. It's a spectacular choice of music as it's my choice and, because it's my party, if it's not to everyone's taste then I won't even notice.

I'm experiencing the inevitable pre-party panic and decide I need more supplies, so I jump on the KTM and go back to Kaufland. Incidentally, they are not sponsoring this book, it's just my favourite of the three supermarkets in town as it has the most choice. I will though, before publication, contact them, so if you see a red K or an advert in the back of this book you will know their contribution kept the cover price down.

Anyway, it's bloody Friday again and market day, so the place is heaving. Knowing my way around pretty well now, I nimbly manoeuvre my trolley down the aisles and get my last-minute tortilla chips and soft drinks. I always forget to cater for kids and grown-ups who don't drink. They are to me like fifty-pound notes: I rarely come across them and, when I do, I'm not sure if they are real or not.

Every need beyond a supermarket shelf is a challenge – meaning, if I can't pick for myself what I want, I have to get my point across without the language, which can be quite tricky. When I rode the length of Russia five years ago, this was a recurring problem. Walking into a hotel in the evening, the receptionist was at a complete loss as to what I might possibly want. 'A room, a room, it's getting dark, you are a hotel, why is it so difficult to even guess what my desire might be?' Some nationalities are happy to play the miming game – *look, I'm driving, it's a big vehicle, now my arms are outstretched, I'm making a rumbling sound,*

160

I'm a plane, yes, I want a bus to the airport. The guessing does not happen here in Bulgaria any more than it did in Russia. I'm happy to make a fool out of myself to get my point across, but I won't perform in front of a stony face who won't even attempt to guess what a foreigner in a bus station ticket office might want. Anyway, I've never done my most inspiring routine in front of an unresponsive audience. Thankfully, someone other than me speaks English and they happen to be proficient in Bulgarian too. So for twenty lev I get a bus ticket to the airport, saving me the taxi fee – a saving that will pay for most of the party supplies. Once again, my lifestyle is justified.

Back home I make burger patties and stuff mushrooms with butter and blue cheese. Polly and Ivo come over to help prepare, make a salad and set up tables and chairs. It's not just their help but their presence, it takes the pressure off me. I can do all the preparation but the pre-party nerves are inevitable and sharing the setting up puts fun into the proceedings. They leave me to it, I put on my playlist and make guacamole, going through the kitchen drawers with hope and expectation for the implements needed. Nothing is lacking. Again, I have to reflect upon what a marvellous purchase I've made. Considering I arrived here on a bike, to be able to host a party and not have to scrounge for essentials is a remarkable situation to be in. I'm so pleased I bought my subwoofer from the UK. Thinking about my panniers, I have a flash of genius. I put them on the table next to the plastic glasses (if ever there was an oxymoron), fill them with ice and stand the wine and beer in them. Inspired, genuinely well-travelled, sticker-festooned, beverage-chilling, ice-cold, super-cool, credibility-assuring, motorcycle-themed, motherfucking genius. Oh, this is going to be an excellent party; I can just feel it.

Right, I'm ready. Ready to worry – what have I forgotten? Ivo and Polly return and any fret of failure is replaced with excitement. They have brought with them the

161

curry-making couple from the next village. We've met a few times. They have bought me a little wooden house plaque, it says *Near Varna*. How cool is that? And so it begins, I'm practically forced to give them a tour of the grounds before the other guests get here. They tell me how lucky I am and how lovely it is. The reoccurring theme is how to keep the extensive lawn mowed. Suggestions have ranged from goats to cows to chickens to ride-on lawnmowers to employing a local. But no one has seemed to grasp that this is my retirement, the greener grass I was searching for. Mowing the lawn *is* my occupation now, and I'm really looking forward to it, just as soon as I get a mower that doesn't keep breaking.

This, however, is a tour request with an ulterior motive. Although I think they genuinely want to see the garden, the real reason is so Polly and Ivo can put up party lights and a welcome banner. My god, what have I moved into? This is nirvana.

The guests begin to arrive: the Bulgarians, the immigrants, the part-timers, the resting riders and the passersby. It's diverse, it's multicultural and multilingual. Among the gifts I'm given is a bucket and towel – a Bulgarian housewarming tradition, apparently. Polly offers bread to everyone who arrives. They break it and dip it in oil, another custom that, although it remains unclear as to exactly what it is the bread is dipped in, creates a genuine transition and insight into the culture I hope to become a part of.

Everyone plays nicely. The playlist seems acceptable to all and exceptional to some. Predictably, I'm manic, running all over the place, meeting needs, swapping sound bites and moving on. At one point, as I go into the kitchen, 'Just Like Paradise' is playing and I stop myself. This song was an anthem of my debauched '80s and, for the next quarter-century, whenever I heard it, it always took me back there. Now it's brought me here. And I *am* home. I think my own personal party has just peaked. I sing out loud, like no one's listening, even better if they are. I'm having a moment. There is talking in my head – how did I get here?

Martin takes photos, the food all goes and the alcohol flows. I'm flitting around, loving being host, everyone has come and it feels fantastic. The demographic is quite old and what eye candy there is, is spoken for, but what the party lacks in available beauty it makes up for in benevolence. The vibe is rocking and there isn't a drop of disapproval or a cloud of antagonism. All good people, and I think there is enough room for every one of them in my new life.

I clean up a bit to point out to the stragglers that the party is over – it always helps me sober up a bit too. I lay out my sleeping bag on the couch as I've given up my bed to a Bulgarian couple. It's over. Well, that went well. I think I can safely say I'm part of the village now. As I recollect the party in my head, the only embarrassing part was how everyone said what a lovely place I have. If you've got to be embarrassed about anything, that's a good one. So much better than being photographed standing on the table with a glass of absinthe in one hand, totally naked but for a half-baked baguette sticking out your underwear. And I know this for a fact.

The perpetual party

Saturday 8th August

I have, over the years, discovered a few hangover-prevention practices. The problem is I tend to forget to implement them when I'm drunk, which is when they are most needed. The best prevention, of course, is to not drink, but what fun would that be? Like never having had a motorcycle accident because you don't ride a bike. When I host a party, I generally don't drink as much as I would as a guest – there is always too much other stimulation and distraction. The clearing up after everyone has left or gone to bed, while drinking a glass of water or a cup of tea, is a dead certainty to waking up with a clear head and, as a bonus, clean surroundings too. Because, regardless of the state I was in when I fell asleep, waking to see empty bottles, full ashtrays and half-eaten food is a morning view that will glare into the clearest of heads and penetrate the strongest of stomachs. At 8 a.m. this morning my eyes open to no regrets on any level. The rewards of being responsible. I'm so proud of myself, I deserve a drink.

There is still no internet so I continue to tidy. I bag up the rubbish, wash up the plates and recycle the plastic cups and cutlery. I see Tabby Cat doing the rounds and coax her up the steps. She's wary but willing. With the offer of some leftover chicken, she overcomes her nervousness as her instincts tell her I'm a cat person and she lets me stroke her. We just sit, me with my chai and her purring at having received a little bonus breakfast. I'm not sure she understands English, but she makes more effort than they did in the bus ticket office – but then I didn't give them chicken first.

At 10.30 my Bulgarian guests get up and chain-smoke themselves back to consciousness as they drink coffee at the table outside. Slowly, their ability to communicate kicks in, and then mine does too. In exchange for the bed,

164

my router is fixed and I have internet again. I cook some sausages on the BBQ for breakfast. CJ the sheikh turns up. He was one of the last to leave last night and he's lost his bike key. We go through the rubbish I'd just bagged up. If I had a hint of a hangover this would have me gagging. Anyway, why am I doing this? It's not my key, I don't even know what it looks like.

Everyone leaves and I have a moment to breathe. In my absence from the internet I had a few book sales, which is always a pleasure to see. I think I'll have a little doze then. The day drifts past unnoticed. It feels like a Sunday, which is fine – I'll sleep through the actual one tomorrow. CJ comes back on his bike, he found the key. Getting home drunk last night, his last lucid thought was to put the key in a safe place. He found it this afternoon under his pillow. He'd looked there twice before he found it, and I've still got decaying burger under my nails from going through the rubbish like a stray cat.

There follows another beautiful sunset that increases the yearning for a west-facing balcony. I walk to Moto-camp. The village is alive, something must be going on to-night. A gaggle of gypsy girls are walking towards me. They are singing and laughing, none of them looking at phones. It's so refreshing. They seem to know my name and say hello in English. The teenagers giggle and the younger ones gaze with intrigue. Predictably, after we pass their giggling intensifies. I wonder what they've heard, probably best I don't know.

The party isn't over, it's just relocated. I can relax, communicate and have some proper conversations. I'm bought beers and it's impossible to go home. Some Germans turn up, they say they met me at a show, and more beer flows. I stand at the bar and the evening passes as swiftly as the afternoon did. The difference is, I'm awake now.

I keep expecting things will change. This pace can't continue, surely. How will I build a shed, write the next book and complete my house when I've got this new, all-consuming social life? The multigym remains unmoved. I glance at it like an ex-girlfriend at a party as I unplug the freezer on my way to bed.

Sunday Bucket Sunday

Sunday 9th August

This morning the water is off. The three services – water, electric and internet – are like sex, drugs and rock 'n' roll. It's a very special occasion when you experience all three together. However, I have a well and can satisfy my needs independently. I have a new bucket too. I look around the shed and find some hairy rope and go down the garden and slide the heavy metal lid off the well. It's deep, it causes a feeling of vertigo. A circle of stones makes up the well walls and goes down about five metres to the water. Just leaning over makes me grab for my sunglasses, as what goes down looks unlikely to come up again. With the rope tied to the handle, I lower the plastic bucket down; it dances on the water and it takes quite a lot of jerking to get it to tilt and fill. However, when water does start to flow in, the bucket fills exponentially and submerges completely. I pull on the rope, it snaps and the bucket disappears into the dark depths. Bucket! Total failure.

Martin comes around, we had a loose plan to go to a car boot sale with Denis and the longest-inhabiting Brits in the village. We all get into my neighbour's people carrier and are driven down tiny country roads I'm not sure I'll ever find again. The route undulates past cows in pastures, and then runs parallel to a canyon and past a sign for a waterfall. I need to remember this road. It's full of potholes but the scenery is spectacular.

I see some familiar faces and tables of junk hawked by keen sellers but I don't get roped in, I just get rope. No one else is as interested in looking as thoroughly as I am. I suppose the same old stuff keeps appearing all summer long, but it's all new to me. We drive back via a bigger town and stop for lunch. Again, it's a diverse, welcoming and friendly group of people I'm with. It's certainly not been

167

difficult to establish myself here. Well, not among the immigrant population, at least.

Back at home I tie a bent piece of metal to the rope and with utter futility I try to fish out the bucket. It takes longer than it should to come to terms with the fact that I'm highly unlikely to ever see it again. It still had the gift ribbon attached to the handle. My neighbours invite me for a Sunday roast dinner but I just borrow a bucket and this time successfully bring up some water from the well so I can finally flush the toilet.

Polly and Ivo have said they would like to go to Italy to see Mötley Crüe. I can't book it by myself, too many unknowns. So I take my laptop to Motocamp and with passports and my credit card I book flights, a hotel for two nights, and three concert tickets for us. It's not cheap, but neither would be a finder's fee, estate agent's commission, solicitor's bill, stamp duty, and all those other extras, expenses and sneaky hidden costs I didn't pay when I bought my house. There was also the ease and speed of the transaction, even when it came to registering with, and sporadically receiving, water, electricity and the internet. I simply couldn't have done it without Polly and Ivo. And, anyway, I want to see this tour and I don't want to go alone so it's not an entirely selfless act and, while on the theme of entertainment, we all watch MotoGP at the expense of the sunset. Going back to the UK will be a break I think I need. I've already stopped referring to it as home. It's not. This is where I live.

Since I arrived here on the KTM three weeks ago my feet have barely touched the ground, even when I got off the bike.

I'm woken at some point during the night as the veins of the house gurgle their infusion. The water is back on.

Tempting scenery

Monday 10th August

In the spare room (well, they are all spare when you live alone), I'll call it the west wing, is an old-fashioned sewing-machine table. The sewing machine is long gone, which basically makes it a table with a pivoting foot plate. It generates nothing other than an irresistible urge to pedal it. I've put it in front of the only west-facing window to write my diary and watch the hills turn orange as the rising sun shines on them.

There is a little town in southern Texas on the Mexican border called Terlingua. Locals will tell you it's a place *where misfits fit in*. It's not ostentatious, it's true, and I've visited several times. I've even taken my mother. The misfits, however, live beyond the town, to the west in deepest desert where there is no building code. Residents buy a plot and build their shelters, living in a post-apocalyptic survival mode.

Terlingua itself has a ghost town – in name, at least – and from the porch of the bar/restaurant/gift shoppe (the 'pe' makes it old, I think it stands for pretentious) you can look east to the Chisos Mountains. This is the only complete range contained within a US national park, Big Bend, which I wrote about extensively in another book. The sunset happy hour comprises residents, 'snowflakes' (the people who winter here), and the sparse but inevitable token tourists. We would all watch the colours change on the rocky Chisos range as the sunset's rays illuminated them, standing with our backs to the sun's low glow in the westerly sky. Well, this is my futile revolution-table of replication; I'm watching the morning rays light up the village (which I'm beginning to discover has its own community of misfits) until the giant pine casts a shadow across my garden. I sit and rotate the redundant sewing machine treadle and peddle my books on Amazon and then manage to finish off the article I've been working on and find some appropriate photos to support it, then lose them again. I clock off to partake in my other occupation. Today I'm a lawn-mower. I can tell I'm going to have to take the bike out first as there is no fuel in the mower and little in the KTM tank – what a bummer. So I ride into the sunny morning on my Kaufland commute. There are some fresh faces in the lay-by today. Maybe they rotate, although you probably have to pay extra for that. I swear, they are to me just like skips: I can't help but look as I go past, and that in turn means I throttle back a bit, the change in exhaust note is their calling, and inevitably our eyes meet. Damn it, it's OK, I was just looking.

Right, what was I doing again? Fuel, and a few supplies of course – a once-a-week food shop shouldn't be so difficult. I managed it for years, and that was before the days of hard luggage, just bungees over bread and bananas. It's not about volume, I just can't seem to think more than a few days ahead when it comes to food. Anyway, it's too late now, I'm flying back soon. As if they knew, among this week's promotions is seventy per cent off of daypacks. Kaufland, you temptress – this is exactly what I need, just one more justified purchase.

By the time I've syphoned petrol and am ready to start, it's lunchtime and the day is reaching its peak heat. Without a plan or pattern, I cut the thick mower-stalling grass, motivated mainly by getting a tan to take back to the UK. I stop to put my head under the running tap and cool my overheating brain boiling inside my skull. Being the place where my thoughts are generated, technically it's my think tank, although right now it's more like a jacuzzi. Then the mower won't start, so with dripping hair I check the obvious with a motorcycle toolkit. It reluctantly comes back to life, but its lack of reliability has taken the pleasure out of the pastime.

Anyway, I have to move the rocks and the roof tiles which had previously been used to level pallets of beehives.

My neighbour has a friend staying who calls over the wall to see if I want to go off-roading with him. Let's be clear, I've just been doing that, but he's not talking about mowing. Another day, more uncharted territory. We ride up to the northern ridge of the valley and follow a track along the top. How long will I have to be here before I can grasp that I'm not doing anything illegal by riding these tractor and logging trails? The only rule is respecting the crops, nothing else matters and nobody minds. We come to the inevitable monument where we stop for a fag break for him and sanctimonious fresh air for me. From here is a full, unobscured panorama of the Balkan range. I'd love to have this view permanently. To glance is a teasing temptation and I've already done that once today.

This is the first proper off-roading I've done on the KTM. It's definitely better at it than I am. There's a lot of power available and the handling is in my hands. I'm not sure I'm in full control of my destiny.

When the day cools, I make an attempt at creating some dinner and then Ivo calls – they are ordering pizza, do I want some? No … well … yes … bugger, I'll come down anyway but don't order for me. The Germans who arrived the other day are looking at my website when I arrive. It feels strange, like I've caught them reading my diary. Still, it must have had the desired effect as one of them buys a book. As well as me, the other popular topic this evening is Kaufland and this week's special offers, which is another subject I'm quite informed about - although I don't think there's a book in it … well, not until now.

There is quite a lot of drinking going on but I'm on water and can see some aggression building due to miscommunication. I could step in, but like trying to work on your bike at Motocamp, there are too many people who think they know better. I'll leave them to figure out their misjudgement.

I find some insects in the sink and on the walls when I get back home. They are like centipedes but with hairy tentacles, translucent grey bodies, incredible speed, and the seeming ability to squeeze into the tightest of crevices. They seem to like drains and dampness. They are repulsive, unwelcome and squash softly with a projectile of pus like innards. Like the nastiest of creatures, they don't seem too bothered or slowed down by losing half their body or having the pulped part trail behind them. They are a cross between a caterpillar and a cockroach and not the sort of thing you want to feel crawling over your naked body in bed. It's unfortunate that this is my last sensation of the day.

Leaving the party

I'm awake at dawn so go up to the ridge behind my house to watch the sunrise on the right side of the day. I've seen more dawns through the screen of an Essex-bound night trunking truck than through the bottom of a glass that wouldn't stay down but I think here on the ridge is my preferred viewing pleasure. I'm not naturally nocturnal – when my working days were dark, it would cast a shadow over my life which only reflected on my health and mood. The night-time shades in my life are now reserved for my favourite clothing and favourite bike, and I'll keep the black theme until I find a darker colour. Anyway, this sunrise is a far more natural, relaxing and gradual start to the morning than its previous uninvited entrance into my darker life.

I find the photos I lost yesterday and I can finally get the completed article sent off. This, I'm finding, is a massive advantage of being two hours ahead of UK time. When I lived in the US, I would turn on the laptop in the morning to be bombarded with a day's worth of UK correspondence. But here I can be the one who gets the last word in first. My emailing is completed and my book orders fulfilled before the UK has got up and the US has gone to bed. It's a very efficient time zone to live in, just a shame the days are so short.

This village has two permanent background sounds: the dogs, which I have to say are a lot less annoying since I applied my mental muting; and the two-stroke engine. Not in the form of off-road bikes but in the strimmer or the chainsaw. From dawn to dusk, and I come to realise, all year round, there is always something that needs cutting: weeds or wood. Like all the other village sounds, the cock-crow, cuckoo and chalga, the notes accumulate and drift up the valley and past my house so I don't miss any of them. It seems there is no antisocial time to rev a two-stroke: if there is a hint of light, it's acceptable. To be fair, the first light of the day, this time of year, is by far the coolest and most agreeable for manual labour. So to blend in, on this dewless morning, I mow the browning and patchy part of my lawn. I watch the sun shine on the tops of the trees that border my garden and then turn back towards the shadow which the house casts on yesterday's freshly mown grass.

If this was employment, I would tell the house owner that mowing this lawn is my favourite job of the week. But no one pays me, it's my property. I am still in awe: this is my house, my garden, my view. It's not mortgaged nor rented, and after Mötley Crüe even the gratuities will be paid for in full. So not only am I revelling in the scenery and the sun on my skin, but all I'm seeing as I pace to the boundary and back again is within my ownership. It's not an evil laugh – *mwahaha, now you belong to me* – it's more an inexpressible elation. This is what I was looking for. I wasn't even sure it existed. I've not only found it, but I'm present in it, not camping and pretending, housesitting and imagining, holidaying and dreaming. I'm living in it and loving it. And every time I look at the shed, I think to myself – *mwahaha, wait till I get my hands on you.*

My neighbour, and his mate, whom I rode with yesterday, are off on their BMWs for a two-week ride. I wave them off as Bruce turns up in his dodgy Lada. I've promised to have another look as it's still overheating. I flush the radiator and I'm not convinced the thermostat is opening, so we jump on the KTM and go into town. His Bulgarian is at a functional level. He replies to the words they say which I don't understand, and picking up parts for a Lada in Eastern Europe is easier and cheaper than lay-by lovin' … probably. I become laddish when I'm in his company and there is a lot of laughing and innuendo. The thing is, as a musician he's toured the US, done the festival circuit and been on some MTV shows, so he truly is rock 'n' roll. I was once introduced at a presentation as 'a rock star without a guitar'. I admit, I embrace aspects of the lifestyle despite being musically inept and tone-deaf. I did, however, find some success in something that puts me on a stage now and again, and everything else is part of my rock 'n' roll fantasy. Bruce's band was dropped by their label some time ago and he's riding a receding tide to obscurity. Our heights are behind us and alcohol and stories are all that's left in their wake. So, with my philosophical view of a planet travelled alone, and his experience of touring in a group, we have common ground and many reckless stories to swap. I take the KTM up to 165kmh on the journey back because it just seems like the appropriate thing to do. Hot and dirty car maintenance soon turns to down-and-dirty drinking habits under the shade of the giant pine – it's Tuesday and the alcohol-free week is already over.

Later, we relocate to his place. It's barely habitable but he has plans for it, like every hovel owner does. However, his being in Bulgaria is, as in the case of so many part-timers, his holiday, and it's not a constructive way to home improvement. There are always better things to do than kitchens, bathrooms, plumbing, heating, tiling and decorating. I know, I've been there and done that. Bringing out the potential in these bargain purchases is a laborious task, best performed with local labour and know-how. Bringing your British standards here won't necessarily bring the property up to standard. The stone and oak construction is built for an extreme climate, making mild Gulf Stream practices impractical. Pipes will freeze in winter; walls will radiate in the summer. Power will cut and water will retreat regularly, there is no reservoir. On top of all that, at this time of year, the garden advances like triffids. Just cutting it back and gaining control will take up your two-week work placement. So it's a daunting task to attempt when you are only here temporarily, and finding a reliable and trustworthy builder to take care of it while you are away is equally difficult. Much like the publishing industry, the ones who say they will are liars and only want your money, and the ones who would won't. In this case, the builders' experience, honesty and credibility has taught them that if you don't work with the homeowner on site then it will become a project of contradiction, leading to blazing feuds based on lack of understanding.

After we have exhausted his beer on the concrete balcony, we move on to Motocamp as, somehow, it's become 5 p.m. and we've not eaten. A German girl has ridden here on an XT500. As we walk towards the communal table, she looks up in surprise and says: 'What are you doing here?'

I look at Bruce, assume she's speaking to him. He looks at me, I look at her. 'Me?' I say.

She's listened to me on a motorcycle podcast and has read one of my books. So here I am with a genuine rock 'n' roller and I'm the one who gets recognised – well, we are in my domain. I compliment her bike, I've had several over the years. She says I can take it for a ride. Since I've got some food at the house that needs eating, I accept her offer and ride home to fetch it. Only I've forgotten the keys, so I have to break in, which involves climbing a wall. I break some tiles getting onto the balcony.

It's a typical Motocamp evening – or, at least, the typical British part-time expat pastimes occur. Everybody's drinking has converged and continued here. The German girl seems most disappointed I'm leaving tomorrow; this is now a disappointment to me too. Someone else has me sign a book. I feel like a drunk celebrity. I'm definitely half-right, and I'm not the rock star here. However, I have a flight tomorrow morning, I don't have a tour manager, and I have not even begun to pack, take out the rubbish or empty the fridge. It's about 10 p.m. when Bruce drives me back promising to take me to the bus stop in town tomorrow morning.

Somehow, I manage to ride the KTM up the bank, round the back, through the garden and into the bee shed next to the lawnmower. God knows how I managed that, drunk and determined, dark and in sandals. As a token act of responsibility, I drink some water. I'm just having too much fun. But I've got to exercise more restraint. In fact, I've got to exercise. If not, I'll become a fat alcoholic in no time. There is no time. I set the alarm for 4 a.m. and pass out.

Little Blue, I've come for you

I wake at 3.30 a.m., have a shower and throw some stuff in my daypack. Money? No, card. Ticket? No, screenshot on phone. Passport? Yes, definitely, but I keep checking it like a dumpee checks their phone. In a way, I have been dumped. I call Bruce and it goes to voicemail, although reception is hazy when you live down in the valley. I empty the fridge and walk into the warm, dark morning. His light is on, that's a good sign; I knock on the window, he's barely conscious, that's not. Turns out he carried on drinking with Peach last night. He's in no fit state to drive, just like his car really. The alternative is Peach, who's equally unlikely to pass a breathalyser test. Friends don't let friends drive drunk, unless you have a plane to catch and they promised last night to get you to the bus stop which is fifteen kilometres away. There is no point in me simply waiting for the bus to pass on the main road – it's pitch-black with no pavement or street lights and the traffic is fast. Likewise, bus drivers are instructed to pick up at specific places, and are not in the habit of looking out for, or picking up, hitch-hikers. So, with a combination of obligation, no other option and the promised leftovers out of my fridge, Bruce finally agrees to take me, or at least let me take him. We board the Lada and trundle desperately to the designated bus stop.

I say goodbye to Bruce and let him return under the veil of darkness: it's the same lawless road we rode as motorcycle ton-up boys yesterday. I wait, it's late but there are others waiting too, so I have hope. I try to decipher vehicle size based on headlights. A bus comes and stops and does not let me on – apparently, the airport bus is behind. I wait alone now, feeling like I let my last chance slip away. An indicator, air brakes, another bus has come. It's full of the sleeping and reclined. My ticket lets me on but reserved seating means nothing. The disturbed spread over their adjacent seats and fake sleep; the true dreamer will wake to find he has my company. An obnoxious TV drowns out the snoring and both keep sleep at bay. However, the journey, like the snoring and TV, is non-stop for the three-hour drive to the airport on the outskirts of the capital. Part Two of the transport back to the UK is complete. I'm early and hungry, so opt for the shit-omelette and free-Wi-Fi café. They are certainly consistent: the password is the same and the omelette is burned again.

I haven't seen or heard the instruction for all passengers to stand impatiently queuing at the gate, despite having assigned seats, but the sheep still push and heave. I sit and read until they are let out the pen to stand in the next queue. In a window seat with no window I rest my head against the fuselage and doze the three hours away.

What was I thinking? Clearly, I wasn't thinking at all. Mid-August in Gatwick is horrendous. The line for the 'chip' passport moves slower than the international arrivals; it's a single-finger welcome home. This helps with the attitude adjustment after a holiday and quickly brings back the mood of resentment. With my compact daypack, I weave through the mindless masses and make it to the station ten minutes before my pre-booked train leaves. At Liverpool Street I have even less time, so that worked out perfectly.

My god it's so cramped here, not just in the airport and on the train but outside the window, along the side of the track, these squat terraced houses, built up with a loft conversion, and out with a flat roof extension. Builders' yards which narrow to a triangle of scaffolding eking out every last available space, edging onto the railway embankment. Big yellow storage taking up prime car parking space; double yellow lines and kerb-parked cars; multi-lanes and multi-stories all with stationary vehicles. They queue like communism, for transport, for parking, for tickets, everything is available here except space, because everyone comes for the availability. There's nothing like seeing with new eyes what I only looked at before. It's uniform and regulated and often out of order. And the noise of it all, a chainsaw couldn't cut through it. I miss Bulgaria already. Once I have my things around me, I'll be even less inclined to leave. In fact, after a three-hour flight I wonder how much I really want to come back here in September and October and December and again for Motörhead in January. It's living in two countries; I've made the move but there's a hidden tie I'm yet to sever. With shows to attend for work and concerts for pleasure, a three-hour flight sounds simple, but it's much more than that and I don't think I want this other home anymore. The choice is easy. I'm not sure if the separation will be.

As I ease into Essex, the high-density population eventually fades and the fields come to meet me - though my mum does not, her car has broken down. For the last part of the journey, the family connection has broken. She sent the neighbour.

The overcrowding continues back into my valley of materialism. I'm in the perfect mindset to see what's important and gets put in the van, and what is just baggage best left behind. The shed is as cramped as London living – how much do I want to bring that feeling back to my liberating new life? The KLR fires up enthusiastically, as does the van. They seem keen to go.

I walk to the Co-op and go back to my old way of selecting a wine based purely on price. I wonder if the government have missed my tax contributions on every bottle I bought.

In the evening I speak to my favourite ex to arrange dinner. She says my new life looks like the one she cohabitated for a while, at the address people still use as their password. And another friend I rode through Ukraine with says I was always a professional at finding a feel-good factor. And that's why they are my friends, as I never feel the need to disagree with anything they say.

My Eastern European body clock wakes me before I need. Actually, I'm not sure when I need to be awake, only that there is a reality that needs to be dealt with. I book mum a flight to Bulgaria for next month and, while she is still asleep, I take the SIM card out of her phone. She has a list of things for me to do and I take the old reclining chair into the driveway and put a 'free' sign on it. The dustmen come, one of them really likes it. It's so good to be able to talk to people – I tell him it's his if he wants it, but his only transport is in the dustcart and it won't look the same when he gets it home.

I head into town. At the phone shop they cut my mum's SIM card down to a micro size and I pick up a new battery for her car. Her little Ford Focus has been the epitome of reliability, but batteries have limited life expectancies and hers has expired. Back at her house there's a lot of mail and eBay purchases waiting for me. I open a box and put her reduced SIM card into the new smartphone and start it up. I just leave it on the kitchen counter and go back to the garage to fit the battery. The car fires up. I call her. It takes a while as she doesn't recognise the ring tone or the phone, but then she answers.

'Happy 80th, Mum!' Brilliant, that worked perfectly.

Her landline has been ringing all morning and her doorbell too, flowers and well-wishers. It's not a competition, but her social life today is as full as my Bulgarian one.

When I got my moving-out date, I called the council. My council tax was summed up to my moving date and the difference refunded. I gave the water and electricity companies their meter readings and my accounts were settled.

But then came the phone company TalkTalk.

They said they needed six weeks' notice. I explained that I didn't have a moving-out date six weeks prior to my leaving and then, over the following two months, I proceeded to Blankety-Blank TalkTalk and their demands.

Today, however, I have to face the situation – because, like hepatitis, TalkTalk won't go away. Over forty-five uncompromising minutes, I keep talktalking and they keep refusing to listenlisten. They offer to transfer the line to my new address.

'OK,' I say, 'have you got a pen? It's in Bulgaria. Oh, you can't do that, you mean my *mailing* address. No, they already have a phone provider, they don't need another one.'

They say they want £50 to transfer the line to the new owners' names, who have been using and paying for the service for the last month. The only alternative is that they put a block on the line. You can never win with a phone company; you can only hang up.

But keeping the theme I try to open an account with Virgin and that doesn't work either. Life is so much easier in a country where I don't speak the language.

I take Mum out for lunch and then have to load the van for the show tomorrow. I can't find my gazebo – it's bloody massive, how can I lose it? When I get the KLR out of the shed, I see it lurking in the corner. The van gets loaded in the way it has been for the last few years: with bike, panniers, books, pop-up banners and all the other things I've accumulated that make my stall irresistible to the passing punter. The laptop goes on briefly to check the setting-up times for tomorrow's show and I see the UK's most prestigious motorcycle mecca, the Ace Café, have put me in their newsletter. That feels good. The night thunders and it pisses down. Tomorrow's event is in the grounds of a private school and I fear a mud bath is imminent. If I expect that, then so will those members of the public who were going to buy their tickets on the gate but may decide to stay at home in the dry instead. This happens a lot with adventures. That's the risk you take hosting and attending an outdoor show in the British summer.

* * *

This weekend's show used to be a five-hour drive away, but this year they have relocated to north London. It has a broader travel theme than many of the motorcycle-orientated shows. Thankfully, its new location means I have to travel less to get to it.

Its wider horizon attracts a greater cross section with a wide-ranging interest in travel. As a bookseller, I meet a varied audience and it's more family orientated too so I'm taking my mum along as a birthday bonus.

With the Ace Café on my mind from last night, it occurs to me that we can swing by on the way for a full English breakfast. For me, it's more about the revered venue than a fried slice of British cholesterol, but they both have a place in my heart. I've checked mum into a hotel nearby as I don't think sleeping in the back of the van is the sort of travel adventure she would appreciate. Being a new location, it's a bit tricky to find, and there isn't a single sign to help locate the entrance for us lowly tradesmen. Nor for the trade area once I'm in the grounds, but maybe that's to add to the adventure travel aspect of the show. However, it seems my fellow adventure traders have found it and many familiar faces are setting up in the allotted, shady, wooded trade-stand area. I show my tickets to a girl with a clipboard who asks who I am, my fellow traders seem embarrassed on her behalf. I'm not phased in the least, until I see I've been completely overlooked and not made it to the list of pre-booked, pre-approved prime pitches. Nevertheless, we find a spot which I'm perfectly happy with.

At the old location the trade stands lined the walkways and every visitor had to pass by on their way to wherever they were going. It was perfect and eventually either their intrigue would get the better of them or you could just wear them down and make a sale due to sheer persistence. It soon becomes apparent (and it's not a big surprise) that nobody goes down to our woods today. It's dark and damp and not on the way to anywhere. It's raining and my unseen display is getting wet. It's a total waste of time and books and dampness are not good bedfellows so it all goes back in the van. The enjoyment is not in sales but in a social event for traders, and when we aren't selling, we all love to moan … and drink. I hadn't intended to start this early, but others clearly had, so what am I to do? It's a washout, and if this behaviour is considered antisocial it doesn't matter as there are no bloody customers to complain. Profit margins notwithstanding, we are celebrating like we've sold out, or, in my case, sold up. Everybody seems to know I've moved to Bulgaria – I'm around my friends whom I've met over the last five years of doing the show circuit. We don't know where each other are from or quite what our weeks consist of. However, at the weekends we are show traders and the bond is strong. The rain is heavy and so is the drinking. I call a taxi for Mum at some point and continue drinking to another point at which point all direction is lost, which at a travel show is a bit of a dichotomy. So much for drying out in England.

* * *

As a truck driver, I would, if I could, hold on until I got to my destination instead of stopping for a wee only an hour's drive away. I've learned that this is entirely the wrong strategy to apply at shows, because the second you arrive there are people who want to chat, and getting from the entry gate to the toilet block is not a direct route. This morning the need is quite urgent and I'm quite late. Oh, for a cloak of invisibility, or a porta-potty in the trader's area. But instead I have to walk across the extensive campsite to the toilet block. A rider pulls up on a BMW and asks me where he should park. He clearly knows who I am and that I'm not a marshal, but with his helmet on, an indistinct bike and my lack of facial recognition, I really have no idea who I'm talking to, and I've got something quite pressing on my mind, and elsewhere.

I go and pick up Mum from the hotel and use her shower while I'm at it, which is just what I needed. As we set up the stand, it's busy. Lots of people want to chat, which is generally the case when you are setting up or breaking down. But once all the merchandise is displayed, everyone goes off to look at other events and, again, we are left alone in the woods. One man comes up and says: 'I've read both your books.'

'Both,' I reply. 'You know there are three, right?' That was an easy sale.

The stand next to me is run by a couple of young, attractive Hooray Henriettas. They seem to be putting the gap in gap year, promoting luxurious travel which avoids local food, guest houses and anything else that might involve interaction with those nasty foreigners. They seem a little out of their depth here and the fact they don't even get up to open their stall until lunchtime says a lot about the dedication they have to their little hobby. The downside of this is that if people see empty spaces or shut-up stands, they don't bother to walk down the aisle and footfall decreases. Considering the count isn't very high to begin with, the apathy of the girls is having a knock-on effect on my stand.

Drob turns up with his wife, who also has a birthday around this time. Being equally unprofessional and undedicated to my cause, and slowly losing interest in the whole bloody shitshow, I join them to find a plastic table where a few rays of sun shine. We open a bottle of Prosecco. Who's the hooray now? Soon enough, it's 6 p.m. and what little life there was has died. I have to see this as a birthday outing for my mum because if I started to count the cost of attending I'd be very angry. One of the author girls, Ants, has locked herself out of her camper van. I have a coat hanger in mine for just such occasions but, where I have Prosecco she has a procession, an army of chivalrous men who compete to break and enter. Well, she knows where she can find me.

It's a very social evening with many faces from the industry: magazine editors, photographers, film-makers and writers, most of whom I know to varying degrees. Tonight all conversations seem to have a political theme, although everyone seems to be of the same opinion: the hopelessness for the future of this country and the planet in general. It's not all pessimism – these are varied nationalities and well-travelled people, can we really as individuals make a difference? I watch the sunset, believing that all I can do is live my little life as independently as possible, under the radar, letting the rest of society go about their business. This event attracts people who seem to know the score, who have witnessed the world first-hand and have made as informed a judgement as their experiences can allow. They are not swayed by media lies, political powers or religious beliefs. They see the planet as an accumulation of individuals who all want to be safe and warm, protect and feed their families. They don't want to be labelled or fight for their rights to survive, they just want the right to survive while the powers that be promote fear and loathing for no good but their own. I don't need a book of religion, I know what good is and generally I am, and if I'm not then I'm mindful not to let my bad affect the lives of others. So now we are all agreed on that, can we talk about something else? Actually, now I've said my prayers I think I'm going to have an early night.

* * *

I feel great this morning, fresh and rested. That excessive drinking is no good, why is there no warning about it? I stride purposefully to the toilet block. I'm Mr. Bouncy this morning. Some people are still sitting round the smoking embers of the firepit drinking. I'm so glad that's not me. Back in the van I fire up the camping stove, make chai and a sausage-and-egg baguette. Feeling fit, fed and productive, I move my gazebo; the Hooray Henriettas have given up and gone home to Mummy and Daddy. So I take their space, facing the imminent hordes of Sunday book buyers. Mum is getting a taxi in this morning, so I man the stand and talk to a fellow KLR rider who buys a book, then I sell all three to a guy who doesn't even want to chat. I love customers like that.

One of the organisers comes around. Other than the state of the planet, the next popular conversation has been the hopelessness of our position on it – no one is coming to the trade area. However, like mouthy school kids when faced by the teacher, no one has anything to say. I bloody have. I'm listened to and told that next year we will line the concrete walkways. He only put us here as he thought we'd like the wooded environment. Yeah, but I'm here to sell, not hug trees. And anyway, I'm a writer, for me trees are more interesting when they are made into books. I'm not sure if it's lip service. I suppose I'll see next year if I come back.

The sales are steady today. The sun is out and so are the wallets. I have a few 'triples' bought, sometimes as gifts and sometimes just by an enthusiastic customer who wants all three books. I really must make up a box gift set. Even Mum is asked to sign a book as she did feature in one on them when she flew out to Mongolia to meet me – actually, that was on her birthday too. My adventure travel mother.

I'm getting a bit tired of the Bulgarian conversations now. Still, it beats the 'where to next?' compulsory end-of-conversation question. The only one worse than this is the 'actually, I've written a book …' admission. It's not so easy to get away from that monologue. A German speaks to me about the possibility of translating my books. 'OK, into what language? Oh right, I get it now.' But I doubt I can afford it and, anyway, how am I supposed to promote them in Germany? I can only say, 'Ich liebe dich', and if I tell a German I love them they'll expect me to give them a book.

As is often the case, there is a sudden exodus. The wandering punters disappear like there's been a primal calling, and for us traders it's the sign to break down and evacuate. I swap books with Ants, the girl who was momentarily locked out of her van, and say goodbye to the organisers – well, one at least, there are a few celebrities here and that's where their interests seem to lie, it's the only connection they feel is worth the effort. I'd probably have ignored the villagers if Lemmy had come to my house-warming party too, not that anyone here is in that league. An older woman collars me to look at her broken bike – where are all the chivalrous men now? I want to go home. Thankfully, a volunteer steps up and I drive out.

Back at Mum's I unload and stocktake. If I hadn't had the expense of flying in from Bulgaria to attend the show it would have been worth my while. It's not viable to do these shows anymore and, after today, I won't even have my van in the UK. Time to admit for me that this side of my occupation is over. Moving to Bulgaria means living in Bulgaria, and England is not a commute away by road or air. Bookselling kept me just above the breadline, I loved doing it, but it has to pay and by sleeping and cooking in my van at shows I could make ends meet. The ends are further apart now and, with no mortgage or place to live in the UK, both the opportunity and incentive have gone. The next time I load the van, it will be Bulgaria bound.

* * *

Perseverance has many motives. Today, vanity drives me back to the optician to try and learn how to get a bloody contact lens in. I try for an hour and a half. At one point, I drop it on the floor and, picking it up, I manage to cut my head on the desk. I get one in, it stings, my eyes water, and then I can't get it out again. My eyes are red and sore and I'm really bloody annoyed. They make me another appointment for tomorrow.

A more pleasurable pursuit should be loading the van for my migration, but that's equally frustrating. Bedding, clothing, books, the van is filling up too fast, and I want to get the KLR in too. The shelving was originally designed specifically for my tools when it was a handyman van. They stack well but are heavy, the density of them can't be denied. It's packed from floor to roof with what I can find, and I still have to pack all the things I can't find. I might have to leave the bike behind.

At 5 p.m. I have to head out. The roads are empty. I think everyone must be on holiday, which means Europe will be crowded. I treat myself to a brand new DeWalt cordless drill – my last one was worked to death and deserves a quiet retirement servicing my mum's minimal needs. I deserve this purchase. The strong box packaging it comes in makes me want to protect it like a suitcase full of money, such is its desire and appeal. I walk out the shop with my much-anticipated power tool. I've considered this moment for many weeks and this is not a drill.

The van has certainly gone up in value with its payload. I won't be leaving it unattended on my way back home. For now, I park it in a pub car park and meet my best ex for dinner. While I'm still in the treating mood, I order a steak. She says I'm having too much fun, it's hard to play it down. When she goes to the toilet, I look at my phone. I have a message from Polly: 'Do you want to join us on a five-day sailing trip around the Greek islands?'

'What? What is it? What are you smiling about?' says my best ex when she comes back.

'Well, you know how you said I was having too much fun?'

Life seems to have gone into fantasy mode and it won't slow down. In fact, I couldn't even dream this – my imagination has limitations, that's why I don't write fiction.

The only immediate restrictions in my life right now are what will fit in the van. It feels OK as I drive it back to Mum's. However, like this unpredictable new existence in which I've found myself, there is always more to try and fit in. I will have to prioritise. I'm already loaded and I can't do another trip.

* * *

Book thoughts. For several years, they were what brought me to a conscious state every morning. Promotion, distribution, selling. It was my passion, my obsession to make my night wishes and dawn dreams come to life, a viable reality of earning a living by writing. Those dreams have drifted to other desires these days, and book thoughts don't wake me so often. But when they do, I act on them.

'Beer thoughts?' That's what my mate Andy, with whom I travelled through Mexico, would say to me as we rode into the second half of the day. 'Are you having beer thoughts?'

'Well, I am now.'

It was his infallible way of calling an end to the riding day. So, be it the power of suggestion or the power of the pen, the thoughts have a driving momentum. Based on that, this morning I email the Ace Café, while my name is still fresh in their inbox, to see if they will stock my books.

Boat thoughts. Polly and Ivo continue to update me about the sailing trip. I really can't think about this at all. I know nothing about sailing boats and nautical navigation. However, the thought of floating around Greek islands and mooring in the evening to eat at seafood restaurants is enough. Count me in. Why not? I could be hit by a bus tomorrow.

Bus thoughts. One of Drob's favourite theories is the very high likelihood of getting hit by a bus. The phrase conjures up images of being hurled across lanes of traffic from the impact of formidable force. He loves to point out that if, for example, you are in a Third World bus terminus, wandering round incapacitated by a backpack with your head in a guidebook, pursued by hawkers and beggars, it's quite likely a shunting bus will nudge you, and technically you have just been hit by a bus. Voiced in such

190

terms, I'm sure I must have been bumped by many Asian buses. I've had haircuts that hurt more. Regardless of the force of contact, it seems like an inevitability and, therefore, I'm going sailing.

Anyway, it's raining and perhaps this is the rainy day I've been saving for. Actually, I've not been saving – well, not money. I've been saving my life for opportunities like this and I'm taking this one.

Blind thoughts. I ride the bike into a pissing wet morning to once again stab my finger repeatedly into my eye with the hope of leaving a contact lens over the iris. This is my fourth appointment and – bam! – in it goes, perfect. After an hour I've still not managed to take it out. The apprentice assistant tries, but she can't get it out either. She's being really brutal too, she pushes so hard my eyeball squelches. She knows she's done something very wrong and calls the optician who takes me into the examination room and finally the lens is extracted. He tells me two blood vessels have burst. He says I'll be OK in a few days. Well, fuck vanity, it all seems a bit superfluous if you're blind. Never again am I going to try and get a lens in my eye. It's over. I ride back in the rain, my right eye blurred and streaming.

Bulgarian thoughts. To continue the theme of things that I can't get in the van, Bruce's drum kit arrives. I'd agreed to bring it over to Bulgaria for him. The day consists of nothing else: back and forth to the shed, filling every available space in the van. Sliding a CD or book in where boxes don't meet. My eye throbs and waters. I'm wet and achey but the van is packed like Pickfords.

Bed thoughts. The Ace Café say they don't have the room to hold a stock of my books. I can empathise. Tomorrow I will leave this crowded island and give it a little more space.

Van gone

I'm awake at 4.30 a.m. It's my dad's deathiversary, ten years today. I'd been waiting for the call: my phone always charged; the bike's tank always full. The Marie Curie nurse rang just after midnight. 'Your mum says don't rush, there is no need. I'm sorry. He's already gone.' Don't rush? I've got a Triumph Sprint 955i, a road I've been riding for thirty-five years, there is no other traffic, no better reason to ride like there's no future, and no better defence than death – but neither it nor the law caught me.

There was a lot of emotional baggage on that journey. I'm overloaded again this morning but in a much better frame of mind. What have I forgotten? You forget a lot when you lose a parent – it's self-defence, a temporary Alzheimer's, but the memory is restored when it's ready to move on. I'm ready now and still forget my headphones and Pink Floyd oil painting. Too rushed for moving pictures, I say bye to Mum. 'See you in Sofia,' are my parting words, a positive distraction for this difficult day.

The van sways over the uneven dirt driveway, and rocks steady onto the road. 1,600 miles to go, with my most valued possessions around me. Back to the ferry terminal, no special-status queue jumping today. Bikes tend to board before the masses, but today I'm not an easy rider, just a lowly driver, with compressed shocks, keeping a low profile. It's only been five weeks since I came this way on the KTM. Again, I look at the house on the mouth of the River Stour. It was never destined for me. No regrets now, just a narrow escape, a light heart and heavy departure.

I contemplate a cabin but go out on deck, up some stairs, find a peaceful sheltered spot and join a few other horizontal passengers. Oh yes, I can doze away the crossing here, and do, until some dickhead with a football decides to have a kick around in this confined space. Stupidity and ignorance should never be underestimated, nor should the universal comprehension of 'Oi!'

I've got some laptop obligations but I'm not in the mood, so I look over the side and see porpoises breaking the waves. Better than writing about motorcycle mindfulness is to travel with porpoise. I manage to avoid the noise of the voyage; it's only when queueing for the car decks that I become aware of the clots inside the vessel.

I started doing European truck driving in 1984. I wasn't old enough to have an HGV licence and drove a vehicle exempt from the driving hours restrictions. It seems as alien as smoking on planes now, but back then I would drive onto a ferry and sleep in the cab as it crossed the channel. We all did. Then, in '87, a roll on/roll off ferry rolled over, capsizing as it left Zeebrugge, and nearly 200 passengers and crew drowned. It left port with the bow loading door open and, with forward momentum, water immediately flooded in. After that, vehicle decks were closed to passengers. As a long-distance driver, I wasn't able to get as much undisturbed sleep, but I never woke up dead either.

I weave my way round the Rotterdam ring road and trundle into Germany, moving away from the border as the sun sets in Holland. I have a coffee connection just off the autobahn, it's a place I could stay but I'm not looking for somewhere to sleep. I don't want to leave the van unattended or abandon my drive. But for a few hours in the company of the well-travelled, I'm the recipient of German hospitality, strong coffee and compelling conversation. The most controversial topic being Motocamp, and I learn things I'd prefer not to know, but which, now that they're mentioned, don't come as a total surprise. Ultimately, it's gossip – I have to live in the village, and a golden rule I have in life is never to react to gossip.

I push on through the night, but routine overrides adventure and I park in the lay-by under the wind turbines and sleep across the seats – not under the stars and hidden behind the KTM like I was last time – embracing my body that still accommodates my hardcore habits.

Habitually unhealthy

This pastel dawn is too faint to photograph and too subtle to define. I sit up, turn the key and pull out. No tea, no food, just a need to beat the traffic. Some jobs never leave you. My destination-driven driving habits would incense my friends when I'd take us to a festival – no, we aren't stopping for a wee or tea. But I could get us non-stop through the night from Glastonbury to Essex as they slept off their delirium. It was the same mentality when we rode: pack compact and, when the roads choked, ride down the centre like deadlines. It's not about speed but momentum. Often the same Mondeo-driving sales rep would pass my speed-limited 56mph as I kept on truckin'. My reaction to delays is not to let them slow me down. This morning, with no company to complain, I brush my teeth as I drive and spit the foam out the window.

The van is going great, always has, a little blue LDV Convoy that runs on LPG, bought specifically as a handyman van. I spent a week panelling and shelving my low-mileage bargain buy before I got it sign-written. Then, embarrassed by having my name in writing, I tinted the windows; you can't even pick ya nose in a traffic jam when ya identity is displayed. My name and number have long since been removed, just a ghost shadow of less-faded paint. Although now, this morning, I have a go-faster fluoride streak down the side. I just want to get out of Germany without getting weighed or waylaid. I'm doing the same route in the same time frame as I did on the KTM and, predictably, I stop at the same place for fuel and a fast-food breakfast, world-renowned for its free Wi-Fi and clean toilets.

The coffee is strong and I have a low tolerance to caffeine so I'm buzzing down the autobahn to a well-crafted playlist with German connotations. My thoughts replay over yesterday's coffee chatter about the dynamics of Motocamp. Gossip is a product of group occupancy, although, in the seven years spent at my last location, I was oblivious to it all. I lived in my house but not the village, everything else I did elsewhere. Now I'm part of an immigrant community, there is an 'us and them' mentality with the natives, not in a nasty way but an inevitable one. Bulgarian interaction and integration will take time, the instant expat inclusion, although endearing, comes with preconceived persecutions of certain people based on village history. I think I'll start my meter at the day I moved in, experience and assess before accepting someone else's accusations and judgements. This is something I will have to learn, along with the language, and keeping on the side of acceptance is going to be a tightrope. Thoughts are secure. When voiced they become vulnerable, shared they become distorted, retold they are dramatised. Proportion is lost in repetition and translation.

This train of thought takes me into the Czech Republic and a welcome break from motorway monotony and subject matter. It's mentally healthier to travel around the hills and villages. Old men on bicycles pass established stone structures – both have time-bestowed character. The skyline is defined by Orthodox churches. There is no peace for the residents until the bypass is complete. I'm sure it's welcomed by most, with the exception of fuel stations and snack shops – this is another village with conflicting desires, no doubt. Weaving through a living community, stimulation coming through the windscreen, it provokes thoughts. An unwavering autobahn just replays them. The unfinished motorway was a slip road into a permanent population, that bridged the gap before being thrust back to the isolation of direct and efficient transit.

I yawn my way round Prague and then doze across the seats. There are a lot of pretty girls hitching as I leave the service station. I'm slow to make a decision as I accelerate, and at the end of the slip road there is no choice left. It would have been good to have a chat, but then the traffic comes to a standstill and I'm grateful for the privacy. Those are the pros and cons of a passenger. I contemplate that doze, if without it I'd be ahead of whatever has stopped the flow. I bought a vignette for this, the corrugated road surface and suspended progress. The rush hour I feared would slow me passes while I'm stuck in three lanes between two cities.

My tummy rumbles louder than the sound of the wheels. It's so easy to eat unhealthily on the road – dinner is KFC in the cab. This is the reason the majority of truckers are in a bad shape, it's usually round.

Slovakia and another sticker for the windscreen. It's valid for ten days and I'm using it for an hour. The light fades and Bratislava Castle is lit up against the dusk sky. Magically majestic from a distance, if it's better up close I'll never know.

I'm past the point of no return now – in distance only, that was never an option in mindset. The cab smells of fried chicken and stale me, it's more noticeable when I get back in with my Hungarian vignette receipt. I could drive on but I've no need, so I pull the duvet out the back of the van and hang a towel in the window. This isn't a European tour, it's just a motorway vein to my heart's desire.

Bring it on home

Friday 21ˢᵗ August

Listening to my body: at 3 a.m. it says wait; at 4 a.m. it says go. I'm in a motorway lay-by dwarfed by artics and less conspicuous because of it. I'll be the other side of Budapest before the commuters are awake. Under the mood-lit canopy of a fuel station, a couple of lads are laughing their way through the night shift.

'Where you go?'

'Bulgaria, new house, new life.'

'New wife?'

I point to the back of the van. 'No. Moto. Better than wife.'

We all laugh. They say my van looks good, and under this artificial light I have to admit it does. Bright sunlight is rarely a friend to the aged and world worn.

Ring road and red sky, Budapest from a dawn distance – I can't capture it through the screen but that doesn't stop me trying. I even leave the motorway for a view from a bridge and a photo of the van in the foreground.

I stop for coffee and Wi-Fi to put the photo on Facebook. It may lack composure but it's clearly captured the mood, or my caption has. My mindful friends seem to get it. I feel like I'm sharing the driving, I've got 200 viewers in the back seat.

I'm very proud of my little van. I maybe pushing my own limitations, but the van is coping well and trundles on, unperturbed by all that passes, and gratified at all we've passed through. I'm on exactly the same time schedule as I was on the KTM last month. If it wasn't for the hold-up in the Czech Republic I'd be ahead. I'm getting hungry and the golden arches don't appeal. Leaving the Schengen zone, there is a token check at the Romania border. I open the back doors, they don't even want to see documents for the KLR.

I need to deal with my hunger. Clouds gather and the rain starts, just like last time. However, now the only delay is the wipers as they take Western European wildlife off the windscreen. The motorway ends, it's single carriageway from here to home, but I still can't make myself stop for food. My tummy is cramping now. There are no supermarkets and I've no local currency. There is no one whinging to stop, except my gnawing stomach. I'm not listening to my body now but I can't ignore it either. I see a popular diner and pull in, so popular there is nowhere to park or even turn around, and with rain-stained mirrors I have to reverse onto the main road.

I see the place I stopped at last time; this journey is the KTM tracks revisited. The same omelette, bread and Wi-Fi, and the same satisfaction and renewed energy. Not the same thrill of the hills and hairpins this time though, but the van pulls without creating a tail of infuriation behind it.

The heater is never quite off. There is always a waft of warm air blowing over my feet. It's never fully on either, it can't create a warmth that thaws the freeze outside. With the rain, the temperature is comfortable and that increases endurance levels for both me and the van. Down to the Danube and now I can calculate my ETA – I just don't believe it, surely I'll be there sooner than that. But the trucks are slow, speed limits low and villages frequent. Overtaking possibilities are few with a right-hand drive vehicle.

One more crossing of river and border and I'm back in Bulgaria. One more fuel stop and I'm given a can of coke. It's like a welcome home present. I must be radiating something other than unwashed to generate such generosity. The last thing to contemplate is Kaufland and I can't face it. I've got bread bought in Hungary and tortilla chips at home, my body can cope with that low-grade, high-carb fuel for one more day. The home straight is a procession caused by one crawling, archaic vehicle which even the obsessive and possessed Bulgarians can't get past. It's not delayed gratification – after forty-eight hours behind the wheel and with my village in sight, this is pure irritation.

The van reluctantly reverses up the driveway – well done, Little Blue. Welcome to the new house that your contents will turn into a home.

The KTM is still in the shed, the grass is not too long and the water is off again. I really need a shower: well-water will have to suffice. It's so much cooler than when I left. From instinct I wander to Motocamp. It's busy tonight, all sheltering from the rain and waiting for pizza to be delivered. It's a varied crowd and I chat to a Romanian father and daughter. If this journey they're on is to form a bond, this dampness and a dying bike may dissolve the adhesion.

I ride the last of my sleep-deprivation high with beer and road tales. It's a chilly walk home, where did the summer heat go? The only thing I unload is the duvet. I'm able to fully stretch out, the length of my sleep, and the length of the bed.

Rainy day display

I just got that duvet here in time. I left in 30°C heat and now the temperature is in the teens, rainy and English. Food is scarce. I microwave some beans and pour them onto a slab of stale Hungarian bread. Just like the loading, emptying the contents of the van is done in the rain. There is no motivation in this weather and the radio fails to rock me, yet even without the desired beat I still manage to revel at just being back home.

Overwhelmed by all there is to do, and by a hallway half-full of capable tools, it only really reveals how much more I need to bring over. It's all too much, I think I need a little doze. I may be present but I'm not over the journey yet. The nap doesn't last long – Motocamp calls, am I going to Kaufland? The Romanian father has a dead bike and a vegan daughter to deal with. Can they come with me to buy some soy milk and tofu? Yes, of course, it's just what I need to nudge me out of this inactivity.

This is the first time I'm taking four wheels to the supermarket. There are no restrictions but I can't think ahead and the trolley gets a token filling, meat for my needs and the vegan finds something sustainable for hers. At the checkout I use my Asda bags for life, to pack my bloody essentials in, to save the planet a little longer.

The father sits in the 'oh-my-god seat'. So-called because, since this is a right-hand drive vehicle being driven on the right side of the road, he has to make the judgement call as to whether it's clear to overtake. And assertive passing acceleration is not really a characteristic my van has.

I tell him I'll take a look at his bike later. I return with older clothes, newer tools and a woolly hat against this damp day. His undercover bike has dried out like rehab and starts again like temptation. I'd hoped as much.

The rain continues and all it's good for is to see if the shed leaks. Its tile roof seems impenetrable despite looking too heavy for its pine pole supports. The dirt floor has a dampness. I'm not sure if it's blowing in or rising. It doesn't appear to be dripping down. Once I build the walls I'll know for sure.

One of my reoccurring queries as I drove here was if the van will fit in the garage. Now it's unloaded, I slowly reverse it. It's looking promising, and then the sound of scraping echoes into the cab. Either the floor is too high or the ceiling too low. The van is gently wedged. So I know the answer to that question now: some of it fits.

This year Motocamp have allocated a corner of the restaurant as a shop and I've bought a shelving unit from the UK to display my books and those of other authors I stock too. I spend the afternoon making an alluring display and drinking equally irresistible red wine.

Stickers, flyers, postcards and key rings all help to enhance the exhibition, and bright price tags leave the browser in no doubt that this is a shop not a library. Polly loves it, and is motivated to display the jewellery she makes too. It's a wet cold night, I get my first insight of what life must be like here off-season. But, while it's quiet, that's when people look for alternative entertainment, like books. Well, that's my optimistic theory anyway.

Rock out of the garage

Sunday 23ʳᵈ August

A Sunday morning is just what I need to adjust back into the house and a less urgent lifestyle. I suppose it feels a bit like retirement, I've only got good jobs to do. I'm still unsure if my income will bear any resemblance at all to my expenses, as there hasn't been a normal week yet. In fact, the only normality seems to be the constant variety. I put on Team Rock and make a sausage-and-egg sandwich, because Sundays are meant for self-indulgence regardless of employment status.

The rain is still coming down so I go into the attic to look for leaks. The dirt floor seems dry. There is still a lot of debris up here. Old bottles and bee-keeping equipment, a spinning wheel and a large pile of bricks too. It seems like a strange place to store them. Every new project provokes the same reaction, it just makes me tired, so I have a little doze. I tell myself it's the drive back here that took it out of me and that's justification enough.

It's time to give the DeWalt drill its first job. I have an overhead cupboard in the kitchen and the door won't stay up. I bought a new gas strut over from the UK, it's an easy job with satisfying results. Now I've got an accessible cupboard it leads to unpacking some boxes. I really need a shed and shelving, I'm constantly moving boxes and it only reveals all the things I didn't bring. There is also a lot of unnecessary stuff in the boxes marked 'Kitchen'. I had a friend help pack everything up. While I was doing a run to the dump, he was diligently boxing and labelling the contents of the kitchen cupboards. I've got flasks and egg cups which I really don't need, yet although they are not practical they come with a sense of history and significance. These are things I hoarded and now they are here, establishing an essence of belonging. It incites the need for another little doze.

I borrow a spade from my neighbour as I want to dig out the garage floor. It's only gravel and I think removing it will give me the clearance I need to get the van in. It instantly turns into a very big job. Beneath the gravel are boulders, deeply embedded into the ground. Digging them out leaves cavernous craters, which at least I'm able to put the dug-out gravel into. I roll the rocks outside and every extraction unearths an increase in workload. This is going to be a mammoth excavation exercise. Well, I've got to start somewhere, and I want to do just one job at a time. This will either be a garage for the van or a secure shed – either way, it's needed.

However, this being the village it is, there is a party to attend and as soon as the sun has made an appearance, I feel I should too. Peach has moved into his house, and this afternoon is the barbecue house-warming party. It's well underway by the time I arrive: same faces, different house to warm. I wonder if this happened when Milton Keynes was built, a new inhabitant and welcome party every week. It's a very chilled gathering, but then this is a village of experienced socialisers. There always seems to be something to celebrate, even a day's sobriety is worthy of a drink. I manage to stay off the rakia so I have recall, but there's little worth recounting. I'm seeing a pattern in people's drinking habits and behaviour. I think I'll just say goodnight, I could probably use some structure in my life besides a shed.

Most stones left unturned

It's a new week. I need a plan, a list, today marks the start of production. I've got a month before I have to go back to the UK and I don't want it to disappear in a haze of alcohol and hangovers. It's time for home improvements, I've got the tools, time, transport and ability. Now I just need to find the ability to implement some self-discipline between the interruptions. There is the sailing trip in Greece and my mum's visit, but I'm sure I can get something done in-between.

There is a noticeable change in the temperature since I've got back, the sun no longer radiates its brutal inescapable heat. At some point, it will offer no heat at all, and that's when I'll do my homework inside.

For now, though, it's a perfect morning, and I ride the KLR lidless to Motocamp to pay my bar bill. It's 9 a.m., a perfectly acceptable time to call on a Monday morning, or so I thought. However, they seem to work to a different time frame. They certainly sleep to one, and aren't awake – until they hear my exhaust, that is. Sorry, my conscientiousness brings premature consciousness.

I'm keen to keep digging the garage floor out. I need to bring it down eight inches to allow enough space for a concrete base. Although, it occurs to me, the rocks I'm digging out will make a beautiful stone floor and reduce the amount of sand and cement needed. What a pleasurable task, all the more so as it's my job. I don't have a customer taking away logical progression, with their personal impractical desires. Just me, my plans, inspiration and pragmatism.

When I worked in the US doing remodelling, I fell in with an interior design company. I was their handyman and would go to an uber-posh house to hang a toilet-paper holder in their granite Romanesque palatial bathroom.

It was profitable work and insightful to see how, when money is no object, the prosperous develop other issues. The neurosis was generally health related, but a few of my clients had some quite unique quirks. My fee would reflect the difficulties of working in the environments they created, rather than how many drill bits I blunted trying to make a hole in half-inch-thick granite. My boss was a very softly spoken, effeminate man who, with waving hand gestures and restrained shrieks of exuberance, would simultaneously calm the client while gently nurturing them round to his visualisation. I occasionally worked at his house too, it was predictably neat, ordered and manicured, and everything was considered and created in his image of perfection. He bought these qualities to his clientele and I always felt he was modelling Denver to his own personal tastes. Hanging pictures was a precision job, and he would stand back telling me, 'No, down a smidge, to the right, no, too much, back a bit … oh yes, that looks positively resplendent …' And so it went on. I could never see it, I don't think such skills can be learned. I certainly didn't have the capacity, it was the creative equivalent to mechanical sympathy, either you have it or you don't, and when I stood back I could see he was absolutely right. A vision of precision.

That's not what is happening in the garage. I'm making it up as I go, but with an abundance of the precious stones that I'm excavating, the job still has stimulating qualities. I'm unearthing the kind of treasure that I would never find digging in an Essex garden. Rocks and stones like this would be expensive and imported. Here they are just a product of the geological environment, and they are going to make a solid floor. Best of all, no one is going to tell me different. My job, my vision, my design from start to completion. Plus, being a garage floor, I can hone my stone-laying skills before I start setting them in more prominent places.

I get a call from Motocamp – they are going into town, do I want to come? Not really. I want to get on with what I'm doing, but I do need their assistance with some things and, anyway, I have the rest of my life to do this. I love that they just drive round to pick me up, it's done with a freedom that my UK life lacked. Everyone had obligations, underlying chores to perform. No one just turned up with time to spend, they were always trying to save it, but never for anything enjoyable, only to rush through another day. As we drive to town, Greece is the word and we discuss the sailing holiday. Ideally, we all want to ride there, but unfortunately practicality wins over desire. We have a lot of stuff to take from Bulgaria to avoid paying Greek euro prices. Also, leaving our bikes unattended for five days on a quayside is not going to be conducive to relaxation. So we'll take the Motocamp car as it's cheaper to run than my van. It's all new to me, whatever transport we take, I really have no preferences.

They take me to meet their insurance agent so I can get my bikes and house covered, but I don't have my photo identification yet so it can't be done. The price is right, but it remains to be seen if the cover is adequate. Inevitably, we end up in Kaufland, which is way more exciting than buying insurance. I buy a new hose. This is a momentous moment – the hose I used for my fish pond had more holes than a water filter, but living in a state of limbo for so long I wouldn't replace it. New house, new hose (as opposed to 'new life, new wife', as the Hungarian fuel attendants suggested).

We decide to stop for lunch. This is the freedom again, no kids dictating or parental obligations. It's just free time to spontaneously and enthusiastically enhance life's essential needs: food intake performed in a more pleasurable manner. To continue the theme, when they drop me back at mine, I have a little doze.

Back in the garage I have to pace myself. Much as I want to see the job complete, tearing into it will have me burned out. It's been a while since I did such physical pursuits on a daily basis and that stamina has to be built back up again.

When I would return from a motorcycle journey back into my labour-intensive working life, it would take about six weeks before my aching body once again became used to the physically uncomfortable pursuits my living demanded of it. Back then, I at least had a bath I could rest and rejuvenate in. Here I can only stand in the shower, and that won't wash away the pains and strains of deep digging and rock moving.

I may still be able to do a marathon drive, but I don't want the garage at the end to break me. Based on that, I use my new hose to dampen the ground to ease tomorrow's excavations.

Deep down

It's time to reciprocate: this morning Bruce has a bus to catch. Being the responsible, conscientious and punctual person that I am, I get to his in the van at the arranged time. Being forever the opportunist, my actions aren't purely motivated by friendship and reliability; I also want to borrow his strimmer while he's away.

We leave the village like it's backstage, into a dry-ice mist creeping down the hillside and floating just above the lake. The sun is shooting beams that cast shadows from the pines that line the shore. There is an unspoken need for a pause, to honour this immaculate combination of elements, light, mist, trees and water. Occasionally, with the right awareness, a sight so magnificent appears that it demands the reprioritisation of the day. The lake is the first impression anyone will have upon entering the village, not that I recall it having a striking impact upon my first arrival. However, it's a sight that gauges the seasons' temperature and rainfall, as well as representing the beginning or end to any journey. I see its subtle differences, and this morning it's got qualities that stop us in our tracks. However, it's unlikely to stop the bus, so I drive up the hill out of the obscuring clouds and into the light.

Living in Colchester, the thing that used to stop the van just a few minutes from home was traffic lights. Here it's terrific light. I don't recall a red traffic light ever generating such feelings of gratitude, unless the police car following me got caught by it.

My elbow aches this morning, it's not something I can put my finger on. I think I jarred it thrusting the spade into the ground, only to hit a rock. Back in the garage the little triangle of stone protruding out of the ground is revealing its iceberg characteristics. At a 45-degree angle, it has unknown depths.

With increasing despondency, every shovel full of dirt fails to discover its limitations. It's displaying JCB needs, or at least implements of mass reduction.

Dancho the Spanish speaking gypsy is working next door and comes over to smoke and surmise. He brings a large crowbar which is much appreciated but still inadequate – this boulder has wisdom-tooth roots. I can usually tell from the sound of the spade how much further I need to dig, but even with leverage I can't force a hint of movement. I'm beginning to wish I never started this job, it's undermining my independence. I find myself thinking of winches, kangoes and, more worryingly, the integral structure of the entire garage. The rock continues to grow the further down I dig, it's already the size of a dining table and a foot thick too. While I'm measuring, I realise the garage is not square, its depth decreases by a foot from left wall to right. This is a crucial foot as it's the difference between getting the van all the way in and having securing doors. I'm knackered, my elbow hurts and the job is beating my body and ability.

Another thing that could beat my body up is the stairs. The meticulously tiled half-spiral steps have no handrail. My night-time needs, stepping bleary eyed into the darkness or blinded by the light, can create a tricky manoeuvre. One slip and down I'd go, especially if I've happened to have had a little nightcap, which has been the case on the odd occasion. I noticed that in Lidl – yes, Lidl, sometimes I do cheat on Kaufland – they had some ideal brushed stainless-steel handrails. So I take the van to town. They have two left. Brilliant, I need three.

Having left the tape measure in the garage, it's not until I get back that I can see if the handrails fit. They do, perfectly. They also tie on the KTM from the crash bar to the pannier rack, not as an engine guard but for transportation. So I ride it to Gabrovo to see if the Lidl there has a railing. It doesn't, but the town does have another Lidl.

None there either. I'm on a mission now, so I take the road to Veliko Tarnovo. It's a new road for me, along the edge of a canyon, through a tunnel carved into the cliff face, which puts my little excavation into perspective. Then miles of sweeping bends, a smooth surface and of course no other traffic. Oh yes, I'll definitely be riding this road again. I find Lidl, but they only have wooden rails, and that will just look weird. However, this town too has two Lidls to choose from and, as I enter my fifth Lidl today, I see a stainless-steel handrail.

'Why is it always the last place you look?' I once exclaimed, stoned and victorious, and then added with the lucidity only an altered state can attain, 'because once you find it, you don't look anymore.' So based on that, I go to Kaufland and, what do you know, the handrail was in the second-from-last place I looked. I strap it on the side of the KTM and ride home trying to think of a link between the handling of the bike and the attached handrail, but nothing comes. Every time I pull in the clutch my elbow aches, what's bloody wrong with it? I try a white-wine-and-ibuprofen cure-all cocktail and sit outside to watch the sunset. Tabby Cat comes by for a little stroke, and the evening lacks for nothing.

Low side low point

An email from Mum tells me the tickets for the Mötley Crüe concert in Italy have arrived. She will bring them over next month.

A nearer but less accessible rock is on my mind and I go back to the garage to try and unearth the project-halting protrusion. I dig out smaller rocks, the hole gets deeper and still there is no end in sight. The water may have softened the ground but it increased the level of humidity, and I'm sweating like a bad liar. Peach turns up to have a look, this is becoming a sight to see. It reminds me of the large cylindrical spacecraft that the Martians from *War of the Worlds* arrived in. Embedded into the soil, it's attracting a gathering of intrigue and wonder. Peach is the third person to have a close encounter with my predicament. However, as opposed to invading the Earth, he assures me he has a method to excavate the rock from it.

Next, Ivo comes around with an electrician and I get a new electricity meter, which fails to generate any excitement in me at all – I'm not sure what my reaction should be – so I go back to the rock.

After lunch, I can't face the garage again. I think I'll fit the handrails around the stairs. I'm going to need some Rawlplugs, it's a ridiculously hard decision as to which town to get them from. Veliko Tarnovo is further away, but I can browse in the DIY shop and choose directly from the display. I consider the difficulties of trying to mime a Rawlplug in a smaller local shop – that's the clincher, I'll ride to VT. I need to get some shoes too; my good trainers are getting wrecked with this ground work.

As I approach the city, the pretty pedestrians start to appear and my Akrapovič exhausts do what they do best: heads turn to see the source of the pulsating rumble. Entering the roundabout, a couple of attractive girls look my way and I'm just considering waving when, halfway round, the bike slides out from under me. I'm dumped on the road, although I'm back up like a bounce. However, the bike is still sliding, and it's like running after a skateboard. It won't bloody stop, sliding on the engine bars and pannier rack, sparking and gliding along with no apparent friction to stop it. I feel like a cowboy running after his bolted horse. It's humiliating. By the time I catch it up, some assistance has come out of the nearby car dealership to help me lift it up and off the road. They were so quick to arrive on the scene. I assess the damage to both me and it. It's minimal – other than the crash bars and pannier rack, the road only made contact with the top box, hand guard and the pillion peg, which has ground away. I couldn't hope for a better result. If I were made to choose which way I was to part company with my bike on the road, I suppose a low slide like this would be quite preferable. As with most accidents, they generally occur in slow motion and, feeling the bike slide from under me, I knew it was going to hurt my wallet more than my body.

I had a similar experience in Guatemala riding down to Lake Atitlán fully loaded and fully clothed. The moped riders were out in force with their pretty pillions sitting side-saddle, their summer dresses blowing in the breeze. I was overdressed for both comfort and coolness. As I gently rounded a corner, the tyres lost their grip and the bike started to slide. *It's OK*, I thought to myself as the angle of the bike dropped to below correction, *it's gonna be a low side, it's gonna be a low side, it's gonna be a low…* Then as the bike and I were both about to make contact with the road, the tyres found traction, and the bike stood up: … *oh shittttt, it's a high side*, I thought as I was flicked up and over the bike and into the air to land ungracefully on all fours. *You little bastard*. The armour in my riding trousers and the protection of my gloves saved my skin and bones;

the bike's landing was more brutal. One of those petite pillions would not have come off so unscathed.

The reaction I have to this little fall is the same as observing someone trip on a kerb and fall – they are really too embarrassed to take a moment to access their ripped clothing and broken skin, getting up far quicker than they would if they had fallen on a stair at home. I, though, am grazed and ripped and the trainers I was about to replace have torn. I'm invited into the car showroom for a seat and a glass of water. I'm shaking a bit, but it's only unspent adrenalin. I can't sit here, I'm anxious to check the bike over more thoroughly and, anyway, what the hell just happened? So, thanking them, I go back outside and look at the road surface to photograph it. The roundabout has an adverse camber and the surface is shiny. It's hard to tell which skid marks are mine. Now I look, the surface is covered with them, there must be a lot of lost traction here. I bet sliding out of your exit is a regular occurrence. No wonder the assistance came so quickly. I take photos of the indentations the incident left on the road, the damage to my bike and the abrasion on the tyres, which I'm supposed to be reviewing.

An incident like that can change your priorities. Well, I certainly don't need to replace my trainers now. I get my Rawlplugs and gingerly ride the big orange bastard back home and inevitably the fall replays through my head. If I still had the handrail strapped on the bike that may have saved it.

The garage is a mess of mud and rocks. I don't have the confidence now to ride the bike up the bank into the bee shed, so I leave it outside. It had been redeeming itself after breaking down on me, but now it's dumped me off I'm wondering if I can ever truly love or trust it again. Now calmer, I look over the bike once more. I check the tyre pressures, they are fine, and there is no damage that will significantly devalue it, but it's still gone down in my estimation.

The mirror reflects a few bloody grazes but nothing worth crying over. The damage to my trainers is the biggest annoyance. The 'all the gear all the time' brigade will shoot me down with this told-you-so ammunition. I'm going to be stiff in the morning – ahem – so now would be a good time to put the handrails on the wall. I open the packaging and there in the box with the mounting bracket are bloody Rawlplugs. For fuck's sake, I went to town solely to get Rawlplugs and some inexpensive footwear and have come back to find I had fasteners the whole time and my good trainers have just been relegated to work shoes. I'm not in the fucking mood now for anything. I put on some music and the bloody iPod dock isn't working, no sound at all. I don't think I'll attempt anything else today. Sometimes you have to know when to just give up.

The feel of stainless steel

Thursday 27ᵗʰ August

There's a completely different perspective to my days now there is work to be done. i've got purpose. I once saw an interview with Sting and he was asked why he still made music and toured; he didn't need the money. He simply said, 'Your work defines you.' It's true, and if you are lucky enough to enjoy your tasks, paid or unpaid, what better way is there to spend your time on the planet? I wouldn't want to spend the rest of my days unearthing rocks, and hopefully I won't be. That's assuming I will eventually extract the Stonehenge-size megalith and create the garage floor I envisage. Once complete, I suppose that stone floor will define me. I'm not exactly sure what it will say, but I'm anticipating a huge amount of satisfaction from the achievement. For now though, I can't even get the honey out of the squeezable container – with the cooler mornings, it's got thicker and my bloody aching elbow shoots pain when my honey isn't runny. It's not a good omen for the task ahead, but I'm not giving up on the day this early. I fiddle with the iPod dock connections, and now I have heavy rock inside the house as well as the garage.

I mark out the positions for the hand rails. I'm going to need a 12mm drill. I only have to write 'I' and my phone, based on my previous messages, predicts the following text correctly: 'was wondering if I could please borrow…' Hmmm, it would seem I've become a needy neighbour.

Despite the walls being two-foot thick, they crumble like a corrupt empire. The drill bit shoots off at an angle. I've whisked eggs with more accuracy. I have to hammer in slithers of wood to fill the elongated hole, the irony being that now I don't even need a bloody Rawlplug. On the plus side, my eccentric drilling means the lining up of wall bracket to handrail is only a matter of rotation.

Clearly, the walls were not built of the same stone that's embedded in the garage floor. More neighbours come to view my mining operation. It's become quite a social event, although only in a spectator capacity. Maybe I should have a 'bring a pick' party.

I pop another ibuprofen and have a shower. That will do for today. It's time to turn my attention to some other things that won't budge. Santander have, for my 'convenience', reinsured the house I sold two months ago and won't give me the money back. My publishers have totally miscalculated my royalty payment. A crowdfunding project I thankfully didn't get too involved in is going to fail as the instigators have made no effort to promote it at all. I bloody hate dealing with issues in England. Give me a steadfast rock any day.

Dinner is a disaster too. The fish is soggy so I just have vegetables and throw the rest in the dustbin as I walk to Motocamp. I tell of my low side fall yesterday. Apparently, it's a notorious roundabout. Why am I only hearing this now? Is there anything else I should know? Does the tap water cause kidney stones? Is the log burner prone to exploding? Is the bee shed structurally unstable? Should I take a weapon if I'm going to walk the streets at night?

Peach will come over tomorrow. He's optimistic that together we will get the rock out, he has some excavation implements. The evenings are much cooler now. I feel a shiver as I walk back but it's not from the threat of being mugged. However, there are predators at the dustbin: Tabby Cat and her kittens have caught the smell of fish wafting out of it. Probably the job of retrieving it from the bin defined her motherly commitments, and the meal was all the more satisfying for it.

It's a long way to the top when you want to roll a rock

Friday 28th August

In the night, it occurs to me that I could mount a vertical handrail in the centre of the staircase. As soon as it's light I check the size and fastening points and see it would work perfectly, even eliminating the need for the other three. Still, I'll buy a fourth, if that last one remains available.

Peach is dead on time and in the back of his van are scaffold poles, crowbars and even rollers. He's clearly got a plan. When I fitted bathrooms, I could usually remove the old suite in a morning. The speed would impress the customer before the pace slowed for the precision installation. Likewise, with vigour and determination, Peach tears into the job and soon there is the trace of movement. My stair rails have more play in them but it's an encouraging start, he's broken the seal. I feel like Uma Thurman trying to get her big toe to move in *Kill Bill* – wiggle, ya big rock. The hard part is far from over, it's going to be a pig of a job.

I bring the sledgehammer down onto another big rock I've unearthed. It fractures into slate-smooth fragments. They are manageable and will make ideal flooring when re-laid. With that gone, we have more access and leverage points; we manage to pry the rock up enough to get some scaffold poles underneath. Now its true size is revealed, I'd love to know what it weighs. There is probably a formula, but for now we don't want maths, just physical strength. I think some choice blows would have this shattering, but Peach wants to get it out of the garage whole, to prove a point, to show the achievement, to define his work. We are using Neolithic methods here – however, when ancient temples and monuments of stone were built, I'm sure they had more than two blokes pushing fifty trying to move the rocks into position. Now with scaffold rollers underneath,

218

we can lever the stone into an exit position. However, as it moves out of the garage the back end falls into the crater it came out of. We have no choice but to lever it up hill past the point of pivot at the threshold of the garage.

Alternately, we force a crowbar under, push forward, then hold the rock in that position and take the weight while the other person forces their bar under, and then we lever it forward. There are only two scaffold poles and two of us, we can't stop, the rock will slide back and we'll lose all of the distance we've gained. It's excruciating. We are giving it absolutely everything to hold it in place before moving it uphill a few more inches. There is no release until it passes the point of balance and takes the strain off us. We have to persist; we can't rest or relax.

Now pointing uphill, it puts even more force on the levers. Fighting gravity, this rock's only desire is to roll back down to where it came from. I've never experienced such relentless strain; our sole motivation is to not let it slide back, we can't do this again. In retrospect, there were a few other options, but sweating and with convulsing veins straining taut as rail tracks, this is not the time so say, 'Ya know what we should do?' I've never been so committed, every ounce of strength is summoned. One last push and it passes the point and pivots away from us. The relief is orgasmic. They say there is a thin line between pleasure and pain. Like the rock, I just crossed that threshold. I'm panting with euphoric joy, I have a rush of rapture, it's like nothing I've ever experienced before. *The reason is, I'm to find out sixteen months later, that this was the moment I broke my back!*

We are absolutely spent. The rock is totally blocking the entrance to the garage and I haven't the strength to even pick up a crowbar. 'Com'on,' I say. 'I'll buy ya lunch.'

You often hear after a long ride on a hot day the rider exclaim how a beer *never tasted so good*. Well, sitting in the roadside café, I can tell you this – if you could capture that taste, that feeling as the beer flowed down my throat, if you could capture that in a commercial, you could persuade the strictest abstainer to take a sip. It was heavenly, and on an empty stomach it bounced a buzz into my head to accompany my prolonged, belaboured exhilaration. There is only one thing to do in such situations, and that's to have another.

The urgency to get to Lidl, before the last stair rail sells, falls down the priority ladder. What just happened was a near marvel, and I need to acknowledge it. I also need chicken and chips to sustain me through the rest of the day. God, I ache.

Two hours have passed by the time we get back to the operation. Polly and Ivo are waiting for us. With their help, our replenished energy, and with rollers and levers, we move the rock to its resting place. It's a plinth big enough to park a bike on. I pay Peach, have a shower, get in the van and drive to Lidl to buy the last stair rail.

It's 5 p.m. as I leave town on this Friday evening. In the UK it's the start of the three-day August bank holiday. I reflect on all those late starts to my weekends when, as a trucker, I got stuck in the traffic of everybody else's holiday, seething and frustrated in stagnant traffic (due, in the early days, to a jack-knifed caravan or overheated coach, but more recently due to the sheer volume of traffic and inevitable roadworks). The unpaid hours ticked away, crawling back to the depot to park up, and leave the captivity of the cab and prison of the road behind me. But here in this principal city, there is no evidence of the time in the traffic flow, no jams due to lack of people, no roadworks due to lack of money, no bank holiday because it's not bloody England and therefore not raining either. There isn't much I miss about my old life, but man, would I love a bath tonight to soak my overexerted body in. That was always an option in my former existence. What wasn't, though, was to sit on a balcony with a beer, listening to cowbells and crickets, and that's not a bad consolation. I accept it happily.

As I sink into my folding chair like Barbapapa, I really don't have the energy to move from this spot for anything. I briefly contemplate the possibility of weeing over the balcony.

I have a friend in the US, a true homebody, he watches football on the TV but never goes to a game, even when I got complimentary tickets. He lives an hour from world-class ski resorts he's never once visited. He drinks his beer, smokes his pot. He lost his girlfriend and driving licence twenty years ago and never tried to replace either. Over that time, I watched him get bigger and his hair get thinner as he wasted his life away. I still enjoyed his company immensely; we clicked and would have guttural laughs as we talked bollocks into the night. He once accepted an invitation to a package holiday in Mexico. Instantly out of his depth, he spent his days at the all-inclusive swim-up bar that was incorporated into the swimming pool of the holiday complex. He would sit on the submerged stool, drinking the free beer and not leaving the spot *all day*. Those actions display an element of decadence, albeit at the expense of everyone else. I don't mind him pissing away his life as long as it doesn't cloud my dreams. Anyway, weeing over the balcony was a brief consideration I had that passed with a trip down the stairs to test the new handrails out.

Polly invites me over for food but understands I'm just knackered. One of the kittens comes over. She's very apprehensive. I call her Echo as her nervousness bounces off every movement. The rock beside the garage is in its new resting place. I go to mine.

A planet aligns

I didn't have blinds when I lived in the bungalow. I did have a wall of conifers outside the window though, which gave me privacy. I don't want blinds over my windows here either. I bought this house for the view, and I'm going to keep my eye on it day and night. Anyway, I don't like the term they imply, my father was blind in his later years. Why would I want to deny myself starry nights, dawn skies and morning sunlight? The numbers on the clock no longer dictate to me, no one expects me to be at a specific place at a certain time anymore. If I wake at dawn, like I have this morning, I'll get up. I'm free to drill holes too, mounting the vertical stair rail will disturb no one. It disturbs me a little, that this one rail now makes the other three obsolete – as a consolation, though, it does have pole-dancing potential.

I've got a Tanzanian friend, he lives very close to the equator, in a permanent equinox as far as the light-to-night ratio goes. He stayed in a holiday home in Scotland one June. Waking at 3 a.m. and seeing how bright the day was, he began working on some plumbing in the bathroom. His English girlfriend wasn't best pleased at the noise he was making, but he found it incomprehensible that it could be light in the middle of the night. We don't have the long winter nights or the extended summer days that I so loved about the UK; in Bulgaria, the extremes are in temperature. The country's position on the globe is geographically further down, but it still rates high to me.

Back in the garage I have one more big rock to reduce. Much like my non-stop journeys here, my motivation to completion is what drives me. I'll pay in pain when the job is over and there is nothing else to think about. The German dog rescuers come down to visit from Hippy Heights at the other end of the village. I like them a lot, they are different

from the other immigrants. Since one of them is a physiotherapist, I mention the pains in my arm and, after a very
short examination, I'm diagnosed with tennis elbow.

'It veal feel better in about a year.'

'A year?'

'Yar, and it veal not eel if you keep verking on dees rocks.'

Bollocks. I go back to verking on de rock and fill a hole
with rubble and dirt.

I've got four missed calls on my phone. The boat people
are at Motocamp. The couple who have arranged the hire
of the sailing boat are there to meet their motley crew. So
I jump on the KLR in shorts and a T-shirt as there are no
roundabouts between my house and Motocamp, and I ride
down to meet them.

The captain is probably about my age, although his face
hasn't been lived in as much, and his wife seems affable
enough with beer on her breath, although no English comes
from her mouth. However, they have a sixteen-year-old
daughter who is predictably pretty, with deep, dark eyes
you could set sail in, and she speaks excellent English.
Doug is back from his ride down to Tunisia where he was
looking at abandoned Star Wars sets in the desert, and his
English isn't too bad either. That's the crew. No, I don't
have any questions because I don't have a clue, no plan, no
expectations, and I feel no pressure. Everyone seems satisfied with the situation; we shall set sail in a week.

There is so much going on, not just here where the place
is full of guests, visitors and friends, but in general. We
leave on our sailing holiday next week. The rock removal
has only revealed how much more work there is to do to
the garage floor. My delivery of winter logs is due to arrive
shortly, as will my mum – not that she will need splitting
and stacking. And I still can't even remember every letter
in the thirty-character alphabet. I don't see boredom being
a factor in my life anytime soon.

When I get back home, where I left my phone, I have more missed calls. Bruce is back, can I pick him up? So I take the van to town and he tells me of his time in Varna – girls, girls, girls, lots and lots of beautiful girls. He's staying at a room in the house that Peach has bought. He offers me a beer and, without feeling too awkward, we drink and watch as Polly, Ivo and Peach work on bringing his garden under control. Unlike Bruce, my garage floor is not going to be getting laid. I never got a chance to use his strimmer either and, like my lawn, I'm soon half cut.

Apparently, we are all going to a restaurant tonight. It's one thing to have a new social life but the cherry on top is that I don't even have to organise it. I was always the instigator in the UK. I didn't mind, but coming up with a plan wasn't enough. I then had to sell it, encourage, persuade, compromise, listen to the excuses – 'can't afford it', 'can't get a baby sitter', 'I'll have to ask the missus'. In the end I just used to say fuck it, I'll go on my own. And that is why I'm a solo traveller. My travel books, I suppose, hearten the people who couldn't get babysitters and have to appease the missus. Anyway, here in my new life I'm just given an itinerary, and I'll always come along for the ride.

I go home, shower, and rock out to the iPod, shuffling through its library as the sun sets. Then, just as the rising moon catches my eye through the bedroom window, 'Eclipse' plays. Fuck me, I'm loving this life and all that's to come. I would have missed that if I had blinds. So what if the houses the other side of the valley get two moons in their sunset?

I'm picked up, and the moon rises over the lake as we leave the village. If I was driving, I'd have stopped, but life isn't running to my itinerary.

Brits abroad

At dinner last night it was decided we would all go to the car boot sale this morning. So, as the moon fades into a lightening sky, I get in the van to pick up the bargain hunters from Motocamp.

I suppose I'm getting used to this now: the enthusiasm, the spontaneity, the company. It's like starting a new school. In fact, thinking about it, I've spent most of my life being the new kid. We moved around a lot when I was younger. As an only child, I had no choice but to make friends in a new location, with no brother or sister for support or companionship. I didn't like it and, even when I went to college, again I didn't know a single face. Then there were the agency driver years, a new company every week. By comparison, I have eased into this place gently, firstly coming through on a motorbike. Alone on a bike, if you wear the right smile, the curiosity you attract will soon turn to conversation, and that has been the case in every country I've ridden through. So it's been a staggered introduction to this village and its inhabitants. Like starting a new school, I'm here to learn, although here there is a lot more playtime. To keep the analogy: today, I'm the driver of the school bus; the bad kid, Doug, is smoking; the whole bus has to wait for Bruce, who overslept; Polly is the prefect; and the Germans aren't coming as their dogs ate their homework.

As I drive our bus through Veliko Tarnovo, we stop at a petrol station for Doug to get more fags. He's so bad. But in the forecourt is an equally bad girl, with a skimpy dress and high heels. She clearly hasn't been to bed yet, at least not hers. She'll be getting detention, or maybe she's had it already.

The playground is a campsite that hosts a car boot sale on the last Sunday of the month. Most of the pupils are Brits, and there's the token Bulgarian-speaking teacher.

I really don't like this environment. The best thing about it is a bacon-and-egg butty from the tuck shop, and a curry to take away from a show-and-sell stall. There is a swimming pool here too, but I didn't bring my kit.

We don't stay long and I decide to take us on a field trip to the DIY store. No one but me needs anything, but everyone buys something. Then at Polly's request we go to a massive cash and carry. I don't need anything else but manage to come out with a bulging carrier bag, inside are some deck shoes and a strap to hold on my sunglasses, as suggested by my crew mates.

Back home, having dropped everyone off, it's time to squeeze the van into the garage. This is not a euphemism. I line it up and gently reverse in into the now deeper but dirtier subterranean shelter. This is very exciting. Slowly, I edge back, stopping to open the van door and stick my head out to check roof clearance. So far so good. I get to the point where I have to pull in the mirrors and back in blind. There is no scraping sound, and then the rear step of the van makes contact with the back wall. I can open the door just enough to get out and go into the sunlight. It's in … mostly. The front of the van protrudes by about five inches. I suppose the doors could mount on the front garage wall as opposed to inside the door frame. Still, for the first time in the five years I've owned it, the van is under cover.

With renewed enthusiasm I move more rocks and soil. The project has found a new level of motivation. While I'm putting vehicles under cover, I ride the KTM back up to the bee shed. The sun is beating it up and the handgrips have gone all sticky, as have I.

I'm beginning to realise that just having a shower is not enough to cool me down. I have to stay in and increase the cold-water flow as much as I can stand for my core to cool. Simply soaping myself quickly is like taking condensation off a bathroom window with a squeegee – it's soon replaced with another layer of moisture, and then I'm sweating again before I've got dressed. *Dharrling, I'm positively radiating,* but not in a good way.

Not that it makes much difference this afternoon. I join the others in the baking clubhouse of Motocamp to watch the British MotoGP. It's absolutely pissing down there and I'm just damp with sweat. One more notch in the 'I love Bulgaria' post, despite the commentary being in a monotonous Bulgarian voice as dull as the British weather.

The race is over and I have to run. I've got dinner at my neighbour's – roast lamb, which is lovely but unsuitable for this 30°C day. It would taste better with rain running down the windows. Still, the wine flows relentlessly and that keeps us cool. Denis is back, he'd taken his van to pick up some books and other possessions from a hovel he owns in France. Keith turns up too making nine of us. It's quite an ex-patty evening, it's fine but very *Brits abroad*, in company and conversation. It's an easy rut to fall into when the day has consisted of a car boot sale, bacon sandwich, trip to the DIY centre, British MotoGP and a Sunday roast, all mostly in the company of immigrants. I'm not integrating, and I've certainly not burned off my food and alcohol intake with the little work I did in the garage. However, it is a bank holiday in the UK, so school's out.

KAT conversion

I hope my mornings this week start with a clearer head than I have right now. I'm fine, but I could be better. Today the immigrants will integrate – well, three of us will. My neighbour will attempt to help Keith through the Bulgarian vehicle registration process, and I'm going to tag along to learn how the process works. After all, it is a school day.

I don't have time for breakfast, Keith is already outside in his van. The first thing we have to do is look up what his van's kilowatt output is. I've never heard of such a thing, it's not an electric heater. But it's a recognised vehicle measurement apparently, and is the scale on which the eco-tax is worked out, a tax every vehicle being registered for the first time has to pay.

We all head to Gabrovo, our principal town and home to the offices of KAT, which stands for Komplete And Total (jobsworths) – although the official abbreviation is actually Kontrol for Automobile Transport. No longer being under communist rule, we are free to call them what we choose. However, it soon appears that this place is a museum for communist practice. Paying the eco-tax is relatively straightforward, and the receipt is our entry ticket into the aptly named complex.

The place has a very Soviet feel: time stands still, much like the long queues in the disheartening corridors of chipped paint and hopeless endings. Strutting, uniformed officials with the stale air of authority break the heaving silence. A weak smile from the faint-hearted is reflected rather than returned as their turn comes to approach the window of displeasure. Toughened glass, thick glasses, hard face, harsh voice. A meek pleasantry falls into the depressions of the nail-gouged counter.

'Документи,' demands the woman with a face as hard as comprehension. She wants to see the vehicle documents and has the power to make your day or take it away. Log-book, insurance, passport, Bulgarian identity card and eco-tax receipt are respectfully pushed under the glass. A form is thrust back, it's in Cyrillic but it's acceptable to fill it out in English. Completed, examined, stapled and stamped, we are now eligible to queue for the vehicle inspection.

Another deteriorating building, it wasn't constructed with splendour, so it couldn't be reformed to it, but still there isn't a hint of an attempt to delay its decay. Abandoned and wrecked cars surround the perimeter fence, it's a place of termination. There is no logical system to queuing, drivers push their vehicles forward like taxis ranking for pole position. When the greasy finger of authority is pointed, we flip the bonnet and the VIN is meticulously scrutinised, the tyres are kicked, the brakes checked with unexpected diligence and, if it's a right-hand-drive vehicle, you'd better have headlights that dip to the right. If they do, the paperwork is stamped and you are authorised to stand in a different queue. They are a bit softer here, not exactly friendly but, having made it to the fourth level, the scorn is lighter. There is Cyrillic writing on the wall in an abrupt font and fading paint. I sound out the letters as we shuffle forward – it's ironic that the Cyrillic alphabet doesn't have a 'Q'. At a cleaner window of thinner glass, payment is requested. Inconveniently, they only take a bank transfer, not cash; conveniently, there is a bank in the building precisely for this purpose.

Behind that door is bright light, beauty and a smile, because the cashier is not a KAT employee, she is pert and part of a franchise. The price is paid and, with the hint of possibility and scent of encouragement, a receipt issued. Then we return to the brutality of regulation and the end of the queue we'd previously been at the front of. This time, when we get back to the front, we're given our

Bulgarian plates. This is not the end; in fact, the rest will continue after the ninety-minute lunch sabbatical.

I'm bloody starving and can see that I'm going to get nothing else done today. The KAT is so far out of town, I can't even walk to the electricity company to register my new meter.

We find a café that doesn't serve food. I'm happy to get bread from a corner shop but, with persistence, I end up with cold sausages and potatoes in oil. We aren't in the KAT complex; this is free enterprise, and it's shite. The conversation is equally negative, I hear lots and manage to say little. I'll assess later. It's mainly directed at Motocamp, and at this point I'll keep the comments to myself. It's also implied that Bulgarians have no compassion, which is somewhat paradoxical after the bitterness I've been hearing. They may be hard-faced bureaucrats in the KAT office, but I bet if you collapsed in a queue, you'd see some compassion. You might lose your place but not your life, someone would check for a pulse and, if you didn't have one, you'd probably be given a job there.

Back to the process, and the KAT man replaces the UK plates with the Bulgarian ones, fastened with a tamper-proof seal, drilled and screwed into your precious vehicle. The floor is a layer of swarf and extracted rivets, the DNA of a hundred-thousand cars. That only leaves one more queue, to hand in the UK plates and receive the laminated Bulgarian vehicle ownership document, simple.

Well, that's a day I'll never get back, but I do know the sequence now and it's something I could never have worked out on my own. So as the day isn't entirely wasted, we swing by the immigration office and pick up my Bulgarian photo identification card. I look good too, well chuffed.

The garage floor didn't need to get laid today; there was, instead, an opportunity to learn a process that I will soon have to go through myself. However, I feel frustration because nothing is happening quickly enough. I have to tell myself, 'Quick enough for who?' I'm the only one making deadlines here. It's the last day of August and everything that needs to be will be undercover before the snows come. I have to take the pressure off, slow the pace. I'm not wasting my days, I'm accumulating all the time. This is how I will gain my independence in this country, one day at a time.

The beauty of this country is not in its crumbling official and abandoned village ruins, but in the nature that its low population has failed to ruin. The sky turns redder than socialism as the sun goes down like oppression. My thoughts turn from shabby KAT to Tabby Cat as she comes to sit with me. I wonder if she looks forward to this part of the day as much as I do.

The cracks are already beginning to show

Tuesday 1ˢᵗ September

There are two people on the planet who are banned from Motocamp, they are both British and both live in the village. Denis is one of them and Keith is the other. There are, of course, two sides to the story of the bannings and the truth may lie in the middle, or possibly it got lost in translation and distorted in time. However, I think it's fair to say that Keith can be his own worst enemy and he can be prone to gunboat-diplomacy tactics which don't do him any favours. I can't help but think though that in some instances translation is to blame, both parties feeling their comments were perfectly clear although misinterpreted by the recipient. I'm becoming more aware that righteous judgement of people in this village is made when the defendant is absent. I will draw my conclusions based on what I experience in the company I keep and events I attend, and then I'll keep the conclusions I've made to myself, for everybody's benefit.

I send off a completed article to a magazine before I start my manual work, then realise I can't do any more to the garage without materials. Keith has been working on his house relentlessly for nearly two years and has offered to show me where various building supplies are available. I'm hesitant to contact him and he obviously feels the same as the 8 a.m. call I get from him is apprehensive. Silly that we are so careful not to offend; clandestine conversations have made us overcautious. I step lightly to the dark side of the village.

It's the first time I've seen Keith's place, and the first thing that strikes me is the standard of workmanship. It's flawless: the precise construction of the stone walls, the pointing between the paving, the sharp lines on the painting, and his colour scheme is positively resplendent. The rooms have exposed beams which I've always wanted and his log burner is free-standing with a mosaic of natural stone behind it. It's all done with such attention to detail, ability and patience. I don't work like that, I'm not exactly envious but I am impressed – oh wait, he has a bath, oooh, now I'm jealous. He says I can use it. What, for three hours, with my playlist blasting, candles burning and beer bottles chinking? No, that's a gratification that will have to be delayed until I have installed my own. The reoccurring contemplation when I sit on my toilet is how I can fit a bath in the room.

For now, though, it's time to put my aching body behind the wheel. We go to the aggregate place. No hard hats, no high-vis, just a spade and sandals like I'm going to the beach. Drive on the weighbridge, reverse up to a pile and shovel like a stoker. More merchants, more materials, cement, timber, filler and paint. You just can't do this on a KTM. Although there is still an element of adventure to the day. Every place I go to is a first, all locations have to be remembered. The company, conversation, projects and plans are all fresh, and the time passes faster than progress. Again, I have to suppress the frustration that nothing happens as quickly as I would like it to, I'll put it in a little box marked 'for England only'. These are moments to live in, it's not a job of rushed completion to continue to the next. I've clocked off, I'm on my time, no charge, no payment, no pressure. I'm building a dream here. One day it will all be done and with wandering idleness, I don't need to see perfection but I do want reflection. So stop ... stop, it's not a race, this is home, my base, the haste stops here, my foundation stone is about to be laid.

However, the looming sailing holiday now feels like a disruption. When shovelling sand appeals more than drifting at sea, I must really be enjoying my work. It's the pace I need to work on: I think I'll take a break.

Polly and Ivo are both helping Peach renovate his place. For the first time, I feel a little coldness. Is my novelty wearing off or have I been keeping the wrong company, have I broken protocol by socialising with the Motocamp *persona non grata*? I wander on to see Bruce but he's busy working on his place too. So I come back home. The lawn needs mowing but I can't face that today. Instead, I fill some holes in the wall and put a bit of paint on the outside of the house to see how it covers. Suddenly, it seems very big.

I don't venture out again after that little kick to my confidence. For the first time, today I feel that the honeymoon period may be over. I was flavour of the month, but tastes change. I console myself by replying to some fan mail. I've always got my anonymous readers who make me feel like I have worth – that's because they don't know me.

I can't help but be influenced by what I've heard, and I'm beginning to see how fragile the connection with Motocamp is, how easy it can be fractured and that crack can't be filled. It changes the whole dynamic of the village. It seems outlandish and irresponsible behaviour has a sliding scale of tolerance based on who is the perpetrator – some can do no wrong, others can do no right, tattoos will fade before the bitterness, in certain circumstances. I'm wondering if my speaking to Keith is causing resentment and if it is then, actually, I resent that. I've got a lot to learn about this community, and playing the part of peacekeeper will require more experience than I have.

I mark some dates on my year planner, it's not over yet. I really think I need a left-hand drive vehicle, which of course makes putting a low stone floor in the garage pointless.

Fix it in the mix

Wednesday 2nd September

Despite my dislike for blinds over the window, I'm not adverse to getting a fly screen. The nights are hot again and, with the window open, the astute insect can smell the blood of an Englishman. I frequently get bitten down at Motocamp (that's not a euphemism): the mozzies congregate around the shaded seating areas. Up here on the north side of the valley it's light and dry, but still the occasional opportunist comes for a midnight feast.

Leaving a bedroom of scavengers, I go to my world of borrowing. Today it's my neighbour's cement mixer. I've cut the shuttering and made stakes out of logs to hold it in place. Now it's time for the concrete ledge around the undermined garage walls. Mixing cement is one of those jobs where having two people makes it three times quicker. However, there is only me, and my multitasking extends to counting in Bulgarian each shovel of sand I throw into the mixer. Thankfully, I hear it straining before I've pushed my limited knowledge. I can count to six in Swedish too – I learned by playing multiple games of backgammon with some Swedish girls on starry nights at the edge of the Thar Desert. Somehow, this sand lacks the allure of those hedonistic evenings, but the counting continues and my back grumbles.

Like the Thar Desert though, proportion is hard to grasp and pretty soon I need more sand. The word for sand in Bulgarian is *pyasuk* but it's not really, we just don't have the sounds in the Roman alphabet to pronounce the word accurately. Now I know how to sound out most of the letters I write the word пясък in Cyrillic. This helps my pronunciation a little, although it's still incomprehensible the way I say it, with the wrong inflection and intonation. But I'm trying, I'm trying real hard in my attempt to speak the lingo.

235

So, armed with only a scrap of paper displaying my crudely inscribed rune-like writing, I head single-handedly to the deserted place of aggregation for more concrete ingredients.

Despite having an impressive windscreen full of European vignettes purchased on my journey down here, somehow, either through pure excitement or perhaps fatigue, I failed to buy the mandatory Bulgarian one. I have been driving without it for two weeks. So, with that misdemeanour taken care of, it's time to overload the van.

I may remember the Bulgarian word for sand but I've forgotten the bloody shovel. I find a corner of broken marble and use it to scoop 300 fragments full of sand into the back of the van. This is not helping my tennis elbow or aching back any more than my counting is helping my grasp of the language.

The girl in the weighbridge office is very pretty and the only left-handed Bulgarian I've met. Knowing that we have that in common, as deliberately as possible I sign my receipt with a great display of our shared awkwardness when holding a pen. I think the only bonding will be the concrete mix I'll make when I get back. Still, she'll remember me now, the guy who spits as he attempts to say *pyasuk* and signs his name with the dramatic pose of a pretentious celebrity. *But I'm an author, dharrling – don't you know?* 480 kilos of sand, paid, best wishes, G. Field.

Several more signatures are required as I go through the process of buying insurance for the KTM. *Podpis*, they say as they point at the dotted line at the bottom of a document. It's another word I've learned in Bulgarian, as I hear it more here than I would its English equivalent at a book signing. I remember *podpis* by association – don't have a pot to piss in.

Failing with the weighbridge girl, the language, the shovel and the vehicle legitimacy notwithstanding, I'm actually quite proud of myself. I got all the materials I needed, all by myself. I've always been dreadfully independent, and it is dreadful. Multiple abilities are the social equivalent of holding a phone in front of your face. People like to help, it gives them pleasure, it defines them. I, on the other hand, am happiest if I can get through my day without asking anything of anyone. Clearly, I'm dependent here, from the borrowing of tools to the comprehension of language. I'm very much in need of others' generosity in possessions and time and I'm extremely grateful for it. I will feel more comfortable, though, when I only leave my house or open my mouth for myself rather than to request.

So back to my single-handed labours, with left-handed lustful thoughts. Now the only mixing is with a machine: four shovels full of sand to one of cement, water from the new hosepipe, pour the mix into a borrowed barrow and place behind the reinforced shuttering. It's shattering but it's progress. The sun is being brutish again, I thought it was relenting into an autumnal retirement but we are having what is called here a 'gypsy summer'. I like that term, it has the romantic inclinations of a low sun glinting off gold-hooped earrings that complement the falling leaves, horses snorting into the mist of dawn as cartwheels run over the first frost of the season. In reality, it's just another sweaty day with a brief respite as I empty the wheelbarrow in the shade of the garage.

I genuinely have a feeling of development today; the physical exhaustion is rewarded with a next stage completed. It's only wet concrete, barely being held back by inadequate bowing supports, but my vision is becoming a reality and, more importantly, the whole structure has strength again.

It would appear I can't mix any more today. There is a new influx of motorcyclists at Motocamp this evening, Finns and Germans, and I can't find a click with this particular crowd. The guests seem starved for stimulation, as my KLR is attracting more attention than it is really worthy of. It's not even the one from the journeys I've written about. I like it, obviously, but it rates low on travel-weary scars, tell-tale stickers and improvised accessories. Its only uniqueness is its US specifications against the more usual European model, and you have to be a bit of an aficionado to appreciate those differences. I've watched many eyes glaze over as I've articulated the pros and cons of distinction. So I don't do that anymore. In fact, I think I'd better go home now.

I've got a response to the article I sent off; they want more. Because it's so good or lacking? I suppose I could throw some facts about the bike into the mix.

The fine art of failing

Despite telling Keith I'd be ready at 7.30, he turns up at 7 a.m., so the pre-calculated morning procedure turns into rushed prioritising, and I missed the list. This early start is our attempt to avoid the queueing, and to not lose the entire day as we try to register our bikes at the KAT office. I only bought the third-party compulsory insurance for the KTM. More comprehensive cover is available, but I'll look into that after the bike gets its new status and registration. Although the basic insurance is inexpensive, there is no such thing as a multi-bike policy, so costs will start to escalate as the fleet increases.

I ride the KTM out of the bee shed onto the wet grass, where the rear wheel just spins. The bike, being so tall, means paddling tiptoes doesn't give me the purchase to push forward so, basically, I'm bloody stuck. Stuck on a dew-soaked lawn; it's not exactly Dakar desert quicksand, vertical dunes and quagmire valleys. It's just grass that hasn't been mowed for a few weeks and I'm stuck like a st-st-ststutter. It's embarrassing. I have to get Keith to give me a push. This model, the 'S', is notoriously tall. I think the 'S' must stand for Scandinavian, as only that long-legged race would be able to touch the ground. Or maybe it's for 'short-arse', because that's how it makes people of average height feel.

Once the challenge of getting the bike out of the garden is overcome, we take the back roads to Gabrovo. I'm still entranced by the beauty, particularly in this morning light. There is a fresh eye-watering chill in the morning air. This, combined with a clear sky and empty roads, generates a feeling that never fails to thrill. Rounding my favourite corner, the full Balkan range comes into view. I have to stop for a photo despite knowing the futility of trying to capture such scale on a phone screen. Scale can't be captured without perspective, like getting stuck on the lawn.

Motorcycles are exempt from eco-tax and this early start means we are close to the front of the corridor queue. We must look English, an elderly gentleman bids us good morning and asks: 'What seems to be the problem?' Rather a surprising way to initiate a conversation.

'Errr, we don't actually have one yet,' I say, thinking – *but give it time, this place dishes problems out like sustenance from a Salvation Army soup kitchen.* It turns out he is a dentist and gives us his card. I suppose asking what the problem is doesn't get such an open-mouthed reaction in his chosen field of expertise.

Like relegated infants, we are back to the first form but, with previously acquired knowledge, we know now how to fill the empty spaces. With a stamp of approval, we soon advance to vehicle inspection. We had the forethought to park our bikes on the front line, not that it makes any difference. Upon our return, there is a row of cars and I'm still unclear as to what determines the choice of selection. We wait for a few random vehicles to be inspected before our turn comes. Keith rides an Armstrong which is made in England, it's a rather obscure motorcycle manufacturer whose bikes are used by the British Army. The make is not recognised here, this would appear to be the only one in Bulgaria and, therefore, they have no trace of the manufacturer in the computer system. The bike cannot be registered. Fail. It's my turn. With their trademark diligence they check my VIN and logbook. There is a discrepancy. My frame number has three consecutive 5s in it. Swansea have put four 5s on the logbook. This will not do. They call the supervisor. Fail. Not for the first time, I've been inconvenienced by the DVLA's incompetence and one wrong character. My middle name is Mark, and a logbook of mine was once returned with the name Graham Mary Field. This, however, is a more significant problem than

240

conflicting genders. I'm 1,600 miles away from the nearest DVLA inspection centre, and getting their mistake corrected is going to be a nightmare.

We leave KAT and I swing by the electricity company to discover my contract is still not prepared, so there is nothing for me to sign yet. I'm beginning to fall out with this day. As is often the case, I'm becoming more aware and aggravated by other annoyances. My elbow hurts, I'm too hot, my jeans are clingy and uncomfortable and I need a wee. I want to go to Veliko Tarnovo to pick up some items from the list I left at home. I was looking forward to taking the KTM around the sweeping bends of the canyon-hugging back road. Now Keith wants to come too, so that's going to slow me down. Not that I'm in any hurry to get to our next destination, a suggested shopping mall. God, I hate them. Predictably, once inside you could be in any country on the planet and oblivious to time of day and season of year. Well, obviously it's not October as Christmas music isn't coming from the omnipresent speakers. It's still horrendous though.

I want a mask and snorkel, but I'm not in the mood for miming and I can't face the task, so I suggest we get out of here. Keith insists and we find a sports store and the day is redeemed a little. Back home I have a little doze. It's 39°C outside. I'm putting a lot of effort into resisting the urge for alcohol. I win the fight, and instead honour an out-of-date request to write my Top Ten Tips for overland motorcycling. It flows surprisingly well.

- Don't rush your morning departure
- Make sure you can touch the ground when you sit on your bike
- Photographing mountains is futile
- Be sure that your paperwork matches your VIN
- Don't wear too tight clothes in the heat
- If you need a wee, stop and have one

- Don't ride with an incompatible companion
- When you get homesick go to a shopping mall, they are identical the world over and such an horrendous environment will renew your enthusiasm for the road
- When your body aches, stop, rest, go for a week-long sailing holiday
- Not drinking may result in completing postponed obligations

Today Motörhead have cancelled their US tour. Lemmy said he just can't do it. That's very sad, I feel the end is nigh. I can totally empathise with how it feels when your body won't cooperate with your desires.

Market forces language courses

Friday 4th September

I'd better have another look at those Top Tips. With freshness in day, body and mind, a stream of genuinely useful, informed, experienced and inspired tips flow from my fingers to the page. Somewhere, perhaps during the procrastination period, I was processing this project, or maybe it's been germinating and today it just burst into life. This is bloody brilliant and I commend it to the internet – well, via the online information organisation which commissioned it.

After this superb ending to my virtual working week, I take the bike to town, realising as I approach that it's market day. However, still being in my top-tips frame of mind, I embrace the unexpected and decide to take the opportunity to have a look around. The problem is, I have to accept this is not just a passing attraction on a road of discovery. This is my long-established local bazaar, and it's getting frustrating now that I can't ask for the price or understand the answer. The irony being that at a Brit-infested car boot sale I can interact but have no desire to.

So I head for the comfort of Kaufland, but only for parking, and walk to the insurance agent. This little office seems to be the place for all insurance needs. Here, there is no 'Go Compare', you just go there. They are friendly and efficient, it's good enough for me.

My KTM insurance is now superfluous as the bike is a perfectly legal British-registered bike abroad. Buying Bulgarian insurance was the first obligatory step to the now-suspended registration process. A refund doesn't seem to be an option and I fork out three times the cost to insure my house. This, however, appears far more comprehensive: flood, landslide, earthquake and storm damage are all covered. I'd like storm coverage for the bike – 'Yeah, I need to make a claim. It looked like rain ahead and I had to get a hotel room.'

I wander back through the fruit and veg market. I'd love to buy some tomatoes but the challenge is too daunting today. I've bought from market stalls around the world, from Iraq to India – it's as simple as pointing and then using a few more fingers to signify quantity. I may pay a little more than the locals do but it's fresh, it's native inter-action and the money goes directly into the local economy. Every aspect of the produce purchase is positive. Here, though, I'm going through a transition; I'm an immigrant, a local without language. I'm embarrassed by my inabil-ities at integration and that isolates me more. This train of inaction is taking me in entirely the wrong direction, only stopping and shopping will change this. I don't, I take the easy way out and go into the supermarket. I know it's wrong, but I've got a little plan. I'm betting that the daughter will be quite bored on the sailing trip with her parents, and having her help me through my Bulgarian language book will keep her occupied and her parents less obligated to entertain her. I can develop my level of under-standing and maybe I can help her English and knowledge of my country.

I consider all this as I slowly prepare to leave my house for a week. This consists of cleaning the KTM, which does-n't seem like an essential preparation but is pleasurable. There could be a hidden motive to this cleaning, as I may be considering selling it. While I'm standing admiring my work, the KLR front tyre pops and goes flat, right in front of my eyes. What the fuck? Talk about spontaneous defla-tion. What a downer.

I remove the shuttering. It's the grand unveiling of the poured concrete in the garage. The ledge looks all right, bends like Beckham and bows like David, but the stone floor by its nature will be uneven, so this reinforcing ledge will complement it perfectly. It's probably a good thing

244

that the base laying won't start until I get back. On the one hand, it could be hardening in my absence but, on the other, I think it's more important that I harden up a bit before I start the next stage. Another advantage is that now I'm able to put both bikes in the garage and reverse the van in. OK, it protrudes a bit, but it's all hidden now and inaccessible – although I'm sure there isn't a single thing I've done that has not been seen, discussed and scorned around the village. It's also probably common knowledge that I'm leaving for a week.

The excitement can certainly be felt at Motocamp. They've even cleaned their car. It's all packed, and I'm packed too. They will pick me up at 3 a.m. tomorrow. Somehow, getting up at that time seems contradictory to the term 'relaxing holiday', but we have a long drive to Greece. Apparently, there is more to hiring a sailing boat then claiming your cabin. Crewing comes with obligations. I'm handed a printout relating to packing and precautions, lessons to learn. It's a bit bloody late for that. It seems I'm going to be working my passage. This is not what I had in mind at all.

From Motocamp to motorway to motorboat (with sails)

Saturday 5th September

My bedside clock has, via some satellite correctional signal, changed from Eastern European Time to British Summer Time, meaning I have to add two hours to the number projected onto the ceiling. That maths is enough to wake me and so I get up while it's still yesterday in the UK.

I play a UK rock radio station via my laptop. The first voice I hear this morning is Lemmy singing 'Get Back in Line'. It's very poignant, is he about to leave the line-up of Motörhead?

Other than moonrises and sunsets, the other light I can see from the house, if I lean over the balcony, is headlights leaving Motocamp. So I turn off water, Wi-Fi and lights. The printout of protocol suggested 'smart casual' as appropriate dress. Being entirely new to every aspect of this sailing thing, I decide to follow the guidelines. I'm not going to drape a sweater over my shoulders and tie it around my neck, but I decide to wear a T-shirt without branding: not mine, Motocamp's or Motörhead's.

However, when they pull up, I instantly feel overdressed. Polly, Ivo and Doug look like bikers in a car, and they are cooler in looks and comfort. Bollocks, with four adults and all their luggage it's hard enough to fit in and now I stand out like a white sheep. I wish I was back in my black T-shirt.

There is a strategically placed fuel station on the way to Sofia. Either tummy, bladder, or fuel gauge seem to need attending to at this point. Knowing there is free Wi-Fi, fresh croissants and coffee, we fulfil our needs. Even cleaning the windscreen with the squeegee makes my elbow ache. How is this ever going to heal?

The southern section of the Sofia ring road reveals a very wealthy and modern side of the city. Glass and steel, neon lights and angular architecture, and a super highway which takes us through modern developments of multi-national names like IKEA and IMAX. This is super-Sofia, but for me the mountainous backdrop has a natural beauty that rates higher than any expediential growth.

Four people, three nationalities, two languages, one stop shop. Apparently, a meeting has been arranged. It happened by phone in the second language with a third party. At the aforementioned food shop we meet the captain and his family.

The supermarket has everything and I can't think of anything I could possibly need for a week at sea. The car is already full and I'm not sure if I should be shopping for myself or whether this ought to be a crew decision. I take the initiative and buy wine and tortilla chips, then I take the wheel and drive us down to the Greek border. Three lanes come to a standstill. I turn off the engine and we wind down the windows and try to avoid eye contact with the hawkers and beggars, all here to capitalise on our captivity. Although I am tempted by a handmade witch's broom. Doug, travelling on a US passport, takes a little more processing than the rest of us. This basically means he has to get out of the car to retrieve his passport.

The Greek motorway is smooth, flat and fast, and the temperature is going up with the fuel prices. The lullaby of the road rocks the passengers to sleep and I fight with eyes that are tired of seeing and thoughts that won't focus. A rest area beckons and the change in engine note wakes me like an alarm clock. Coke and crisps stimulate me back to alertness. Oh yes, I can see myself coming back with some excess ballast from this holiday. The coast and then Mount Olympus come into view, such significant scenes are just half a day's drive from where I live now. However, the stimulation of those sights fades into a long flat stretch of inland-bound motorway, punctuated with tollbooths. The air conditioning has been struggling, and every time I pay a toll, the blast of air gets hotter, now exceeding 40°C.

Volos is signposted. There is a hot sigh of relief. This is the port we will be leaving from. In retrospect, riding in this heat wouldn't have been any fun, and the advantage of getting through the border traffic would have been lost in this sweltering discomfort. Also, it soon becomes apparent that there would have been nowhere safe to leave the bikes. We drive down a seafront of glittering boats, one of which, I suppose, is ours. We see the Captain, double park and make an untidy pile on the pavement. I make the unwise decision to leave my sleeping bag in the car, it's so hot a sheet will suffice.

Having eventually found a space for a week's free parking, we meet the boat owner, who is showing our captain the ropes. If this were a house, the Greek owner would be the landlord, but the rental property being a boat might make him a sealord. Our captain says this hiring process will take a long time so it's suggested we go find a supermarket. I try to change some money.

'Pounds?' I'm asked.

'No, Bulgarian lev.'

The Greek literally laughs in my face. The country is still in a state of economic crisis, possibly due to a cash economy; no receipts are given and credit cards rarely taken. Only US dollars are a possible bartering currency and I don't have any of them.

Back at the boat we fill up the cabins. I will be sharing with Ivo. I don't have much to compare this boat to: camper vans, canal boats and sleeper cabs being my only other transient accommodation. This, though, beats them all. Outside it is white and bright, wires, cables, ropes and pullies everywhere. I haven't got a clue what they do. Inside, though, I can judge the quality. It has a kitchen which is probably called a galley and wooden cabinets curve around the hull of the boat – unlike my bowing concrete ledge, this is calculated carpentry. The seating area is filled with immaculate white cushions that will accentuate the slightest stain of sweat or suntan lotion with deposit-taking betrayal. There are four cabins just big enough for a double mattress and every conceivable space has been utilised for storage of varying accessibility. There is one shower/bathroom which is cramped but adequate. Classy though it is, I intend to spend the voyage on deck, although moving around is a bit tricky. There are places to sit on the bow beyond the reach of swinging booms. The cockpit has a canvas cover and two steering wheels, which will be useful if decisions differ as to direction. There is a throttle as the boat has an engine but apparently no brake. Lots of digital gauges tell the speed, depth, wind speed and direction. On the side railing is a dinghy and a spare wheel. Oh wait, it might be a life ring. Either way, I hope we don't need it.

Well, it all looks shipshape to me.

Signed up and filled up with fuel, water, food and beer, at 5 p.m. we fire up the engine and break all ties with the land. I'm about to find out what this sailing thing is all about, we are going to sea. Volos is in the Pagasetic Gulf, which is where Jason, in his ship the Argo, left from to embark on his quest to find the golden fleece. We open the amber nectar, there appears to be no rules concerning drinking in control of a boat. Anyway, it has auto pilot. So this is sailing then? Seems quite straightforward. It's just drinking at sea really, surrounded by the decadence of the boat and the grandeur of the scenery. The islands are hills on the calm sea and, as the light dims and the drink and conversation flows, we condescendingly wonder what the poor people are doing now.

We set the controls for the heart of a tiny port for dinner but there are no mooring spaces, so while we make sandwiches the captain backs the boat up a bit and we simply drop anchor. This is where we will spend the night. There is wine and laughter and no one to annoy. The lights of the land blur on the surface we are disturbing, it's hot but there is a little movement in the air. We are immersed in the surrounding beauty. It's perfect. I blow up my camping mattress and place it precariously on the bow deck with a pillow and a sarong. The water laps, the stars shine and the chatter drifts away on a cooling sea breeze. In the night, I move down to the stifling cabin. I muse about crews of trading boats, how they coped with the conditions during the age of discovery, what hardships they endured, in diet, confines, labour and length of time at sea. Where did they go, I wonder, if they wanted a wank?

Shallow recreation

This morning I need a little privacy, to get the self-satisfaction of catching up on my diary. I felt the boat sway at 5.30 a.m. and thought maybe people were getting up, but I think perhaps I misinterpreted the movement. So I remain undisturbed in the stern seating area, writing with my head torch on. Every time I look up from the page the sky is lighter than before, obvious really but spectacular nonetheless. At sea the dawn creeps without shadow, and lightens with delicate tranquillity. I've got the daybreak all to myself, and it's all the more powerful unshared. The light brings warmth. I packed with cooler expectations. I think the majority of my clothes will not see the light of these hot Greek days.

After a cup of chai, the anchor is raised, the key turned, and the motor breaks both the silence and the water's mirror reflection. We rumble on past chalk-white hillside houses with private beaches. The contours of the coast create multiple idyllic bays. I consider the road that is cut into cliffs, sweeping bends and camp-able beaches. You can take the bikers out to sea but you can't stop them recognising a good ride. We are still in the gulf so these roads are accessible from the mainland. This was never meant to be a good route reconnaissance, but I just can't help myself. My life has been about overland travel, by backpack, bicycle, motorcycle and camper van. Boats have only ever been a way to join the gaps. Gratuitously avoiding land is new to me, and inevitably I find my mind contemplating the dry dreams a seaman wouldn't entertain.

With a little wind the sails are unfurled, this is where the captain gets his kicks. For him and his family this is, after all, a sailing holiday. I've had to declare myself unfit for duty – winching, ratcheting and pulling on ropes are not conducive to my tennis elbow and aching back. I'm given the wheel – well, one of them – and suddenly I'm the helmsman. There is a digital screen and I have to keep the boat heading towards a certain point, which I suppose is a watermark. It's definitely not a landmark. The wheel needs turning constantly, direction corrected to keep us on course, but it's not too challenging. I say I'm heading for the restaurant with the breakfast special, but the wind is taken out of the sails and we find ourselves in the doldrums. It's not all bad, we switch to motor power and autopilot while we eat cheese, tomatoes, dried meats and bread. At 10.30 the captain and his wife open their first beer. It's tempting but I think I'll wait. Polly and Doug are not drinkers at all and I'll pace myself somewhere between wet and dry, which I suppose is damp or moist. With nothing on the horizon, I press-gang daughter Zoe into giving me a Bulgarian lesson. It's mainly just asking what different words mean and writing them down phonetically. With her help I can count to ten, beyond the needs of shoving sand into a mixer or playing backgammon. I will have to practice daily for these easily forgotten words to imprint on my memory.

I think I can justify a beer now. Actually, this stuff they are drinking tastes awful, and there I was thinking they were doing it for pleasure. We enter a bay with snorkelling possibilities, a gust of wind blows my baseball cap off. I wish I'd jumped in after it as, from the boat, I would have been easier to spot and retrieve. By the time we turn around, it's sunk, and anyway, other than our drifting wake we really don't know where the incident occurred. The sea is clear, scarily so. I can see how far away the bottom is and that makes me wary. It doesn't bother me that I lost my hat, just that I can't stop looking for it. With the title of my first book embroidered on it, the cap was a one-off. Now it's just blown off.

We moor up and jump in. There's no gentle transition and the exhilaration has me gasping. So much so that the snorkel is restricting my inhalation of air as I take deep breaths. The whole hull is visible, the propellers, the rocks far beneath us and, of course, the various inquisitive fish. I calm mind and movements and control my lungs to breathe at a more regulated pace. I then paddle towards the shore for some warmer, shallower water with a greater concentration of fish.

Polly is just bursting with enthusiasm, which is endearing, and what we are doing and seeing is good, it's excellent. Perhaps she has no comparison. I do. I have dived the Great Barrier Reef. Although it was twenty years ago, the memory of it is as clear as the water.

We took a two-day liveaboard diving excursion. Having already qualified, my girlfriend and I were certified to dive on our own, leaving the instructor and his school to teachings of lead, follow and other exercises. We saw all the usual stuff – giant clams, rays, hand-fed barracuda – but the most exhilarating memory was due to my constant struggle to equalise. I've always had difficulty getting my ears to adjust to the pressure of the depth of water. Having descended significantly, my girlfriend couldn't get her mask to seal, so, breaking all protocol and every rule in the safety manual, I continued my descent alone and sat on the huge concrete block the boat was moored to, watching as she followed the rope up towards the distant hull of the boat to correct her ill-fitting mask. It was surreal, just sitting alone at the bottom of the sea, trying to breathe as shallow as I could to conserve the air in my tank.

The waters here are equally clear and it's been a long time since I strapped a tank on my back. I really have no desire to again. I had a bad experience in the Philippines that involved poor visibility, strong currents and dodgy equipment. Unlike motorcycling, diving is clearly not in my blood. I prefer fast bends, but I'm perfectly happy to splash around with a mask and snorkel.

The snorkelling comes at the cost of shore leave and lunch: we have pot noodle as we plod on. Where did the bloody decadence go? We are deckhands on reduced rations. As we sail on through the day, the heat becomes inescapable. There isn't a lot of shade at sea. We reach this evening's port of call near Glossa, which is in the middle of the three islands we are sailing round. It's very fraught, this parking bit – there is a lot of yelling and revving of the engine as we squeeze in between two other boats. There doesn't seem to be the bond that us bikers bear. We attract stares from other boat owners – like the ones you get when you ride a bike into a caravan site – and no one offers to catch a rope or lend a hand. I go down to the cabins, it's humiliating to be part of this. I'm not drunk enough, I'm not drunk at all, I've only had one beer. The captain, however, has been at it for eight hours.

There seems to be a bit of confusion as to what we are doing now. Their beer supplies, not surprisingly, are running low and replenishing stocks is top priority – although strangely not mine, I'm just hungry. After much discussion, the majority of which I don't understand, I give fifty euros towards the shopping expedition. I'm a bit concerned how this will all be worked out. I've had one beer; I'm not funding their drinking. There is also some tension over the lack of land time we are getting. Polly and Doug want to do more sightseeing. I don't have the language and I don't have a care, I'm happy.

We go to a restaurant and finally I get my seafood. The waiters speak the language well – my language – and the menu is in English. So are the bloody prices. I get a replacement baseball cap as the restaurant has a souvenir shop and a bit of Wi-Fi. The whole restaurant is on it, staring at their phones, which makes me even more reluctant to partake. I check briefly, nothing urgent, no book sales, so I turn off and tune in to the world beyond the glowing screen. Anyway, the Greek food is delicious and I want to give it my full attention.

Back on board I sit with Doug and Polly and the conversation turns to old Harleys, a subject I can talk about until the manatees come home.

I sleep on deck again, my bedding so light that I have to find a coil of rope to hold it down when I get up for a wee so that it doesn't blow off into the night and out to sea.

Apparently, they like it rough

Monday 7ᵗʰ September

I must have dreamt about hard-physical labour – my elbow is screaming for ibuprofen, and so that's what I have for breakfast. Even holding my pen is hurting now. At the restaurant last night, I noticed a Greek version of a full English breakfast on the menu, but annoyingly I'm still full from my seafood dinner. I settle for the staple of tomato, cheeses and bread which is just fine, especially here, it complements the climate, scenery and even the company. I volunteer to go to market. It feels good to just wander off to top up our tomatoes and see what else is on offer. None of those self-conscious inhibitions like I get at my local market, I just do the point-and-pay like I've always done. In fact, everyone speaks English. It doesn't feel touristy here, but I would imagine they get their fair share of immigrants from a variety of vessels.

Water is readily available wherever boats are moored, there seems to be a universal key to access a tap and hose-pipe. I wasn't brilliant at physics in school but I know restricting a flow increases the pressure. It may shoot further and feel more powerful, but if the captain just took the nozzle off the pipe our tanks would fill significantly quicker. It seems to annoy the others more than me. I think my reading of body language and facial expressions is improving faster than my comprehension of Bulgarian – perhaps I can use this insight to be the diplomat.

Today we are sailing into open waters, around the north of the middle island and into the big, fat sea that hasn't had the restriction of land to tame it. This point of the trip has coincided with some cloud cover, it's much cooler and windier. As soon as we leave the shelter of the island the boat starts to dive and raise and water comes spraying over the bow. It takes all my concentration to keep my tummy under control, so I sit attentively staring at the horizon. I can't let my eyes wander to anything else as the boat pitches and rolls, it's exhausting. I realise that saying this would make any mariner take the piss relentlessly. I feel my eyes drop and I start to doze but the unpredictable violent motion of the boat does not have the effect of a swinging hammock. It's taking its toll. Doug goes down to the cabin to sleep and puke, Ivo is next and throws up over the side. There's nothing like hearing someone being sick to induce the same reaction. Luckily, I can't smell it, that would be the clincher. I just focus on the land. Not seeing breakfast again is my motivation. The captain and his wife are loving this, these conditions haven't even slowed their drinking down. The greater the swell the more they swill, they laugh and drink more. We don't seem to be making much progress. We pass the church that was in the movie *Mamma Mia*. I've never seen it, and we might as well be passing the Millennium Falcon, since I've never seen Star Wars either. That said, the church seems less out of place than a sentient starship would. Much like looking at the stars, the bloody church doesn't seem to disappear from view, this is how I gauge our progress and it appears to be slow. Zoe is the next to puke, and I'm not sure where Polly is, so there are only three of us left on deck. I'm only just hanging on here. All day the boat has been battered like a cod fillet and eventually we sail into the port of Skopelos. I'm thinking all I want to do is just sit quietly somewhere for a few hours. However, with the calmer waters the feeling of seasickness disappears like a blown-off baseball cap.

There is resentment within the crew. There is too much sailing and not enough snorkelling and shore time. The captain is close to putting an end to his reckless drinking by wrecking the boat – the attempt at mooring today is atrocious. I know nothing other than I am embarrassed by his ineptitude. It's the equivalent of an artic driver who

257

can't reverse onto a loading bay. This inability to moor at the allotted spot would be less humiliating if not for the screaming and swearing, like we want to attract even more attention to our inabilities.

While I'm below deck there is a calamity outside. Zoe has fallen off the gangplank. She didn't fall in the water but she's cut her nose and has rope burns on her hands. The poor girl isn't having a good day. She's shaking from the adrenalin; her drunk mother is absolutely fucking useless, so I adopt the role of doctor and give her some ibuprofen, telling her it will cure everything, and some antiseptic cream for her cuts. All she really needs is the calming voice of responsibility, it says a lot about the company when that person is me.

The Motocamp Four go for a walk around, which starts for me with a great big beer, and here endeth the responsibility. This is another tiny cliff-hugging community of stone paths that lead us through the pastel-painted dwellings of hanging baskets and basking cats, stone buildings, slate roofs, terracotta terraces and, of course, Greek urns. There are wedding-cake tiered churches of open arches and exposed bells. These sights are all the more appreciated as we are all feeling so much better after our arduous voyage today. In fact, I think I would like another beer. Thunder rumbles and shelter is needed – oh look, a bar, that will do nicely.

Back at the boat everyone has calmed down. Music is playing and Zoe is dancing, which seems a little strange, but I'm a little drunk so can take anything but the gangplank in my stride. I'm glad she's feeling better. It would be hard to know what to say if I had the language. Without it, I find a sixteen-year-old girl strutting her stuff in front of her parents a bit of a tough topic to find the appropriate comment for. I go off to bed. Later, Ivo comes in and I move outside on deck, but then it rains so I go on the couch – like Goldilocks, this one is just right. There is resentment brewing in the ranks, I fear a mutiny. I'm OK, I'll be the peacekeeper, we've already seen today the results of walking the gangplank.

Seeing the sights, avoiding the sea

Tuesday 8ᵗʰ September

Goldilocks gets up for golden light; I grab my camera for some dawn shots. Up the narrow stone paths into a whitewashed world, a labyrinth of the long-established, the first participants of the day are stirring. The thrill is in being here rather than capturing it, which is just as well as the camera is an excuse, like having a dog to walk. It wouldn't matter if I didn't take a single photo, I'm seeing not just looking.

I took several photography classes before the instant results of digital were available. Every week we were given an assignment: shadow, light and texture were a memorable homework. I found a crumbling barn wall, soft red brick, decayed by frost and falling from neglect. Every brick was unique, the light caught the contours and cast shadows over the corrosion. Having the limitations of film exposures, I found myself looking more than I was photographing. It was just a wall; I would have strolled passed oblivious on any other day. That's what the course taught me, to not just look but take the time to see. If it can't be photographed it has to be recalled verbally and that exercises our powers of description and vocabulary. Too frequently these days, a phone is thrust into our face to show, rather than tell, the recipient what the topic of the conversation is about. No one can remember phone numbers anymore, many can't find their way without GPS, and now we can't describe what we saw when we go there. A picture is not worth forgetting a thousand adjectives. On handing in my homework, I said to my teacher, 'I thought only LSD brought about such awareness of light, shadow and texture, but I've found now photography does too.' I think he understood.

This place was made for dawn exploration. I can't get lost, all paths lead uphill and, when I'm there, all paths lead down to the water. I feel the reward, three restless beds have got me to one solitary sunrise. What a peaceful place to live, assuming it doesn't get infested with hordes of tourists like Dubrovnik does. As I walk back to the boat, Doug is heading out for a coffee, so we find a café with Wi-Fi. I feel justified in my phone-staring, having already seen the best of the day. My top tips have been published and they seem very popular. I'd hoped they would be, it was one of those rare occasions when the words flow and you just know what you've written has value. Again, we talk old Harleys – it's not our only common ground but it's a topic that's been lacking in my life. Travel and metal enthusiasts are easier to find.

Back on board, everyone is preparing for another rough ride. I don't take the pills but I try the acupressure wristband: a rubber placebo.

I'm given the wheel when the water gets bumpy and sails need adjusting. It reminds me of the compulsory football matches at school. Knowing I was useless, I was put in goal until the ball came up my end of the pitch; then I'd be replaced by someone with capability and concern. The thing I'm beginning to learn about sailing is that I don't like it much. Also, that it's best to go beneath deck and stay out of the way when there are things occurring that I don't understand. Today I try the horizontal approach to rough-sea travel, and it works quite well. I wedge myself in the bed, my feet pushing against the dividing wall and, with a pillow for padding, I push my head against the inside of the hull. I doze and dream and think and watch clouds outside the porthole as time and distance pass.

We are allotted an hour for snorkelling. The water looks cold; the day is cold. I decide to spectate from the boat – after all, I wasn't the one demanding more time in the sea, so I don't feel obligated to play today. Indonesian, Thai,

Philippine and Hawaiian Islands have spoilt me, along with the Dead Sea and Great Barrier Reef. I'll sit on deck and recall those times in depth. When they are ready to leave, I go back to the cabin and happily assume the position. Now we travel by motor power and into the port of Patitiri, on the third island.

The other thing I have learned is to hide in the hold to contain my embarrassment at our inept docking procedure. The diversity of the group is beginning to show, the wants and needs differ as much as the language and are as uncompromising as the conditions. I genuinely have no preference. I'm experiencing that rare feeling of contentment – this is all new, we've only got three more days and, as long as I have food, nothing else matters.

It was a majority decision not to bring laptops, and five minutes of Wi-Fi a day is all I need. Strangely, being with heavy drinkers makes me drink less, and in the company of some inflexible people I become even more easy-going. I've found my balance and I'm happy here. Which is why I'm not going to pay six euros to get a connection at a coffee shop.

This is a bigger port, the town lacks the back-street charm of intersecting paths and seclusion – that is, until Ivo and I venture to the highest restaurant with the best view. The place is empty but for pretty waitresses serving suggestive tagliatelle with a hot white sauce and cheesy innuendo. Availability is questionable and the company is not encouraging. We'll never know what else was on the menu.

Drowning of democracy

I get up for a sunrise to myself, scurrying around the deck like the ship's rat, looking for the best angles as the low light shines. The gangplank is up and I can't get off. Can't get on either, trapped in the confines of some conflicting personalities that are emerging out of five days at sea. I make a chai and sit and watch the port come to life.

We are not sailing this morning so, once the boat wakes up, we walk into the town, mainly for souvenirs. The arrangements are not something I'm directly involved in, and as long as I'm informed as to the plan that's good enough. Apparently, we will be snorkelling before we eat. I see a very tempting, freshly made cheese-and-ham roll and decide it would make an excellent keepsake: I'll keep it in my tummy for the sake of storage. As opposed to jumping off the boat, today we can walk along the bay and then wade into the water. I find some colourful fish-infested coral and wave to the others, but they are following Doug, so I float around like driftwood and go against the flow back to the boat.

I was under the impression we were to dry off before going for a restaurant lunch, but actually we are setting sail. I'm glad I ate that sandwich when I had the chance. I can see I'm going to have to fend for myself here: there appears to be an every-man-for-himself mentality arising.

The sea is calm as a conveyor belt, the motor hums and, with nothing to do, I opt for a shower and shave. Everyone is dozing, so now, stainless and still, I feel I can sit comfortably on the white cushions without leaving my mark. To add a degree of excitement, I make chai and dangerously dunk digestives. It's a dull, overcast day, everybody seems to be self-isolating, and so I have solitude in a communal area. Which doesn't make me look as antisocial as I feel.

The day drags like a useless anchor and by 5 p.m. we are back on the middle island – or, at least, by it – as we moor in the middle of a remote but not unpopulated bay. Without onlookers, the embarrassment levels are lower, but still incompetence reigns as ropes are dropped into the sea, secured things come loose and knots won't come undone. The dinghy is used to take a securing rope to a rock on the shore as the anchor doesn't seem to be working. Despite the clarity of the water, no one can see why it's failing to keep us from drifting.

We harness some roaming Wi-Fi. Briefly, the mood is upbeat, but then it rains and we lose the connection despite our landline. Once again, promises of going ashore to a restaurant never materialise, and the boat appears now to revolve around one person's wishes.

This bay reminds me of Sweden and the islets around the east coast, with a wild rocky shore, dense forest beyond, and isolated houses sitting in secluded bays. I open my wine and try to avoid the drenched deck and wet cushions soaked by a discourteous seaman. Dinner is salad and bread, which is apparently deemed adequate. It attracts wasps and to add to an evening of dampness and disruptions a fish is caught and sacrificed in an inedible way, leaving only stench and scales which attracts more pests on the wing. I let the wine take me away as the only conversation is spoken in Bulgarian, then I go to the cabin to read. Cigarette smoke drifts through the porthole and the rhythm of tinny music from a phone is tapped out on the floor which constitutes my ceiling.

A variety of views

It's a dull morning, so I look at photos I've taken. The authentic smiles from the beginning of the boat trip seem a long time ago. I go out on deck, say good morning. There is no reply, so I say it again. Nothing. Not even a grunt, which is ironic as this is the only other person on the boat who is a native English speaker.

The clouds clear and, although there is no sunrise, the mood lightens. The captain and the rest of the Bulgarians get up as the sun comes out, oblivious to the sullen start, as they have been to every tranquil dawn and personal sunrise I've taken from this trip.

The water is bouncing rays with a squinting blaze and a morning clarity. Eight metres below us, the sea bed has a deceptive depth and an ambiguous temptation. It's clear there is nothing harmful in the water but equally easy to see a predator approach. This only encourages the Motocamp Four. We venture in. I'm surrounded by a school of tiny, bright fish and am thrown a waterproof camera from the boat; the fish disappear like flavour in a frozen prawn.

The captain and his family take the dinghy and go ashore, leaving us with the opportunity, but inability, to sail off somewhere. Like an open door in a birdcage, unease enters, obstructing the freedom beyond. When everyone is back on board, I volunteer to row the dinghy ashore to untie us from the rock; now putting myself in a position of abandonment. The rowing makes my elbow ache, after it had been OK for a few days. I let the winch pull me back to the boat.

My chores are not over: I'm given the wheel. I really want to give it back, I'm not convinced I'm taking us in the right direction. I do what I've seen the captain do and start drinking – it takes any unnecessary conscientiousness away, and I've learnt that, if you don't want to do something, do it badly and you won't be given the task again. It worked for years with dishwasher loading. The sky has clouded over, it's cool and we sit at a steady three knots, which is about five and a half miles an hour. Trying to keep a bike in a straight line at that speed would have me losing my balance, that's my excuse for our weaving wake right there.

We are heading for the big port of Skiathos. The approach is very exciting. There are cruise ships and freighters, and the ramp of an airport runway meets the sea, the black skid marks of initial contact giving it dragstrip resemblance. There are the kind of high-end boats that I associate with the super-rich: sleek designs; tinted windows; bulbous satellite communications protruding from their elegant lines; expensive women with dark sunglasses and cosmetically enhanced curves, draped on the deck like they are drying out, but holding a cocktail. Through a zoom lens there are signs of too much sun for too many years, all best viewed from a distance. Although an invitation to board for canapés is as unlikely as us mooring without a drama. Today we find a new level of disdain. We have to squeeze between two other boats, we rub fenders and are levered away with loathing. I'm not feeling the love from our fellow sea fearers, we are not welcome neighbours as we ram our way into an ungiving gap. Our amateur abilities and scary tattoos attract covert stares of unfathomable intolerance – we are as inexplicable as the superyachts are inaccessible.

It's good to stand on a hard promenade and watch the ferries and freighters roll in and out. Boats seem to have more dividing qualities than uniting ones: freight, food, commute, pleasure, charter, livelihood, lifestyle, it's no wonder it was so hard to fit in.

I don't do much better in a coffee shop. The waitress fails to understand I want food, so I settle for Wi-Fi and get critiqued on Facebook by a fellow travel author, Ants, for being an international playboy. 'Looking for an international playgirl' I reply, as this particular girl would certainly fit the bill, although perhaps not be able to pay it. Anyway, if she'd seen the size of the vessel I've just witnessed she'd realise this is little more than a deck hand job.

From the top of the hill we take in the view of the town. The Motocamp crew opt for a tourist thoroughfare and I for a back-street fish restaurant, where I chat to the owner and enjoy a peaceful meal which is eventually paid for on credit card.

This is a party town and I'd prefer to feel the buzz from a distance than be in the centre of the attention-seeking. So I grab my stuff and sit on the bow deck out of sight but able to view. Boats and planes come to port through a darkening sky of tenacious stars and landing lights. The light on the land has a squinting glaze of alcohol and candid conversations come close enough to hear. It's like sleeping on a park bench under a cloak of invisibility. I'm unseen with an unrestricted view of sky, sea and passing life.

Thinking of the box

Friday 11th September

This is the best dawn of the trip – despite wanting a wee, I watch it all from my blow-up mattress and white duvet, becoming more conspicuous as the day lightens. When I can't hold it or hide anymore, I pick up my bedding and walk to the stern. The captain is already active and trying to top up our water tanks. He can't figure out the hose connections so I help with that, now bursting to top up the waste-water tank.

Still unable to get any kind of confirmation or commitment as to time or plan, and no longer caring, I take my last ten euros to a restaurant for a bacon breakfast and revel in the decadence of my decision. There has definitely become an 'us and them' divide on the boat. Again, without the language I'm unaware of what has occurred, but the Motocamp crew seem to be separating from the captain and his family, and within our party there is an internal pyramid of power too. I suppose it was inevitable. A student anthropologist would have more than enough material here for a thesis; we have cultural, linguistic, philosophical, economic and even biological differences. Being September the 11th, I mention the significance of the date and the conversation briefly gets political. I'm shocked to discover that Doug genuinely thinks Trump would make a good president. I'm not going to argue and I'm certainly going to steer clear of any further political discussions. There is no trace of anyone else being even dimly aware of a certain unease, so I'm on my own with that one. Perhaps because I look further than the bottle, phone, iPod or book – although I'm not adverse to any of those forms of escapism. I am, however, at least aware of what it is I'm escaping from.

Speaking of escapism, Polly and I discuss the possibility of riding to Morocco this October. I'm not sure if it's the ride that appeals or the significance: this would put an end to my wondering how to spend my fiftieth birthday.

The sails go up just before the wind drops, so they come back down again. The motor goes on along with the autopilot. We are going back to Volos, it's the final day of the trip. There is a spontaneous snorkelling stop – well, for me. Perhaps it's been discussed, a clandestine consensus. I try to encourage Zoe to come in; the poor girl is bored out of her mind. I talk her into the water with promises of fish and coral views, and when she does come down the steps she swims in the opposite direction. I can't make a connection now, it's broken beyond repair. I've got a place to go, and spend the afternoon with a wine bottle. Those same tempting cliff-hugging roads reappear, this time on the starboard side. My mind goes back to motorbikes and then the upcoming nine-day motorcycle show in the UK. Last year, one of the authors put his books in brown cardboard boxes as a gift package, thereby selling two books in one go. I should do that for my trilogy, but I want a theme printed on the box, something that will encourage someone to pick it up, that will look good on a bookshelf. I can't really use the planet, it's the wrong shape. What else is associated with motorcycle travel? A pannier, a pannier, a fucking pannier, oh my god. A replica of my beaten-up, sticker-festooned pannier, scaled down to contain the three books. I've just had an epiphany, I can sell the books for less than their individual cost and … and, wait, if I get sponsorship from various companies to have their stickers on my three-book boxset pannier that will pay for the production of it. This is truly a Eureka moment, if I get nothing else from this trip it was still worth it. That only took six days at sea, followed by half a bottle of wine; a necessity, an inkling, a concept, a solution, the invention, all in the space of ten minutes, bam

bam bam bam. My work here is done, take me to the horizon, I've got a plan to implement.

Some people are superstitious about inspiration. Writers in particular will have certain rituals and locations for creativity to flow. I don't know where it comes from; like luck, it's sporadic but still it finds me. Sometimes there is a bottle nearby, but like today, it's not necessarily half empty, and sometimes I wonder if it was always there, gifted to me like being left-handed and word-blind. I may be lacking in some common senses, but the shortfall is compensated for in the occasional creative flash of brilliance. OK, you have to wade through a lot of bollocks to get to that cherry, but it is a fruit so sweet once found.

The captain puts on a Dire Straits CD. The irony of the actual meaning of the phrase is lost on him. It's a live album, there is a version of 'Sultans of Swing' I've not heard before. I know Mark Knopfler is rated as a talented guitarist, but it's never come across on the radio-played hits everyone knows. After all these years, I'm hearing something previously missed, this is spectacular. The sun is shining, the coast is visible and the scenery is stimulating. There is a good vibe, the crew seem content. I think I'm having a moment, and this song will forever remind me of it. This is perfect, I need to capture it, enhance it, I need a cherry on top. I opt for putting my most expensive product in my hair. After a week of sea and salt air it has the effect the advertisement implies. Swish whoosh, shine, body and form. Fuck it, I'm gonna have another glass of wine.

I drink all the way back to port, where we meet the boat owner. He seems satisfied with the condition of the boat, although we have to wait until the morning when the bottom inspector will come with his aqualung looking for pieces of a broken hull.

Well, it's certainly been a voyage of discovery – inward, outward and sideways. Would I do it again? No, but I won't dismiss it either. What happened at sea will stay with me, and I'll harbour the memories.

Racing the clouds home

I'm not really sleeping much on this deck, but it's such a stimulating and rare bedroom that closing my eyes seems a waste. On the industrial side of the dock is a tower with a time and temperature display visible from the whole town, it's my bedside dockside clock and the alarm is set for dawn. I decide to stay under the duvet and view the bobbing boats and shrieking gulls. I'm comfortable and content, all I have to do today is go home, so I prolong the moment. I've made it through the week without a hangover or any confrontation. Which basically means my mouth was opened and closed with responsibility and respect – how quaintly uncharacteristic.

The Motocamp Four are packed and ready to leave, the only thing stopping us is obligation. However, no longer confined by being at sea, we bid bon voyage to our captain and his family. I had a chat with Zoe this morning – she seemed relieved it was over. I had feared the tumultuous tantrums of teenage angst, but the childish behaviour came from grown-ups.

The money is still not sorted out, the boat has to be re-fuelled, and the cost of supplies is a clusterfuck of incalculable contributions. I like things to be even and fair, it's a Libran trait. I don't live my life by the zodiac but, like having a birth sign represented by scales, there has to be some fundamental characteristics I share with one twelfth of the planet's population, who all have a birthday coming up in the next six weeks. But another trait is not liking confrontation, so with my concerns suppressed like a suppository we head for the car. I always drive whatever seat I'm in, it comes from all those years as a truck driver. So I offer to take the wheel. It also happens to come with the most legroom too.

We get to Bulgaria on fumes, of fuel in the tank and

smoke in the car, the considerate vape replaced with the obnoxious toxic cigarette. The roads are now noticeably rougher and the pace slower – that, though, is why I choose to live here. The temperature drops and the scenery improves as the road north to the capital runs through a valley. The country's prestigious ski resort, Bansko, and the pristine Pirin National Park, the nation's pride, is just to the east of us. However, the biggest and strongest attraction right now is a KFC in Sofia. I drive us into the centre, where common sense conflicts with the satnav and there is no compromise or love lost between us. The Saturday city traffic flows through the streets unhindered and everything is affordable again, if not desirable, but apparently there's only one choice in the city.

Every time a fag is fired up, I wind my electric window down. Then, like escaped air round a lung, the window collapses into the bottom of the door. The light fades, the clouds come and cold air blows into the car. For the only time on this trip, we reach for the fleeces and long trousers as I try to beat the rain back home and drop myself off.

I close the door on seven days of social exposure, open wine and Facebook, and unpack. I share my top tips for overland travel. I've got some over-sea travel tips now. That's golden hindsight for ya.

Window can't be recovered from wind down

Sunday 13th September

The bed isn't moving but I'm swaying like indecision. It would appear I've found my sea legs. The horizon won't stay still, but then I've never really wanted it to.

In the two months since I bought this house I've only lived in it for four weeks, but it is undoubtably home. The upstairs has concrete floors and cardboard mats; the walls are still the insipid pink they were when I purchased them. It has a distinct smell – I've not smelt it in any other Bulgarian home, it's unique but only noticeable after a week away. There are no fly screens on the blindless windows, but still I feel a privacy and security here. Even more so now, as I had no quarters on board the boat.

I've never been so detached; I can play music loud and disturb no one. Absurdly, without the resonant tinnitus of a terraced house or the constant flow of traffic, I prefer to listen to the silence. For years I yearned for a place where I could be a slob and turn my amplifier up to eleven, and now I have the opportunity I'm unplugged and uncluttered. I pad barefoot on the tiles and make my chai. The kettle boils to its crescendo and then clicks off for the crickets outside to pick up the beat.

I'm a little embarrassed at posting my top tips on Facebook last night, done with the bravado of the bottle. Thankfully, it's been well received, forty-seven shares, and not a negative comment, not yet anyway.

I pick up the Motocamp car and bring it home in an attempt to fix the electric window. The structure behind the door panel seems specifically designed to cut into probing arms, wires are twisted and plastic rollers disfigured by strangled rotation. Just as I get everything in place with one more cable to hook over a drive pulley, the tension breaks and the window drops back to the bottom of the door. After three attempts, with forearms looking like self-harm, I admit defeat and wedge the window up with some custom carpentry.

The routine is quickly re-established and Tabby Cat comes round for sunset. She relishes the affection and I get the feeling she knows this house better than me. Perhaps she was doing the rounds before I was around. Now all I have to do is get her approval on the improvements.

Like brushing my teeth, Facebook, after a week of sporadic Wi-Fi, is checked first thing in the morning and last thing at night. My post has got 128 shares and reached 28,000 people. I've never come close to such figures before. Annoyingly though, it's not reflected in any book sales. It's all been very quiet. It's not the kind of tranquillity I want.

The pros and cons of virtual commerce

Monday 14th September

I don't usually go straight to the laptop but it's Monday morning and I've had a week off. There is a mental list of chores, among them the need to start the process of producing the pannier book box set. I've got an email though, and that takes priority. The PayPal facilities on my website are not working. I try a phantom purchase, it's impossible to check out. Motherfucker, my post now has a reach of 30,000 and not a single sale from it. There hadn't been any last week – which I saw as convenient, seeing as I was at sea and couldn't get dispatch organised – but it's not bloody convenient now. I bet it's been like this for a while. I contact my IT man and he confirms it's been down for a week and fixing it is not straightforward. Ouch, the frustration. The best, most shared, most popular, most credible post I've ever written, and for all the traffic it generated to my site I've not got a single sale. It's the missed gear on the drag strip, the caravan in front on your favourite corner, the flat spot on a fistful of throttle. All that momentum amounted to nothing. It's a despondent way to start the week.

Six hours pass in front of the screen – well, I'm certainly making up for the laptop time lost at sea. Rations are low, and they have probably been worried about me, so I head to Kaufland. With the conscientiousness of true consumer allure, they have fly screens this week. There are only two left in brown, but that's the bedroom sorted. I buy a bottle of rum for Keith too as it's his birthday, and also because I will want to borrow more of his tools.

Drob calls to try and arrange a visit. I'm a bit non-committal as I've got Mum coming, a possible ride with Polly and I have to go back to the UK again soon. He too has many unconfirmed commitments so he doesn't feel like I'm giving him the elbow. Speaking of which, while I've

276

got him on Skype, I ask about my mine. Apparently, ice is the answer for tennis elbow. Great, that golden bit of information has come about two weeks too late. The entrapment of the internet continues, and I decide to order some new tyres for the KLR as well, just in case the trip to Morocco materialises.

I force myself away from my e-commerce to mow the lawn. The bloody mower won't start. I spend more time repairing it than I do actually mowing. I give up on it, it's knackered. I'm going to let Mum buy me a new one when she gets here. She said she wanted to get me something for the house.

It's another Tabby Cat sunset, followed by some swatting before bed. China has woken up and I'm getting some printed pannier box quotes coming through. How could I do that without the internet? Location is nothing more than a connection; the trick is finding time to disconnect.

Contracts and contacts

Tuesday 15th September

There is an unmistakable autumn chill in the air now, not the crisp crunch of frost or the soft crush of leaves but a respite from summer swelter, at least in the morning. Today all Bulgarian children go back to school after the summer holiday. Traditionally, they all take flowers for their teachers, huge bouquets bigger than the children in some cases. The floral parade approaching the school gates takes the misery out of what can be quite a daunting day. Not that this happens in our village: the school building is abandoned and derelict. This is also one of the few villages without a church. I can only assume this is because we don't need no education or thought control. Anyway, as a grown-up, all today represents is the start of a season of calmer shopping in Kaufland.

I put a pile of ice cubes in a towel and wrap it round my elbow. Having no carpets in the house, I plod around leaving a trail of drips as I go about my morning ritual, and settle in front of the laptop where a puddle starts to form. China has come back with box prices which are higher than I'd hoped – the whole point is to give them away as enticing packaging. After I take into account the freight and import duties, the financial losses are too big to bear, but the idea is too good to give up on.

There is mainly disappointment on the screen. Plans that required the commitment and co-operation of others are looking unlikely to materialise. This is why my motorcycle journeys are mostly solo, my books produced with minimal outside input, and I suppose why I live alone. My expectations often seem higher than the obligation I ask for. Company for pleasure and companies for profit don't seem to share my drive or, worse still, dampen my enthusiasm. I have a track record of achieved dreams, perhaps driven by a single-minded vision, but my plans usually come to fruition in the bright light at the end of the tunnel.

I wave off my neighbour. He's riding to Bosnia. I've not ridden for over a week and I won't be any time soon. Life has got in the way of my lifestyle. I take out the fly screen kit and slowly measure and cut. It's a straightforward project and very satisfying, and like anything that gives me pleasure I want more. Conveniently, I get a call from Ivo. He's taking a delegation of new immigrants to Gabrovo to try and sort out our electric contracts. I wonder if I should take flowers. Apparently, another house in the village sold to Brits while I was away at sea. Incidentally, the captain has been in touch – there is no balance left to pay, he hopes we enjoyed the trip, and he even hinted that we didn't drink enough. Ha, my mother will be so proud.

My contract is finally ready. It's been the slowest process of the entire house purchase. Not that it's been a problem, but I'm surprised at how good it feels to officially be part of the national grid. Then to Kaufland and from grids to grills – although it's the wrong colour, I buy the last of the discounted fly screens. And finally from contracts to contacts: Polly takes me to her optician who has no qualms about selling me contact lenses over the counter without me having to prove I can fit and remove them. The optician thinks I'm her boyfriend so I hold her hand when we walk out the shop. That's contact best not seen.

The excitement of contracts, contacts and screens is topped off with the new roundabout being open on what was a tricky little junction in the centre. This is a thrill the traveller doesn't get to witness. I'm settling down, I'm signing up and securing, I'm establishing myself with local historical facts. I can now recount to glazed eyes of a time before this junction had a roundabout and the in-car entertainment it generated the day it opened. I don't think there's a book in it, *Last Exit to Kaufland*, but the trucker in me has always been thrilled by an upgraded road. I couldn't sleep the night before the unveiling of the QE2 bridge over the Thames, and narrowly missed being the first artic on the A14 Catthorpe interchange as I dozed in a Lutterworth lay-by waiting for the radio to announce access was imminent.

As well as his hundred beehives, the previous owner of my house had hunting dogs too. They were kept in crude kennels made of old pallets and tarpaulin, I don't know what happened to the bees or the dogs but the kennels stand abandoned at the end of my garden. The Germans, being the saviours of abandoned dogs, can put them to good use and come with their trailer to pick them up. I get more elbow guidance, and am told that on no account should I attempt to lay a stone floor in the garage. I know this is good advice, but I just want to get it finished. I'm out of time now anyway, Mum arrives tomorrow, and an author friend is passing through. I'll have to satisfy myself with smaller projects, like fly screens.

Now assembled, I want to install them, so I go and borrow a ladder off Bruce. He's quite envious of my fly screens. He doesn't even have windows yet, just plastic stapled over the frames. He does have a really lovely stepladder though; he never knew his real ladder.

I could go to Motocamp this evening but the sunset calls louder. It's obscured as ever by the satellite dish. I was told the communications company was going to come and collect it and I'm tired of waiting. Since I have the ladder here, I take it down. It's remarkably easy and that only makes me more frustrated that I didn't do it two months ago.

Meeting my mother for the first time (in Bulgaria)

Wednesday 16th September

Tabby Cat has come round with one of her kittens, the long-haired tabby who is cute but clumsy and brutish, with bull-in-a-china-shop tendencies. I call him Blump because he is a cross between a bull and a thump. He's an outside cat born and bred. If I can coax him inside the house, he looks for his escape route with anxiety in his eyes. Outside, he's just a roll-over furball that I can't stop photographing.

China shopping is looking more likely. It seems the box makers want to play the haggle game. I'd politely declined their offer, thanking them for their quotation, and then this morning they seem to have found a cheaper method of production – well, it's the same method, but produces less profit for them. I see how it's done now. I try to get in a contact lens and fail. It seems they only go in when it doesn't matter, in much the same way as how I can only speak my Bulgarian words and be understood when they are superfluous.

Time to go. I'm taking the van to Sofia to pick up Mum from the airport. Being a right-hand drive means I get stuck behind trucks a lot. I can only edge out when I see someone ahead overtake. The van has acceleration like my learning and pronunciation of Bulgarian: it's slow and beyond comprehension. I mostly follow obediently and it takes me two and a half hours to do the 135-mile journey. The airport parking is a weed-infested area of cracked concrete, abandoned vehicles, flat tyres, missing parts and number plates, the ones that have identity are mainly British. A scrapyard of broken dreams perhaps, the relocation that resulted in a flight back to Blighty, abandoned belongings and left longings.

On the plus side, the slow journey means I only have a five-minute wait until Mum is pushed through the arrival's door by an attentive wheelchair driver. On her lap is a Sofia Airport duty-free bag: I had informed her a bottle of Jura was her rite of passage. So airport assistance tipped and mother loaded, I pay the paltry parking fee and head back the way I came.

Mum has her boundless enthusiasm with her as well and the new Motörhead CD and Mötley Crüe tickets. I've met her off planes in Mexico, Mongolia and even the US. She hobbles along on her crutch through the terminal, often overtaking the perfectly able. She'll fit right in with the driving habits here.

We stop at the now customary snack café; I order kebab and salad but get chips and bread. Which wouldn't be so bad, but the words for kebab and salad are *kebapche* and *salata*, so not that different. Chips and bread, however, are called *purzheni kartofi* and *hlyab*, which sounds somewhat different. There is no logic to the driving, the roadside restaurants, the language or the food-ordering system. And, what's more, it's all on bloody display, so even pointing doesn't work.

Well, welcome to Bulgaria, Mum, this is how it will be. If you have a finicky diet, a nervous disposition and no patience, this place may not be for you. However, when two people can eat for a pound, if you are low of funds then all of the country's shortcomings are soon forgiven.

The drive home takes even longer. I can't rely on Mum's 'it's clear if you're quick' overtaking encouragement. I need to get a left-hand drive vehicle.

And this is my house. She has seen lots of photos, but nothing could prepare her for the vastness of the garden, the view from the terrace, the freshness of the air and silence of the surroundings, dogs and strimmers notwithstanding. 'So make yourself at home,' I say. 'I've got work to do.'

China are relentless, don't they ever sleep? The price is coming down like it got a virus, and in other news Adventure Bike TV has nominated me for a prize in the viewers' awards: 'The most inspirational expat-absconded-motorcycle-garage-floor-builder's category' or something. It's very flattering anyway, regardless of the lack of competition.

I have a friend in the US. She used to have some high-powered position in the corporate world, and flew all over the place, all the time, doing things that caused stress and earned big money. Eventually, she decided to give it all up and make jewellery. She approached this artistic, leisure-motivated enterprise in her same headstrong business-orientated manner, and predictably made a success of it. However, I don't think she relieved the stress aspect of her life. She'd check the price fluctuations of precious metals daily, purchasing with calculated prediction. Anyway, the point is, while displaying at a craft and jewellery fair, she was standing outside the event having a breather and was approached by someone who said: 'You're one of my favourite jewellers, I've purchased many items from your website.' She told me later that she'd never been called a jeweller before and it felt simultaneously foreign and a validation for all the work she had put into her desired new direction. Well, today I feel like what I've done as a travel author is actually of interest to some people.

I put on the new Motörhead CD and give Mum the tour. Downstairs is brief – yes, that's gym in the corner, we're not speaking. She finds the stairs a bit tricky but worth it for the view. Then outside, and the circuit deliberately takes her past the broken mower on the way to the overgrown lawn. If it were obligatory to be in awe of the house and garden she wouldn't be flouting any laws. My appreciation hasn't faded, but with every new guest and their complimentary comments, it renews my wonder – how did I get here? I only came to do a talk at a bike meeting; was only passing time before my UK house sold; was only escaping the despondency of a broken bike. And now I'm a Bulgarian resident, with a lawn of the greenest grass, as far as you can see. Let's have a drink.

One of the Germans has a birthday today so we go to Motocamp for cake and German nibbles. It's all vegetarian, it could be wurst. Polly and Ivo are excited to see the Mötley Crüe tickets. Mum buys a Motocamp sweatshirt as the temperature drops. I have tape put around my arm to help support and repair my tennis elbow. It looks a bit obvious, like a dayglo tourniquet. Motocamp has something for everyone: mothers, veggies, rockers and raspberries.

Both being invalids, I make the couch into a bed; Mum will be a ground-floor guest, and those stairs are going to be my escape route if I need a bit of time alone. The water is off again, but it's OK. Now, where did I put that whisky?

Mother, should I mow the lawn?

Thursday 17th September

Thirteen years ago today the phone rang in the middle of the night. I let it go to the answer machine. The call was from the US and the message said I was now a father. It wasn't the proudest moment of my life, but as my daughter has grown we have connected and disconnected over the miles that separate us multiple times. Her mother either loves me or hates me, there is no middle ground and my daughter tends to follow suit – presently, I'm not rating very high in the popularity stakes. Anyway, hopefully today the present I sent will arrive at her door. I've spoken to many estranged fathers and they all say that their teenage kids came back in their twenties, so I have that to look forward to.

There is still no water and the toilet is getting smelly. I have a store of ten-litre bottles for such situations. I fill up the cistern and flush, then fill up the kettle and boil. Responding to China has become my morning ritual, it's like tai chi, with a cup of chai tea. My IT man has been in touch. My website checkout is now up and running, though unfortunately my popularity is down and falling. Nothing lasts very long on a fast feed. 'Hey, wait everyone, come back, it's me, you all liked and shared my post four days ago, remember? Do you want to buy a book? My website is working again.' I'm only as popular as my last post, and no one is going to share my despair.

We get in the van and head to the big DIY shop; Mum doesn't want to do sightseeing in historic Veliko Tarnovo, she only wants to see me happy, and today I'm going to get a new mower. Some purchases I research to the point of paralysis, and considering conflicting views leaves me assessing the reviewer to work out whose views are valid. But there are others where I do not. The house was purchased without research and it's possibly the best thing

I've bought in my life. I will adopt the same method with a mower. The difference being, instead of getting the biggest bargain, I'll just get the most expensive. The salesman agrees with my philosophy wholeheartedly and extols the virtues of the top-of-the-range self-propelled mower, flaunting guarantees and workmanship like a car salesman. I've never had a new mower before, or bike or car or couch or washing machine – in fact, it's probably my second-hand lifestyle that has afforded me so many first-hand experiences.

I've always harboured a venomous envy for people who go to a dealership for a test ride, quoting magazine reviews, statistics and making a purchase based on colour. My life has never been like that. Colour has never swayed my decision. I even rode a 'metallic mauve' Harley for eighteen months in the States – the colour was a faded lilac and could, it's fair to say, in certain lights appear to have a tint of pink. However, it was a spectacular bike, my only transport much of the time, and the most reliable Shovel-head-powered Harley I've ever owned. Anyway, I didn't really notice the colour when I was riding it.

Today I'm going to make my purchase based on the black-and-orange colour scheme. It will match the KTM, it looks gorgeous. I never thought the day would come when I saw sexiness in a lawnmower. This one is dark and sleek, it has orange highlights in the form of hubcaps and branding and an aluminium heat shield over the exhaust. It's got a black, soft optional bag to collect the grass cuttings – so, basically, it's a convertible. You could probably pull chicks with this model. As we drive home, I'm wishing I had a pick-up truck so people could see it in the bed. Cars would honk and wave – hey baby, wanna trim my pasture? Instead, it's locked away like chastity in the back of the van.

Back home we have lunch on the terrace, using the mower box as a table, and once we've had lunch together it's part of the family. I start the assembly. Man, it's a sexy beast, a virgin blade without a trace of grass on it. It's immaculate, so I take photos of it, fill it with fuel and oil and it starts first pull, first pull! The day is hot and sunny, I'm sun-blocked and taped up, clad in panama hat and cut-off jeans. With a purring four-stroke engine and a self-drive power train, I take it to the prairie, past the stripped and dejected old mower that in the bottom of its heart knows it's had its final cut.

I have to confess it's been five weeks since I last mowed – come on, baby, gimme some turf topiary. Eager as Edgar, it cuts the grass and hoovers up the cuttings into the collector box. Up and down, there and back, seeking pleasure in the process for the first time. Mum is fervently taking photos which I imagine will be proudly displayed on the mantel next to my first day at school. The grass is long but the engine is strong. It doesn't faulter. With the bottom third done, I stop to survey my work. The lawn has the lines of a pre-season Premier League pitch.

I down a pint of water, top up the tank and move to the next level. This is the flattest part of the garden. I can feel the wind in my hair as I fly past the fledgling Christmas trees. Then to the incline of the banked cherry-tree terrain, and finally the long stretch, the area I left as meadow for wild flowers. They are all dead now and I happily pass my time in the grassland away, only dimly aware of the time passing. The entire lawn is done; I have a pile of cuttings you could hide a car under. It's taken two and a half hours and I've walked 5.8 kilometres. I've never mowed so much, so hot, so new, so excited, so pleasurable, so overdue. So same time next week? No, sorry, I'll be out of town. Man, the lawn looks good. This is how it was when I first viewed the house. I didn't appreciate the work that went into it, but now I get it. I won't be needing that multigym now, I'm bloody knackered.

We go to the big tree just beyond my boundary and pick some walnuts to add a little more idyllic to the day. If that's not enough, I open some wine and put on my new favourite album: Dire Straits live. Tabby Cat comes over. The sun is going down noticeably earlier every day. I've got internet obligations. I want to ride my bike, paint my walls, do the garage floor and the bike shed, but I have to rest my arm. The thing is, I'll be in the UK for a month – where does the time go? Right now, I can just about see it at the bottom of this bottle of wine.

Monumental obligation

I got a new bin for the kitchen yesterday too, but one has to have limits and it felt vulgar to mention it. It's impracticably small and this is for a reason: there is no recycling in the village. After two months, the immoral feeling of putting plastic, paper and glass in the dustbin is growing less sinful. I'm hoping a small bin will encourage me to take my less rubbishy rubbish to a cleaner, greener place.

I'm swapping images of boxes with China like we are dating.

'Here photo of box printed, this one bare, no design, you see raw material.'

'I found this one on Instagram, can you do this?'

If only my life were as even as the lines on the lawn. It all feels a bit chaotic at the moment, there is no structure or routine. I'm not sure where I am going, how I'll get back and when it will be, plus I've got visitors coming tomorrow. All these uncertainties combined give me an increasing desire to just stay here in the house and get things done, to make my nest for winter. But my arm continues to ache, even strapped up, and I need to rest it.

The girl who asked to share my Buzludzha photos last month has been back in touch. She says she's read one of my books and wants to swing by to get it signed, but she is in the UK. She tells of how she got ripped off by a British builder whom she flew in from the UK to Bulgaria, and her house is not liveable in the winter. So how will she 'swing by'? I don't really get it.

Tabby Cat and Blump come and introduce themselves to Mum. They seem more confident now, but don't stay long – they clearly have somewhere to go, as do we. I take my plastics to town for recycling but I think I put them in the wrong receptacle. In Romania they are made of mesh so you can see what's inside; here there is just a tube to push the bottles through. Maybe it's to stop people taking the contents and re-recycling them for profit.

I think Mum should see something significant while she is here so I drive us up the mountain to Buzludzha. It's not the best of roads on a bike and with four wheels it's impossible to avoid the potholes. The going is slow but the corner that reveals the surreal flying saucer monument makes it worth the effort. Against the dark blue sky, the Soviet architecture is as striking as the brutal design intended. Sometimes I feel it more than others, but this day doesn't allow for projection into the dark times of the Iron Curtain.

The sightseeing feels forced. Mum is happy to just sit on the terrace, but I feel obligated to at least leave the village and go beyond DIY shops and supermarkets. The majority of Bulgaria remains undiscovered to me. I've seen the Black Sea from just about every coast it has except that belonging to the country I now live in, and I'm equally close to the capital as I am near Varna. The journey, though, would be more enjoyable on a bike, and I've not ridden for two weeks now. It's a subtle yearning, not the full-blown withdrawal symptoms of a denied drug or the pink cloud of abstinence. More an irrational, creeping dissatisfaction with everything. Then I realise I've not had enough bike in my life and, once the diagnosis is discovered, the craving for the cure overrides all. That's probably why I enjoyed mowing the lawn so much, the pull of the engine and the late summer breeze in my face is the closest I've got to a ride in ages. This evening, though, I will have to settle for white wine, a big red sun and the sweet smell of newly mown grass.

Does he look like a bitch?

This morning's internet obligations are to persuade the viewers of Adventure Bike TV to vote for me. I bloody hate this. It's bad enough doing blatant self-promotion on social media. All the authors do it with varying degrees of sickening, sanctimonious immodesty. However, this award comes with credibility, and so I embark on my meek crusade. The deadline for this month's column is looming too. I'm losing enthusiasm for the online magazine as emails are never answered and I'd like some response for my efforts. However, the lounge is off limits until Mum gets up, so I may as well sit up here and bang something out.

Mum has no preference as to what to do with the day, so I decide she can watch me paint the house. Or, at least, see how much of it this can of expensive white exterior paint will cover. The day is bright and the paint brighter, one coat seems adequate but it's hard to say for sure as the reflected sunlight from the pristine white walls is burning my retinas. I do the front ground floor before the paint runs out – that's one eighth of the house. I'll need seven more cans and the price of paint doesn't represent the Bulgarian cost of living; in fact, I think I can get it cheaper in B&Q. It really is dazzling – the white bounces sunlight back onto the terrace with tanning intensity. I know they paint the houses white in hot countries to reflect the heat, but if you are an outside person you've just bought your surroundings up to a level of singe. Before I buy more paint, I think I need to decide if a white house is such a good idea. The house is glaring like interrogation and I can feel my will wilting.

It reminds me of those miners in Chile who were trapped underground for two months: when they were finally evacuated, or excavated, into view of the world's press, they were made to wear dark glasses, which seemed particularly strange as the first ones to be unearthed surfaced at night. Still, I feel I should hang welding goggles by the steps for the viewing protection of visitors.

My friend is running late and has only just crossed the Romanian border. So we attempt to clean the house up, which is not easy with Mum living in the lounge, which is also the kitchen and dining room.

I reply to the Buzludzha-photo girl. The painting of the house being foremost in my mind for some reason, I send a photo of my bike boots and an empty Bulgarian wine bottle in front of the virgin white wall. Other than bike riding, there is something else lacking in my life, and corresponding with an attractive stranger has something stirring in me that, due to the thrill of my Bulgarian transition, was suppressed for a while.

But there is hope. Helen the hardcore travelling girl who is coming to visit is bringing a friend. The water is back on too, so I shower the white paint off of what is becoming a tanned body – although it's a shame about the high-vis tennis-elbow tape.

With wine on the terrace, we watch the sunset, awaiting the sound of motorcycles. I wave them up the drive with wine glass in hand. Luckily, it's only my face that drops when her friend's helmet is removed to reveal bushy sideburns. Back to the bottle then.

They will be camping in my garden, appreciating the mown lawn as little as I did on my first visit. I'm a little concerned how Motocamp will react to this. It's not my intention to take biker business away from them, but, equally, Helen and her sideburn-sidekick perhaps would not even be in the area if not to visit me. I show them the banked off-road route to ride up into the back garden, a bit too late, a bit too dark and a bit too drunk. I'll leave the house unlocked, but I know they won't be trudging all the way to the toilet in the night, and I don't like the thought of them pissing on my perfect lawn.

Host with the least

Sunday 20th September

This isn't my escape route. I feel like a prisoner in a tower now. I can't get to the kitchen to make chai or breakfast and I've got squatters in my garden.

Once everyone is up, I feel pressure to be host. No one appears to have any plans for the day so I'm entertainment manager too. I suggest we go for breakfast just as the long-awaited log delivery arrives. He's a local guy from down the street and drives an old Russian Gaz 66 truck, which appropriately runs on LPG. It's four-wheel drive and lumbers up my back passage swaying on the uneven embankment. I supervise the unloading, which basically involves designating which part of lawn is going to die. There is a second load coming which will be a total of twelve cubics – that's how firewood is ordered and quantified.

From my very first visit to Bulgaria, I've been warned of the horrific winters here, the sub-zero temperatures and prolonged isolation due to vast snowfall which can last from October until April. The lowest temperature of the winter as recorded on the most dramatic thermometer is taken, along with the date when the first and last snowflake fell. From those statistics the inaccurate threat of a frozen hell is miscalculated. These exaggerated tales of two ice-covered seasons are generally told by Brits who, perhaps before moving here, only ever witnessed a Gulf Stream winter. I've spent many winters in the high altitude of Colorado and I've coped before with deep snow and immense cold. However, I'm aware that my only form of heating in the house is the log burner. Although every room has a double radiator, without a fire to heat the water all they will radiate is a scolding rebuke. So I have taken the village advice this year and ordered the recommended amount of wood to see me through until spring. If I don't burn it all, it will be all the more seasoned for the following winter. It's comforting to think long-term; after spending the last seven years knowing my house could sell at short notice, I've had a no-permanency mentality for too long.

If I could speak Bulgarian as well as my log man can English, I would be happy. His grasp of the language is appalling, everything is wrong – tense, plural and pronunciation – but he is understandable, and that would be a milestone for me. I tell him I'm going to town to get his money from the ATM. What I lack in linguistics I make up for in fabrication, and we all go for breakfast leaving the log money in the kitchen drawer where it's been for weeks.

Our regular restaurant is closed so we go to the one I was warned away from. They have a menu in English, good service and tasty food, so it must have been a personal vendetta that provoked the bad review. We arrive back home as the second load of logs arrives and I'm told there has been a bike accident. The German who taped up my arm had a car pull out in front of him. I call Ivo, who is on his way to translate with police, ambulance drivers and the emergency department at the hospital. It doesn't sound good; I offer my help, but the picking up of the bike has already been arranged. It's never easy to find yourself as a guest in someone else's crisis, and I'm just discovering that having guests in your crisis is equally uncomfortable. They appear to have no inclination to do anything today and the conversation is drying up. Mum is nagging, I'm feeling pressured, everything is becoming chaotic. I have to work out what to pack, for how long, and how I am even going to get back here. Am I riding to Morocco, catching a flight or finding a left-hand drive vehicle to bring back? I've got no time to consider any of that.

I suggest a barbecue and go into town for supplies. We leave Helen to go over her new book, it's just come back from the copy-editor and she has to check the changes. I know how important this is. When I was in Mexico last winter, New Year's Eve passed me by as I went through the track changes of my book that was published this spring. I finished the work about lunchtime on the first of January; just as the hung-over were stirring back to life, I was ready to party. It's a great way to beat the crowds.

There is a low-quality shop in town that sells Asian imported rubbish. The best thing about it is the mountain view behind. I buy a cheap charcoal barbecue because this is going to be my first and last of the year. I'll get a better one next summer. There is nothing else to do but drink. The alcohol does exactly what it's supposed to and chatter flows. Helen cycled and camped through Siberia in winter. I met her when she was speaking about this at a travellers' meeting. One night, it was so cold she calculated that taking off her gloves in -30°C to erect her tent would be colder than sleeping without it. So she slept alone, exposed by the side of her bicycle in bleak, desolate eastern Russia. That's pretty hardcore, if you ask me. On this current trip, she and her new male friend Jimmy are riding their motorbikes down to South Africa. It should be a bit warmer there, I think.

My neighbour comes round bursting to tell me more about the motorcycle accident and then, in too much detail, about the cyst on his bollocks which I hope isn't as eager to burst. I fail to stop myself visualising his growth. He will be picking his wife up from the airport on Tuesday and can give us a lift, which is swell. I think this would be a good time to go to Motocamp. Helen and Jimmy can buy some beers, thereby helping the local economy, and I can see how my German friend is first-hand.

It turns out no one has any money on them, so the drinks go on my tab. My physiotherapist friend is in bed at the Motocamp apartment, he is in great pain. The house he lives in with his wife and rescued dogs is far from complete and comfortable. So I offer my place, I'll be away for a month, he can sleep on the couch if he can't manage the stairs. He's in too much agony to really take it in, but it's an option, although I think hospital is his best bet. Why is he even home?

Ivo tells me off about my driving. I was going too fast when I brought us back from Greece, apparently. Well, anyone else was welcome to take the wheel. They were happy enough to let me drive the whole fourteen-hour journey, especially when the driver's window collapsed into the door and the cold wind was blowing in. I just wanted to get the trip over with, I think everyone did, and whenever someone yelled 'Speed camera!' I always slowed the pace to regulation. Right, well, I'm not buying you lot anymore beers, so we may as well go back to mine and the barbecue. It breaks as I assemble it. I've had disposable ones with more longevity.

Mum nags and doesn't help, I drink Jägermeister and steam corn on the cob, but then get distracted and boil the pot dry. The room is full of smoke. I'm glad I'm not sleeping down here.

I've got no time for me at all. I've got mounting messages to reply to – that girl whom I randomly sent the photo of my motorcycle boots to has been back in touch, saying she loves a man in boots. This is becoming intriguing. However, I've really got no desire to go back to the UK. I just want some space here. I've still got no idea what to do for my fiftieth or even where I'll be. I might just let it drift past me as innocuously as a speed camera in the night, or like the smoke from boiled-dry and burnt food.

Logs in, sign out

I'm now losing sleep over this looming birthday, still unsure as to which country I'll be in and if I should just let it pass by alone and without ceremony. Solitude seems so much more appealing than company at the moment. Creeping round my house in the morning is getting tiresome, as is being unable to get to the kitchen. We are going to have to come up with a better arrangement next time my mother visits.

I am now getting daily messages from Lilly, the girl who asked to share my Buzludzha photos. She's posted a selfie, soaked from Welsh rain – apparently, that's where she lives. She looks pretty hot despite the dampness. With the confidence of a day's drinking I may have said as much last night. She asked why my books are not available in an audio version. I replied I was concerned about pirating, to which she responded that her business has been a victim of counterfeiting too.

When I am able to get into my kitchen, Mum asks when my guests are going to leave. That triggers me. I explain that, in fact, everyone is a guest, I'm trying to spread myself as evenly as possible, and I've got work to do in preparation for my trip to the UK. If someone bothered to express a preference as to what they wanted to do with the day we would do it. Saying 'I don't mind' is not being easy-going, it just puts the onus on me to decide everything from what we will eat and when I will cook it, to the places we will go and whom we will see. And with that little eruption the pressure is released. There is cloud cover this morning; it looks like it might rain. I can't be arsed to host breakfast, so we leave a note on the door for Helen and Jimmy and go to town in the van.

I need to get some plastic to cover the logs up. As we drive past the pedestrian area, I see a parking spot and spontaneously pull in. That is the only advantage of a right-hand drive vehicle over here: parallel parking is performed with kerb-hugging accuracy. I take Mum to a street café for a coffee. I order two cappuccinos for ease and get one and an espresso, which is ideal as I'd rather mix milk and alcohol than milk and coffee. Despite the caffeine hit, I feel myself relax and the tension lifts. This is some me-and-Mum time and it pacifies her.

Back at the house my other guests have gone to Moto-camp. Not having a secure shed, I start to store outside-implements in the van; the mower, my new precious, is now locked away. I put the plastic over the wood. It's not big enough, but it will have to do. We go to visit Keith. Mum loves to chatter and he's more responsive than I am after a week of constant company. My neighbour calls – a gypsy is outside my house with a chainsaw, come to cut my wood. The village voice is swift and efficient if not understood.

I've left the place unlocked so I hurry back. He is a skinny but muscular man with penetrating eyes which are as hard to read as Cyrillic – not that I need to, it's obvious what's going on here. I have logs that need cutting and he has a chainsaw. Let's get to work. He has brought his wife and daughter too. The wife has olive skin – not the green olives, the other ones – and beautiful long, thick, straight black hair. Hair is the first thing I notice about a person, then teeth, and the longer a girl's hair, the more attractive I find her. She keeps smiling at me, which at first is comforting but becomes disconcerting by about the fifth time our glances meet. Luckily, I have a can of coke in the fridge and give it to their little girl. She receives it with excitement equal to being given her first new pair of shoes. With an aching elbow, I take one cut log at a time into the shed. Jimmy returns and is obligated to offer a hand. Actually, I'll take them both.

299

The strange thing about a log delivery is that, when they arrive, I'm concerned if I have enough. As they are cut, I wonder if the fee will be higher than the quote as the quantity seems to have increased. As I stack them, I go from calculating if they will last the winter, to how they will all fit in the shed, to *for fuck's sake that's enough now*. The shed is full and the wood is cut and under cover. This is super-cool. The guests have earned their pitch fee.

In the evening I round them all up and drop them all off at Motocamp for dinner. I have my house to myself and concentrate on some packing without distraction. It's done in a manic manner of necessities versus Ryanair-weight-restriction awareness. There are too many unknowns to decide what to take. When I go back to Motocamp there is one less unknown. Polly says she can't ride to Morocco, there isn't enough time. I agree, I can't see how I could fit it in, but rather than taking off some pressure it just leaves a little disappointment. We say our goodbyes, and leave a spare key for the Germans. The bikes are in the garage, the lawnmower is in the van, the wood is in the shed and the guests are in the garden. I have no idea when I'll be coming back home, but I do know I'll be older.

Oh and by the way

50th minus 3 weeks

Motorbikes and Pink Floyd, my tastes haven't changed since my teens. The only difference has been the methods of earning the money to afford these obsessions. Presently it's books. I spend my first two days in the UK stocking Amazon, sending out orders, completing my column and canvassing votes for the Adventure Bike TV awards. I insure my KLR, which incidentally comes with ninety days free European breakdown service – oh, the irony. I photograph the original panniers that accompanied me on the long journeys which inspired my books.

I may have had the inspiration to make a box to put the books in, but it's my IT and graphics friend who has the ability to create a 3D image of the panniers for printing. He is such motivating company; we bounce ideas around and every one we come up with is a winner. I miss company like this. The problem with living in a village of retired expats is they may still have bikes but many have lost their drive. I'm told of a mutual friend whose wife has left him for a childhood sweetheart after twenty-five years of marriage. I blame Facebook. It's not the first time I've heard of this happening. I've met up with some old flames myself that way. I've been able to connect my graphics man up with several other travel authors. I love being the conduit in such situations. It's certainly more useful than the connections Facebook can be guilty of.

I go and see my longest friend on the planet. Actually, she's shorter than me, but I've known her since I was nine. She was literally the girl next door, and despite being shorter, she's a few years older than me and was a big influence on my impressionable youth. She is to be blamed by parents, and thanked by me, for my lifelong obsession with two-wheeled transport and my musical tastes from Motörhead to Pink Floyd. She has just got her results for a university course she's been doing for the last three years. She tells me the grade – it's just numbers, it means nothing to me, but apparently it's almost a first. I'm very proud of her, and offer her my spare ticket for David Gilmour in London tomorrow. But she won't go on the underground or lend me her van, is no longer a fan of motorcycles and fears for me in Bulgaria. For fuck's sake, how can she be so educated yet so ill-informed and fearful? I say it in jest, but she really needs to stop reading the *Daily Mail*. There is always one on the table, like a skid mark on the toilet pan that can't be pissed off. It pisses me off though, that her judgement is based on the scaremongering she is reading, and that my recounted, verbal first-hand experiences have no credibility against printed lies.

Her text wakes me in the night. *I worry about you, like it or not. Your (sic) like a little brother to me. So fuck off, enjoy yourself and take great care in all that you do x.* I worry about her too. Is she content in her confined horizons or afraid to look further? I get another text saying she hopes she didn't offend me using the F-word, she just didn't want to sound too gushy, and can I send the link to David Gilmour singing Shakespeare's Sonnet 18? Glad the English Literature degree isn't being wasted.

Lilly wants to know how long I'll be in the UK for. I'd like to know that too. She is messaging me every day now, inviting me to visit and saying she will come to the show I'm signing at this weekend to say hi. My reply is short, the space bar and 'm' have stopped working on my keyboard. I think she has been fooled by the public persona I project on social media. If I truly was a successful author, I wouldn't have to pimp myself out. This current campaign for votes is, in reality, just an award from a YouTube-based production company, who are craftily getting their nominees to increase the programme's popularity. Cynical as it may sound, that's how I see it, but if it gets me laid or a trophy on my mantel, I would like to thank Adventure Bike TV and Facebook for presenting me with this coveted award ...

* * *

I send my newly divorced friend a text as soon as I wake up: *Pig Dude, call me.* He's been in the police service since it was called a force and adapted to the changes of political correctness. His retirement is as imminent as my fiftieth, slightly further away but with far greater reward. This was supposed to be his happy ending: daughter off his hands; comfortable police pension; still young enough to pursue any dream. He has moved up the ranks, gone far, flown high and is now a detective inspector. He called me from the office one particularly hot summer's day to say: 'We're all sweating like pigs in here.' He is definitely a cop with a conscience, and a Pink Floyd fan too. He calls almost immediately; I tell him about the ticket and without hesitation he accepts. That's what I want. Enthusiasm. Nothing else matters.

I ride the KLR to his in the afternoon. I want to hear everything about the break-up. Unlike Raymond at Moto-camp ensnaring me with an undeterred and detailed account of his divorce, having Pig Dude getting it off his chest does not get on my tits. Obviously, there is another side to the story. He is struggling, but he's smart, reliable, balanced and always good company.

We had intended to get food before the gig but time has slipped away and we head straight to the Royal Albert Hall. We walk the long Kennington pedestrian tunnel towards the source of reverberating and atmospheric guitar, which stops conversation in exchange for musical appreciation. This is something me and Pig Dude share – back in the day we would visit each other with some new vinyl or CD discovery, and we would just listen.

There is a calming vibe as we stand outside the Royal Albert Hall, amongst fellow Floydians. The chatter is easy and we all prove what authentic followers we are with a combined encyclopaedic knowledge of where, when and whom. This for me is why the band, or the solo performances, never have a support act. This interaction is the warm-up to the main performance. I have so many memories, over forty years of the conversations and occurrences, warmth and camaraderie I've experienced before I go to a show. I'm wearing my ironic 'Which one's Pink?' T-shirt, produced for a Roger Waters solo tour when his ego was mutating. I think it works regardless of which incarnation of the remnants I'm watching, even the Australian version. We rush a beer, it's time to go. I'm feeling OK. The lights dim and my god walks onto the stage. I am once again engulfed by his presence. Oblivious of everything – body pains, plans, pressures, obligations – the sight and sound envelop me.

When they toured 'The Division Bell', David played a version of 'Com-Num' that, along with lasers and mirror-ball, automated intelligent lighting on a projection screen suspended horizontally over him, it made for an overwhelming sensation. There were tears on cheeks, the uninhibited emotional reaction to the most powerful guitar solo this planet will ever witness. And I was there, at Earl's Court, for three consecutive Fridays. Life and live music were never quite the same after that. But right here, right now, in the company of the equally affected, I can feel something once again so powerful it makes my eyes moist.

At the half-time break, I grab us a drink. Pig Dude is an aficionado and an excellent choice of company. I see the guy who runs the magazine I will be working with on the nine-day motorcycle show in two months. He drops the bombshell that they will be having another permanent guest author on the stand this year. At £3,000 for a 3x3-metre pitch, it's precious real-estate – how are they going to fit everyone in? They aren't, it's a physical impossibility. So am I just going to be selling their magazine for them then? The 'oblivious to everything' feeling is a delicate state.

The second half of the concert is even better. Too potent to compare, too exceptional to share. Some things are just personal.

On the train home I show Pig Dude Tinder on my phone. After a quarter-century of marriage, he no longer has his finger on the pulse. I am more in awe of his reaction than the unlimited London faces I'm swiping left and right. 'So this is what dating is now?' he says. Life and love will never quite be the same after this discovery.

* * *

A wealthy Arab once said: 'If you have something that gives you pleasure, get another and double your pleasure.' I've used this philosophy several times. Tattoos and motorcycles are two things that immediately spring to mind. David Gilmour is playing a second date at the Royal Albert Hall tonight. As I have to pass London to get to the overland show I'm attending, it would seem rude not to drop by and see him again.

Mum is going to lend me her Ford Focus. It's going to be easier than trying to get books and all I need for an adequate outdoor stand on my bike. I fill her car. It's far more comfortable than the bike but the radio doesn't work so, like being inside my helmet, the only music to be played is in my head. This, of course, gives me time for reflection. The thing that strikes me the most is how I have instantly switched back to my British lifestyle; as easily as driving on the other side of the road. This, I suppose, if nothing else, proves I'm adaptable. I'm not sure exactly why I need proof of this – depending on what constitutes 'living in', whether it's a van, tent, as a prolonged guest, or house-sitting, I have lived in multiple countries. I feel I'm currently straddled between here and Bulgaria. My 'work' – the shows I continue to attend in the name of book sales – were mostly booked before I emigrated. I'm not sure if I can justify travelling so far for the limited sales the shows generate. Which is all the more reason to make the most of every moment and go and see David again.

The issue tonight is the safe parking of a car that is packed to the roof with valuables. Having a hippy Indian blanket over my bulging belongings is not making them any less conspicuous. In Knightsbridge I find a hotel and spiral down into a parking area. It's £27 for four hours, £36 for six. Hmm, is an encore worth another £9? Yeah, of course it is. For the cost of three books I can keep them all safe. It's not really a choice. I park up and walk to the event. I don't have a ticket for tonight and, what's more, the purchaser's name is printed on each ticket – they are allowed a guest but still have to prove their identification to avoid the black-market markup. Despite this, there are touts outside. I'm not adverse to using them, but in this situation they require more trust then I'm prepared to give them.

I need a sign. I go back to the car and make a two-part placard. On the top it says 'One ticket needed'. Once I catch someone's eye, I fold down the bottom bit which says 'I'm really nice to sit next to'. Wearing the same T-shirt as last night and a smile as authentic as my needs, I get a lot of response. I speak to security just to make sure they don't have a problem with me being here doing this, and they don't. My aptitude has bought a multitude of offers, now all I have to do is decide with whom I will share the show. I want to pay less than face value as I have parking to pay for. For half price, I decide to buy a ticket off a French Canadian who flew here specifically for the show. His friend didn't make it and I get to occupy his private box with him. Once he's got me inside, I give him the money for the ticket and buy him a beer. The saving soon disappears.

We get talking to a girl who is an avid David fan. The Canadian and this girl are connoisseurs. I'm challenged by their expertise and this would be my chosen subject in the

Mastermind chair. I show a photo from last night's performance. Looking at his guitar, the girl points out he has a Jimi Hendrix strap on. 'As opposed to a Jimi Hendrix strap-on,' I say. *Ahem.* No matter how highbrow the debate, I've always been able to drag it down to my level. 'I'll go and get some more beers in.' I'm approached by many faces who say how pleased they are to see I managed to get in, and that is the loveliest warm-up you could hope to have before any show.

When the house lights come back on, I say that the performance seems to have passed faster than last night's. 'Perhaps your friend was not as good company,' says the Canadian. I never even knew his name but, like a one-night stand, we shared a few passionate hours, exchanged mutual appreciation, and then went our different ways. Mine is up the M40 to a racecourse in Stratford-upon-Avon for an overland show. There might be 101 different ways to sleep on top of a Land Rover, but the only way to sleep in a Ford Focus is curled up in a foetal position across the front seats.

* * *

I may not be sleeping vulnerable and exposed in the wilds of frozen Siberia, but in the last five nights I've gone from floor to couch to across the seats and I'm driven by the challenges I'm facing. This is the travel author at work: inadequate sleep, bad diet, ringing ears and a smelly tour T-shirt, it's as rock 'n' roll as my musically inept existence gets. I've definitely got that side of my lifestyle down. Next it's drugs, and love is the drug I'm thinking of. Today Lilly will come to the show and I'm going to be the headliner. Well, at least with a full house of pop-up banners proclaiming 'Book signing today', I'll certainly look like I must be someone. I go to the toilet block and shave. It's time to change my T-shirt too. I put on one of my own branded shirts because, today, I'm Pink.

I find the organiser whom I'd clocked in the early hours when I arrived this morning. I knew that to have announced my arrival then would have meant getting involved in a drinking session, and I've never been able to sell a book hung-over, let alone impress a girl. I'm recognised and welcomed and given a pitch between stone carvings and aloe vera remedies: two travelling 'essentials', but attractive stalls nonetheless. Once my stand is set up, I go and fetch a full English and take it back to my gazebo. I'm so glad I didn't drink last night. So I did learn something from the show when I was with Mum last month.

Now that I've stretched, unpacked, set up and walked around, my cramped, sleep-confined body has become fully functional again. People shuffle past and say hi. I think I know them. I respond like I do. I only see a few of the traders and authors who are rumoured to be here. The boyfriend of Ants, the girl who had locked herself out of her van at the last show, comes over and introduces himself. I'd hooked them up with my graphic design man, so I go and check out their stand with the new pop-up banner. Only the owner of a pop-up can truly appreciate such things beyond the design: the casing, the fold-out feet, and whether the edges curl on a damp morning. Suitably impressed, I start my working day. I see the headline speaker from the Irish show. I know he sees me but makes no effort to show acknowledgement, which is absolutely fine by me.

I get chatting to a couple of girls about books and travel. Out of the corner of my eye, I notice someone approach the side of my gazebo, but I can't look away from the conversation I'm having. I can feel her: like a solar eclipse without protection, I want to look but I can't. The girls leave, I turn my head, it's Lilly. A hippy chick, slim and pretty, flowing red hair, no make-up, natural beauty, a little pierced, a little dyed, no tattoos I can see, but I'd like to research more. I give her a kiss and a hug and can't seem to let go of her hand. Oh my god, she's lovely, she has a creamy Welsh accent and smells of … well, it's not a well-shagged scent. Her face has ever-changing expressions. She is so lively, pure energy. I can't understand a word she says, but then I'm not really concentrating, I'm just looking. Look at this girl, she's striking, I just want to hold her. She's got a skinny waist and flat tummy, her body goes in and out at all the right places. Her figure, her face, her smile, she's mesmerising. It's like watching a David Gilmour solo. I'm oblivious to everything else around me, people could be stealing books from my stand. I should listen, she's talking, what is she saying? Something about a dog, a talking dog, this isn't making sense. All I can think of is how much more of her I want to see. She must be able to see it in my eyes, it's louder than words. Listen to her, work out what's she saying, you will have to retort soon. Definitely a talking dog, the dog said this, the dog said that, then the dog gave her the all clear … oh, *doc*, the doctor gave her the all clear. I just caught it in time, my turn. So she just happened to ask the right person where she could find me – a trader who knows me, and who has a picture of me wearing his product on his trade stand. He is also under the misconception that I'm better known than I am. Perfect. I just want to shut up shop and take her somewhere, back to Bulgaria. After an immeasurable amount of time has passed, Ants comes over, and Lilly says she's going for a walk around.

'Was that your girlfriend?' asks Ants as Lilly walks away.

'Not yet,' I say.

'Oh shit, sorry, did I scare her off? Wow, she's got a lovely arse.'

'Hasn't she?' But I'm not ready to see the back of her yet.

Back to book selling. I glance at my phone. I have a bunch of missed texts from Lilly, *I'm here, where are you, I'll be there soon.* I message her back because I can think of nothing else.

In the afternoon she comes back. She'll be camping in the Cotswolds tonight. I could do that, I could come, but there isn't a hint of an invitation. Nevertheless, overall I think I've not done too bad. I don't think I've said out loud what my mind was imagining and I hope my eyes didn't betray me. Every disastrous date, every meeting I wanted to run from, and every girl I clammed up in front of has got me to this point. I put all my lessons and all my luck on this first impression and maybe we'll meet again.

The footfall fades away. I'm undecided as to my plans. Avoiding drinking here is … well, you can't avoid it. But I have another show to attend tomorrow. I think I'll head out. The other motorcycle-orientated traders are heading that way too. It's like a Beaujolais run. Tomorrow's event is a resurrected bike meeting, a one-day event with an attendance of 3,000. It sounds too good to miss. I drive down the M40 into a rising moon as the sun sets behind me – it's the perfect evening to be camping. I head to Guildford and the fire station that will host the event tomorrow. The night watch let me past the gates so I can park safely inside. With a Chinese takeaway and a bottle of red, I sit alone in the concrete courtyard and contemplate the day that just passed. After dinner I manoeuvre the contents of the car and put a wooden placard over the books and sleep on top of that, nose inches from the roof. I still can't stretch out. This is not comfort, it's compromise: the Focus foetal.

* * *

The inside of the car is wet with condensation but it's not as cold as yesterday morning. The firemen let me into the station and I'm able to shower, but I've lost my toothbrush somewhere, and a finger is so unsatisfactory. The fire engines are pulled out of the garage and, being the only one here, I'm able to set up inside. Slowly, the others arrive. Ants and her man make me extremely powerful coffee and interrogate me with questions about Lilly. One of the firemen, a young lad, has made a video and insists I watch it. I'm led into the labyrinth of the complex to a recreation room, and on a big flatscreen TV he plays his production. It's a harrowing shockumentary drama, the aftermath of a drink-driving accident. He acts in it, his girlfriend crushed in a mangled car. Makes sleeping in the Focus seem far preferable. It's hard-hitting, poignant and beautifully filmed. He's rightfully proud of it and, once again, I'm misjudged to be more than I am. He thinks I can pull strings to get his creation a greater audience. I tell Ants about it; she's far better connected than I am.

So where are these 3,000 people? As the morning progresses, it becomes obvious that this figure is utter crap. We are lucky to attract 300, and the majority of them are bores and idiots, the posing Harley Owners Group chapter who won't buy anything that isn't branded. As is always the case in such situations, the traders, bored and frustrated, chatter among themselves. A paramedic does an excellent demonstration of post-motorcycle-accident protocol. I speak to him after and he buys a book. These people see the trauma of life on a daily basis; I'm not sure how much awareness I want. It's not *Daily Mail* scaremongering, but it's still a consciousness I'd rather ride without. I know my lifestyle could cause the end of my existence, but it's not a thought I want inside my helmet.

I see the Bulgarian I met at my last presentation. I say hello in Bulgarian. He's not in the least impressed, but the invitation to visit at Christmas is renewed. The raffle is called with utter disorganisation. How difficult is it to call out numbers? Apparently very. It's the final flaw in this disastrous show. The hosts have been spectacular; it's the organisers who are inept. I'm given a survey card to fill out. 'What would improve the show?' 'Attendance,' I write. They clearly didn't put as much effort into promoting it to the public and attracting riders as they did traders.

The day is saved for me when I see the editor of a magazine who requests a review copy of my latest book. His publication always generates some interest.

As I drive back, I consider future shows, accommodation, logistics, diet. This isn't working. Without a van, I can't do the show circuit with any professionalism. It's work and I can't function to my full potential eating junk and sleeping curled up across the seats of my mum's car.

There is a lunar eclipse tonight but I can't stay awake to watch it. After I've unloaded the car I have to crash, but at 3 a.m. I'm wide awake and walk to the beach to see the blood moon. What a week, what a summer, what a life. What's next?

The gravy train derails

50th minus 2 weeks

Last night the planets aligned and the shadow that cast the eclipse seems to have stretched into the daylight. Memories of the weekend can be moulded and manipulated into the glamour of being on tour. Now there is a dim light of despair, a week of reality awaits. Down to earth with the broken space key, the replacement keyboard has arrived and soon my words will stop running like a hashtag. I watch the YouTube instructional instalment video fully – once my computer is apart, I'm committed to completing the task.

The weekend's book sales don't tally. Overall, the takings were OK, but that's if I don't take into account the expenses and hardships. I have three calls to make. They are all difficult and I'd rather not make them, so I don't. Instead, I text and flirt with Lilly. This will not do. I've got to get motivated, so I head off to see my graphics and IT man. We look at the pannier artwork and put it together in a way that the Chinese companies can make sense of. Then we have to do some work on my website. It is laborious and boring. I just want an email address that comes from my website domain. The back end of the site is beyond me and all I can do is make my request and see what will appear. Something happens and suddenly every email I've ever written or received starts to load onto my laptop, it's using up too much memory, too much bandwidth, the internet is going to break, how do I stop it? Abort, abort!

It's late afternoon by the time I send the design to China. That will do for today, too much screen time – but it's soon replaced with phone time. The messaging with Lilly has passed the thoughtfully composed and strategically timed phase: we've reached a level of heavy texting. Even in script, I still find her conversation hard to follow. But, unlike my website, incomprehension only heightens intrigue, which can lead to dangerous dreams of misinterpretation.

* * *

This morning's emails confirm I'm not the only one failing to grasp what's occurring. China doesn't get it, nobody understands me. I find some more suppliers. It's much easier with a space bar. Today I'm going to have to make those three calls. I opt for the easiest one first. Adventure Bike TV have, for most of the summer, been promising to do a feature on my bike. I don't want to push it, but that appointment is the last obligation I have here and I want to go home. I wonder if they can bring the date forward. I chat to the producer, it's an easy conversation. I can't help but pry about the award. He says he can't tell me how the voting is going, but he'll text me if I need to book a flight to attend the live Christmas award show. Next, I have to call the magazine I will be working with at the nine-day motorcycle show. It goes to voicemail. I leave a message and my call is not returned. I can't face calling my accountant, and look at eBay instead.

It wouldn't hurt to contact some UK box makers just to see how their prices compare, and also because, based on opinion polls for next year's vote as to whether Britain should leave the EU, the pound is plummeting in value which makes overseas production look less attractive. The Essex couple with whom I crossed paths at the Irish show have invited me over. They want to hear about life in Bulgaria, they are considering emigrating. It's a night of heavy drinking – oh yes, they'll fit right in. Another night, another bed. I end the evening sending a drunken text to Lilly. It's a compliment if not completely coherent. Basically, it's bottom appreciation.

* * *

It's just getting light, I may as well try for a dawn escape. I ride into the sunrise, disguising myself as a commuter – live to ride, ride to work. I feel more tired than retired. This work thing looks awful, all queuing to spend their day doing something they'd rather not. I hope never to be part of that game ever again. However, I appreciate their presence: I'm diluted in stagnant traffic and it helps to conceal the mid-week toxic breath that's misting up my visor. Back at Mum's, I brush my teeth and hope I can continue to conceal last night's excesses as I walk to my dentist appointment.

An acquaintance of mine was reprimanded by his dentist as to his habit. 'How can you tell?' he asked. 'Is it rotting my gums?'

'No' said the dentist. 'I can see the white powder on your nostril hairs.' Busted.

I need a filling and the soonest appointment means I'll now be stuck in England for my birthday. That's it, I'm committed, my stay prolonged. With every obligation I've tried to reschedule, a later one has come along and filled the space. That's how you get stuck in your life.

The UK box companies are utterly out of touch, and it can't be blamed on translation, so I'll persevere with China. I Skype with a lovely Chinese girl at a box company. I think we are finally making progress. It certainly saves us a lot of emails. Of course, all this effort is for the nine-day motorcycle show, which is now shrouded with uncertainty, and with every unreturned call I'm hearing what they don't want to tell me.

I look at left-hand drive vehicles, bikes and houses on the internet: something I need, something I want and something I should consider. Decisions are not coming easily. Generally, the reason for that is there is something in the way. I've got some truths I need to face, and the best place to address them is inside the helmet.

After lunch I get on the KLR and head for Southampton to see my riding buddy Andy. I'm still running the bike in after its 685cc conversion, so I take back roads the entire way as I'm in no rush and the sun is shining. I need to straighten out my plans and make some changes. I reluctantly have to admit I can't do the show scene anymore. It's impractical, I would have to have permanent transport in this country for haulage, sleeping and cooking. That's how I was able to make book selling my living, by living in the van. This would require me to have a vehicle permanently in the UK with MOT, insurance and tax. Even if I could justify that expense, I still have the flights to take into account, and getting to and from the airport on both sides of the journey. Yes, for a nine-day show the travel expenses may be offset against sales, but that's no longer the case for smaller shows. 1,600 miles of travel is too far to take the losses of the badly organised, low-attendance and bad-weather events.

The thought process is therapeutic, but the cost is that I manage to miss my favourite road: the A272. This comes to my awareness when I see the sea. The A27 it is then. It's pretty and everything but, bollocks, I was looking forward to some twisties. It's a disappointing mistake, plus it's colder on the coast. The sun is not as warm as it looks, and I'm feeling a chill to my bones. This is the longest run I've done with the upgraded engine. It's smooth at 70mph and, as the journey drags, impatience rises and the motorway entices. I take it up to 80mph and it seems perfectly happy, so that's a quirky bonus. I meet the afternoon rush hour as I approach Southampton. There are those damn workers again, messing with my pleasurable ride.

My mate and his wife have several properties they rent out and are keen advocates of that source of income and security. I've been looking at properties for sale but something about buying to let feels wrong. I'm not necessarily against such immoral capitalist ways, it's more a gut feeling, of risk. Yes, the return is about five per cent and I'm getting less than two per cent on my savings. However, the rental property only has to be without tenants for a month or in need of expensive maintenance and that attractive return disappears, and that's my living money. My friends are keen on new builds and coach houses, whereas I've been looking at properties that would suit me if I had to come back for some reason. We look at the houses I've saved on Rightmove, and I listen to their advice. I get it, I do get it. But I don't like estate agents, don't trust the housing market, rental agreements, maintenance fees, contractors, tenants, landlord's insurance, finders' fees, lost deposits and all the other variables and vulnerabilities. I would be an absent landlord and, what's more, houses are fetching their asking price right now and I never like to pay face value for anything. I'll sleep on this new angle they have suggested in yet another different bed.

* * *

It feels so good to wake up refreshed and with no hangover. It's almost as good as drinking … almost. But it is my birthday month, so I imagine this will be the exception. I've slept in this guest room many times over the last five years. It looks out over the back garden, and a fir tree as big as mine in Bulgaria. The shed contains multiple bikes, and machinery capable of miracles. I've seen wondrous things occur in that shed. The dysfunctional is pushed in and with intuition and ability function is restored and ridden out.

This visit, though, is not about mechanical enhancements. It's about financial security, from sheds to houses, and there's no time to consider a favourable quote from a UK box company. Andy takes me to see a coach house he owns that is in between tenants. I have all the enthusiasm of a teenager forced to go for work experience. The property is cramped between a bunch of other new builds – however, inside it's OK. Spacious and light, it even has an en suite. Then, when I see the garage, I start to feel its potential. OK, this could work. As we drive, I consider the possibility of buying here in Southampton, rather than Essex. Andy could manage it and his wife who works for an estate agent could find what I'm looking for. I put it to him. He's ahead of me. I think he and his wife have already discussed this. Well, this could change everything. It's quite exciting: relocation, delegation and peace of mind. Andy and his wife are one hundred per cent trustworthy, I'd get good value, and I wouldn't have to deal with the scumbag wideboy Essex estate and letting agents.

However, I'm still not fully convinced. I have an inner niggle. Despite my faith in Andy and his wife, I still don't trust the housing market. I feel the prices are generated by agents and inflated by investors. There is an unsustainable greed and I predict a crash. Even if all those fears could be put to rest, I can't shake the unease I feel from seeing a copy of the *Daily Mail* in their kitchen.

Anyway, all that aside, we have to drop by Andy's place of work. A massive estate of horses and staff, the grounds are so vast I can't even see the manor house where his boss lives. There is a state-of-the-art horse transporter, superior to any truck I've ever driven. Its value is twice the price of the coach houses I've been looking at. That puts things into perspective, too much perspective.

It's a beautiful autumn day and a long walk is suggested. We wander lanes and paths of the undulating Hampshire countryside. Huge trees and rolling hills, Friesian cows and ploughed fields, big houses in little villages. Inevitably, we find a pub, and beer-thoughts come to mind. It just feels wrong to drink lager in a place like this; a locally brewed ale on a weathered bench in the beer garden is aesthetically perfect. The triple chimneys of the old pub cast sundial shadows across the unkempt grass. Old England is alive and well, secure and serene: there is character, tradition, respect and the feeling of reflection that autumn light and light ale induce. I consider the ghastly construction of new-build housing, a multitude of tasteless terracotta uniforms, trapped and detained, cramped and suffocating, airtight and lifeless. Do I really want to buy into that blot on the landscape? If I want to maintain these afternoon delights, I do. On the way back I pick up some conkers and roll them around in my pocket. I'm still looking for answers.

When Andy's wife comes home, we tell her about the house idea and she jumps on Rightmove with enthusiasm and knowledge. With instinct and experience, she finds some places we will look at tomorrow. I appreciate the eagerness, I feel the excitement, I have the incentive but not the conviction, something isn't right. I want to buy motorbikes. I might get hit by a bus tomorrow.

* * *

I'm going off the boil with Lilly. She's attentive to the point of obsession – whatever I mention in a text, her lengthy reply comes with relevant links. I don't want a written relationship, a pen friend, a messenger romance, I've got time to invest but not in the virtual world, and not today. I think this comes from the days of dial-up connections. Knowing I was paying by the minute, I would speed-read the essential and delete the rest. I still get frustrated reading lengthy text on the screen, scrolling my life away. The unattended is getting restless in my inbox, and other Adventure Bike TV nominees are creating momentum in their endeavours to earn the honour that will leave me with nothing to put between the candles on my mantelpiece.

I look at Rightmove and do calculations. The income can't be guaranteed, headaches and hassles can. Also, financial obligations can have a ferocious effect on a friendship. We'd have to have a written agreement as to input, payment and support, and I don't like the thought of having binding obligations in our bond, it makes a friendship inflexible.

We head out to look at houses – first, a coach house which has a £900-a-year land-maintenance fee to maintain a garden it doesn't have.

'Is that too much for you?' sneers the estate agent, confirming that it's not just Essex, they are all insidious cunts.

'No,' I reply. 'It's just too much.'

The place we most wanted to see sold overnight, which is ominous. I don't like buying in a sellers' market. We drive into some cramped estates, where cars are parked on pavements, prams block doorways and satellite dishes take the community out of communication. Seeing my disdain, I'm taken to some more established estates. Nothing appeals, nothing excites me. I know I'm supposed to see it as an income-generating, capital-increasing investment, but the money will feel dirty if I spend it on this shit.

Possibly at their wits' end, Andy says I should go with my gut, and although it's proved to be unreliable in the past, its cautious character has never left me at a total loss. I've been overloaded with uninspiring properties, nothing more than brick-built boxes stacked haphazardly in the confines of overpriced, but apparently affordable, high-density housing projects. Perhaps if they had seen where I've come from, and what it cost me, they would be able to think beyond the inflated prices of southern England and see how far that money will take you in another country. I invite them, and I'm pretty sure they will come; I need to return some hospitality.

Today I take the A272 and happily wind my way east at modest speed under blue skies. No rich Arab to my knowledge ever advocated tripling your pleasure so, although it's an option, I don't divert into London to see David Gilmour again. Anyway, I too have another show this weekend. The tour continues and Mum will help me accommodate the last of this lifestyle.

* * *

I've been going to the Copdock Bike Show since it was held in the Copdock Village Hall. It's since expanded to the Suffolk Show Ground in Ipswich, so it's only just up the road. The fee is reasonable for both punters and traders and for that reason there are lots of both. It's a massive one-day event held on the first Sunday of October and, because the profits go to charity, there is no greed factor and always a friendly vibe. Only a few well-connected trade stands get a pre-approved pitch, and over the years I've pulled every string I can find, but to no avail. I don't mind, other than the fact I have to do the journey twice. I like to be at the gates at 9 a.m. on the Saturday morning, when they open to trade, and get myself the prime spot, because there is nothing worse than having a bad pitch at a good show. Well, except cancer maybe – oh, and bike theft. Actually, there are lots of things worse, but when you are on the last row of a twenty-aisle-deep trade area, even if people do venture to your pitch, they are zombified from too much input. With glazed eyes and lethargic demeanour, you could be giving away lines chopped on the pert bottom of the latest celebrity heart-throb and the only reaction you'd get is, 'Naaa, it's a long walk back to the toilets.' I've not actually tried that, but it's equally far to carry a book back to the bike park and no one buys anything from the last aisle in the line-up.

So, based on that hard lesson learned, Mum is going to follow me on the KLR to go and stake my claim (that's me on the KLR, Mum's following in the car with the gazebo). Our early morning efforts get us a perfect corner plot near the ice cream van. All I have to do is half-erect and secure the gazebo, chain the KLR up, and that's it. A fifty-minute drive and ten minutes to bag a good spot; the rest of the day is my own.

Back at Mum's, I need to figure out box prices. The UK ones are OK until I put twenty per cent VAT on the price and then China becomes competitive again. There isn't supposed to be VAT on printed goods, that's why flyers are handed out everywhere you go, and books that last a lifetime are the same price as two festival beers. The pannier box replicas must fall into a different taxing category, so I put all the prices down on a sheet of A4 and on Monday I'll make the jump and choose a company.

I see a lovely, old but immaculate camper van on eBay. I bid £500; within an hour it's up to £3,000. I've got good taste, I've definitely got good taste. With no transport now and no interest in looking at houses, a drink is on my mind, but I decide to clear out the garage. Then, I split and stack Mum's winter wood for her. It plays hell with my elbow but it's a winner on every other level. The wood is now drying and accessible, I've had some exercise, it looks great all stacked up, Mum is pleased, and I can definitely justify a beer now.

An overland website has asked me for an inspirational quote. Perhaps they were hoping for something as exceptional as my top tips but I'm dry and all I can do is shoot back a much-repeated line from one of my books. *Motivation and inspiration are everywhere. So are distractions and excuses. A dream made into a plan has a momentum; it won't drive itself, but it has the ability to entice, exhilarate, encourage; and I believe all dreams are born to become realities.*

It's OK, but out of context it sounds like pretentious bollocks. Once again, the car is loaded to the roof, but tonight I don't have to sleep in it.

* * *

Pulling into the showground on a Sunday morning, two hours before the gates open to the public, we see the place is predictably packed. The lines for trade stands reach back further than I want to walk. It's time to turn my pitch into an irresistible place of commerce. I say good morning to the trader who has set up next to me and get a grunt. That's the only downside to low pitch prices, it attracts all sorts. The cheap tools and bulk-buy bargains, the low-quality items, the market mentality and the lack of integrity, it's all more suited to a Sunday car boot sale. 'Twenty spanners f' five pand, come 'n' get 'em.' It does dilute the bike-orientated traders, but most people know shite merchandise when they see it. My stand has authenticity, intrigue and, once the dew has dried up, a plethora of pop-ups that don't curl or sway. Book signing today motherfuckers, and maybe never again.

We have a routine here, me and Mum. Once set up, I run to the autojumble, with too much excitement to concentrate, in search of the kind of bargains that don't get yelled out in an Estuary accent. 'Shovelhead belt primary drive with clutch, light use, hidden in a box of rusty chains, come and have a rummage.'

'What price you got in this?' I say, pointing with my foot to convey indifference.

'I paid a monkey f' that, gissa ton and f' rit.'

'Will ya take fifty nicker?'

'Naa, fak orf, stick a couple a ponies on that and it's yours.'

'Awe white, 'er ya go, have a good show.'

'Nice one geez, you 'n' all.'

Mum calls. 'Someone is waiting here to get a book signed.'

'I'm on my way,' I say, and then, a few moments later: 'Hi, sorry to keep you, was just hunting round the old bike parts. Now, do you want a signature or an oily finger print?'

'Nice belt drive, that's gotta be worth a monkey. How much did ya pay for that?'

That has never happened, I just wanted to see what it's like to write fiction. There are a few other 'adventure authors' here whose imaginations are bigger than their journeys. But, like the marzipan mole grips next door, people generally know genuine when they see it.

The locality of this show means I was coming here for years before I was a best-selling, internationally known author. Oooh, I can see the addiction to fiction, once you start. Anyway, it's as much a social scene as a work environment. Before, I might have bumped into a few familiar faces at the bar by the stage. Now though, the show has grown to such vast proportions, I probably see more friends while I'm staying put behind my products than I would wandering round. Plus, I've got my name displayed so it can be seen from every angle. Thankfully, most of my mates recognise it as my living and don't give me too much shit for projecting my supposed celebrity across the walkways of potential purchasers. A few still don't get it.

'When ya gonna give me one of ya books?'

'What do you do for a living?'

'I'm a carer innit, you know for old people and that.'

'So you wipe arses to earn money?'

'Yeah kinda.'

'Well I sell books to earn money, but I tell you what, you wipe my arse and I'll give you a book.'

'Oh com' on, you got loads of 'em there.'

'Yep, and Tescos has loads of cans of beans, but I doubt just because they have a lot of stock they will give you a can for nothing.'

This is a meeting of the clans. There are my fellow traders, my professional friendships whom I'd meet nearly every weekend around the country. This show tends to represent the end of the season for outdoor events, and therefore I'm unlikely to see them again until next year, or maybe ever. Then there are the locals I know, ex-tenants who've rented my house when I've gone travelling, people I've bought and sold bikes to. Faces from the past, school friends and various pub and rally scene acquaintances. There are the now obligatory Facebook friends and followers and the more current people from my present, at least when I'm present in the country. Even a few Motocamp guests stop by. I see Martin who helped me mow my lawn this summer, he buys another T-shirt. My favourite people, however – apart for the paying customers, of course – are the ones who just swing by to say hi, who saw me do a presentation, an interview or heard me on a podcast or, best of all, simply feel they have a connection as they rode with me while reading one of my books and something I said resonated. See, that never happened in the kitchen-fitting business or as a trucker. So I realise, to a degree, that I'm putting myself on a platform, but it's not a pedestal. I like to think I keep it real and the conversations I have all seem genuine, even if I'm not always sure who I'm talking to. I don't stand out in the walkways handing out flyers, I hate that. The KLR sits, inviting curious eyes and captivating comments. It's my icebreaker and my flyer distributer – people can pick one up off the seat and, without pressure, read what they may feel intimidated to ask. Now informed, they can ask without embarrassment, 'How far did ya bike go, mister?' The speedo broke years ago, the reading doesn't represent the miles or justify the road scars. They'll regret it if they get me talking about the new 685cc conversion.

The day passes in a non-stop parade of people. As usual, I see nothing of the show other than what passes in front of me. I hear the stunt bikes' bouncing of rev limiters, smell the smoke of burned-out tyres, recognise the tireless commentary from the Wall of Death as it drifts by. I've been hearing that at various events for over thirty years. A girl gave birth outside it one intoxicated evening at the Kent Custom Bike Show in the late '80s. That kid could be a parent now. Time is passing, people have stopped, we start packing up. Looks like my neighbour is going to leave all his boxes and rubbish behind him. I'll bite my lip, such a positive day will make the smallest of inconsiderations stand out like a Snap-On sign on a plastic tool box. Yep, he's in his van, and he's going to leave all that rubbish on the grass. And then, he reverses into my mum's car.

'*Oi!*' I'm after him, open his passenger door. 'You just reversed into me car.'

'Well I ain't got no insurance.' That's his first response, the fuckin' reprobate.

'I'll have these then,' I say, taking a pair of new motor-cycle gloves off the seat. That gets him off his arse. The guy has all the integrity of the shite he sells, good for nothing.

'Well, I'll give ya twenty quid,' he says.

What, for a split bumper? I'm speechless, a whole day of positivity and now this twat. I could be a dick about this, get security, get names, but fuck it, I take £40. Let him take his arrogance and negative karma back to the environment that spawned him. Looking around, I see a distant audience, many of whom witnessed the event from the initial '*Oi!*' announcement. The general opinion is 'what a wanker'. I take a photo of his number plate before he leaves, and report the incident to the organisers. *Incidentally, the next year trade tickets come with a warning that anyone leaving their rubbish behind them will incur penalties.* The damage to my mum's car isn't that bad and her vehicle is far from perfect anyway. It was his shitty attitude that grates and, annoyingly, I take that with me on the ride back. One fucktard can ruin ya whole day, and then it makes me angry that he's on my mind. I know full well I'm not on his. I ponder what is – nothing enlightening, that's for sure. I wonder how many compliments he got for his products. 'Love ya Allen keys, they rounded off and bent first time I used them, make great pipe cleaners.'

Not including the damage money, we took nearly £500 today. There is actually a profit margin, and a massive karma credit too. Too tired to do anything, I sit in the lounge. Mum is watching *Cheers* on some classics channel. Oh shit, look at Norm, he's younger than me. He was the old drunk at the end of the bar when I last saw this show. Well, that's depressing. I haven't seen a weather forecast in months and, as soon as I do, its predicted doom plays on my mind like a Monday does on a Sunday night.

In the Flesh

50th minus 1 week

This is the first day in ages without any demands. That doesn't stop me getting up at dawn though and, as last night's dismal weather forecast predicted, it's grey.

I unload the car, restock books and keep accounts. The pop-ups get put away for an undetermined amount of time. When the working day officially starts, I walk to my appointment with the local physiotherapist. Yes, it's tennis elbow and, apparently, it's chronic, because it hurts when I write. She wires me up and gives me electric pulses which send my body into involuntary shrugs. She recommends I wear an armband and shows me one in her book of body supports. I wish I knew of such things five weeks ago.

Out of habit, I look at left-hand drive vans on eBay. I suppose I don't need a van now, just a four-wheel drive for the Bulgarian winters, a left-hand drive for safety, and a big American V8 for my midlife crisis. I order a tennis elbow support and decide to start this month's column soon as I have a subject in mind. My call is finally returned from the magazine about the nine-day motorcycle show. Apparently, this newly invited third guest author is flying in especially – just like me then? 'I booked a flight specifically to honour the invitation you sent me in July,' I tell them. They offer me one day as guest author, so I guess I'll be selling their magazine for the other eight days – or do they not even want me there now? To top it off, the other permanent author who will be on the stand, and with whom I'll be sharing the hotel room we booked three months ago, is all over Facebook promoting the other guy who's 'flying in especially'. I've got more books and re-views than the new special guest author. However, what he has that I don't, I find out later, are contributions in his book from the people who are promoting him. So my independence has come back to bite me and attendance now may not be worth my while. I'm sure he's totally unaware that he's barging me out and is excited to be attending the show – clearly, I'm no longer flavour of the month, not flying far enough, I think I've just been shafted. This is what happens when returning adventure riders try to make a living from overlanding, it's a road to bitterness.

I suppose having contributions from names of note in your book increases your credibility. It's promotion by proxy, which broadens your audience. I might retell a tale, like Ants and her comment on Lilly's bottom, but that isn't really worthy of a credit in the acknowledgements. However, a rule of thumb I have is, whenever a friend asks me, 'Do you mention me in the book?' my default answer is always, 'Yes'. Then they buy it. People belittle vanity publishing – well, that is vanity purchasing: they are more interested in what I wrote about them than my actual writing. Many of them now, realising they are nearing the end of the book and are still yet to see their name in print, have just had an epiphany. I bet you think this book was about you, don't you?

China are not responding to emails as it's a Chinese national holiday, and the UK box companies aren't responding because they are UK companies. I've got little interest in seeing Lilly. I've chased, I've caught and I'm not sure I can be arsed to consummate.

Drob calls and asks what I'm going to do for my fiftieth. I don't bloody know. He suggests organising something with a couple of old friends. I don't think so, I drifted away from them years ago and it would feel contrived. If I don't come up with something, this is going to be really depressing. I need to buy a left-hand drive 4x4, drive it home, then bring the van back with the KTM in it, and sell them both. That's what I need to do, spend a little money, make decisions, take control, have my birthday on the road. I like that idea, and I can take some stuff back home with me. Looking around the room. There isn't even that much I need to take back. I just want some space, just want to cook my own food in my own kitchen and listen to my music.

* * *

OK, I've slept on it and it still seems right. I want a left-hand drive 4x4. I need to get back home. I'm aware this is quite a spontaneous decision and could have consequences. In my haste, I may end up buying something unsuitable. I have a message from Lilly inviting me over tomorrow. I'll see. I've got little else to do.

I've got the Chinese-made boxes down to a viable price delivered to my door – well, my Mum's door; the shed door, I suppose. I'm considering paying for my own stand at the nine-day motorcycle show, then I could be the one getting guest authors to subsidise the £3,000 pitch fee. The magazine is not communicating. I suppose they are doing what's best for their interest, which is fine, but it's my living too and I need some confirmation.

The tennis-elbow support arrives. It's been five weeks since the strain and twenty-four hours since the suggestion and the relief is instant. My new debit card has come too. It's so black. The old one was fading, and I like to keep my transactions dark. I rewrite my column; it comes out so well I decide to submit it to a few of the big bike magazines. It's got wider appeal than the online exploration-based magazine requires. Reorganising the shed, I'm thinking, *yeah, I can definitely get two bikes in here*. If I end up bringing the KTM back, I can store it here waiting for a spring sale.

I can't abstain from drinking. The soap operas on TV are so aggressive, and I can't face the laptop anymore. I think I'll put my camping stuff on my bike and just disappear for a while.

* * *

Still waking at dawn, I can't help myself. A Manchester bike club has requested a write up of a bike show they invited me to last spring. I do it immediately, it was one of the best shows for sales I've attended. My optimism always has me taking more books than I ever sell, but at that show I sold out. Wary of the northern-bloke image, I was somewhat apprehensive about going. I needn't have been, there was a variety of stimulating and memorable conversations. The bike club even made me a large wooden placard listing all the countries I've ridden to on the bike. I still use it; it saves me repeating myself and gives the bike credibility. As a bonus, it's what I slept on in the car when I was parked at the fire station the other week.

I find myself thinking of that show. I'd just got back from my Central American trip, jet-lagged and red-wined. I saw I was tagged in the show's invitation so I accepted. It came with a house stay, hospitality and a welcome that bridged the north-south divide. So typing the review of the show is now the most pleasurable thing to write since I filled in the paying-in slip to deposit the cheque from my house sale and, thus, freed myself from a twenty-five-year mortgage which, in turn, led me to my new life in Bulgaria.

While I'm in the writing mood, I sign a contract with a Chinese box-making company. We have finally agreed on design, material, price, time frame and shipping. The dentist calls, they've got a cancellation – can I come in now? Yes, absolutely, that can bring my leaving date forward. As I walk to the surgery, past the primary school I went to, I see an old friend whom I went to that school with. She's a dinner lady there now. She's bought into the public image and asks me not to forget her when I'm rich and famous. I say of course not, err, what's ya name again? The filling is painless until I get the bill that, combined with one from the physio on Monday, is most of Sunday's profit margin gone. My god, how do people survive in this costly country? The heavens open, and as I hurry back to Mum's

I see her gutters overflowing. So, since I'm already soaked, I get a ladder and clear out at least three winters' worth of leaves and moss. Being a bungalow, it's an easy task.

Well, that's a positive little morning, I think I'll ride to Swansea. The A12 - M25 - M4 journey doesn't exactly fill me with enthusiasm. I used to do night trunking to the Bristol fruit and veg market: coast to coast and back again through the night. Driving into the rising sun on the way back with already tired eyes could turn a squint into shuteye. I can proudly say I've never fallen asleep at the wheel; I've known the signs and the cure, but man, I've had some horrific prolonged journeys back to Essex in stop-start sleep-beating resilience. By comparison, this is just a dull, grey ride to Wales with more than one agenda, and isn't that how this book started? But that was North Wales and on a twin cylinder bike to see an ex; this is a single to see ... to see what happens. It's 1 p.m. by the time I'm ready to leave. The journey is as dull as I predicted. Cold, dreary but dry, and by 4 p.m. I'm halfway. I've run out of things to think about. Yes, I should see if I can get my own stand at the nine-day motorcycle show. Swansea is the home of Adventure Bike TV; perhaps we can do my bike feature while I'm there. I definitely need a 4x4 to drive back to Bulgaria.

There is a hint of excitement in crossing the Severn Bridge, is that a river beneath or a fault line, because a fault of mine is falling for Welsh girls. The smokestacks of Port Talbot almost look picturesque against the setting sun. A beautiful brutality on the skyline, that's the extent of the sightseeing. The rest of the journey has been nothing but big blue signs with names and numbers that are not decreasing as fast as I'd like. Finally, I leave the motorway and ride towards Swansea. On the KTM it would have been so much quicker, and perhaps I could have got the DVLA to correct the discrepancy between my VIN and V5.

Lilly's house is easy to find – a kiss and I'm invited in. Whisky is poured and then she shows me how to get my well-travelled transport down her back entry (this is not a euphemism). The chatter starts. She is pretty, I kind of forgot that with the bombardment of messages we've been exchanging. I'm trying to focus on what she's saying, but there is something about her that takes my concentration away from her words. My mind is moving like narration, like I'm already writing in my diary what didn't happen tonight. It's not written, not yet, I have the power to control my destiny, if I could just pay attention.

She's cooked some dinner, I'm not eating or drinking too much, don't want to fart, don't want to forget what I'm saying mid-sentence. I'm trying to gauge her age; her wrinkle-free face conflicts with her life experiences. She clearly looks after herself, although she does smoke – well, she a has a vape.

She's smart too, really smart, academically at least. She has a chaise longue in her house – actually, it's not her house, hers is full of dogs, this is her mother's place, who is on holiday. What is it with being in a Welsh girl's mother's home? Chaise longue, this is a challenge, I wish I was more familiar with Noel Coward's work. We are touching now, getting knee to knee, holding hands. I've reached a comfortable level of confidence, of alcohol-sedated inhibitions. I have a Welsh phrase that I pronounce as *'Dewy esure suss'*. It means 'I want a kiss'. It turns out she doesn't speak Welsh as well as I do, but it gets the desired effect and it's perfect. Teeth don't collide, arms aren't trapped, hair stays out of mouth. I've never kissed a vaper before, she doesn't smell of ashtrays, more like a joss stick, she has flavour, I like it.

Her body is enchanting, there is no part of it that's a turn-off to touch, no beer belly, she's firm and formed, pert and proportioned. She's got her hands under my T-shirt now. I pull her top off, it doesn't get stuck over her head, every obstacle from past experiences is being overcome tonight. The bra is always the combination lock to success:

sometimes with the snap of the fingers the clasp miraculously comes apart; other times it can be as frustratingly inaccessible as triangle cheese, a foiled attempt at reaching what's inside. Neither outcome occurs, she takes her bra off – looking good, so that's an amber light. Then her hands are down my waistband. Green light. I peel off her leggings with lustful eyes.

I don't want to rush this but I don't want to lose it either, I wonder if I should get a stand to myself at the motorcycle show, noooooo, get back in the moment, uh-ho, where ya going? Come back, what if I do this, ah that works. I want Marillion in my head, 'That time of the night', but I've got 'Skater Boy' by Avril Lavigne. Despite not being able to engage my default mental soundtrack, there's definitely a chemistry and not too much wine. At 3 a.m. we get water; at 4 a.m. I'm hallucinating from sleep deprivation – if there were a steering wheel in front of me now, I'd be looking for a lay-by. She snores, we stink. I think that, from this night on, when someone says Swansea, the DVLA won't be my first thought. Log this VINdication in ya book.

∗∗∗

It feels so good to run my hands over a body without flaws or apologies. If this were art, the eye would be fully fed. Strange, I have to force my mind back in the moment to perform; in less seductive situations, it's a vivid vision that's kept me going. Wind can be held in but my tummy can't be silenced. I need refuelling.

It's a short walk to the café and our timing is perfect, they are having a lull. The students aren't up yet, breakfast is finished and the lunchtime crowd are yet to arrive. This is shaggers' hour – roll out of bed for a full English, it feels like being twenty-three again. She has multiple coffees and I fill myself with a full Welsh breakfast.

I need some laptop time. She has to walk her dogs, and doesn't have any qualms about leaving me in her mum's house alone. Hey, Adventure Bike TV, guess where I am?

Maybe I can see your house from here … but they are out on a shoot. However, they will be in Essex next weekend. That will work. The motorcycle show says yes, they have one booth left. I look on the event map – I know they think I've moved to the arse-end of geography but they don't need to replicate my living location with this pitch in the show. Lost children and skiving cleaners will be the only footfall. Yet the price is fixed.

China now tell me they won't accept PayPal and I don't want to wire money upfront. We settle on a deposit. In more fulfilling fantasies, I narrow down my vehicle criteria as I do the washing-up. I want an American pick-up, four-wheel drive, LPG, crew cab, air-conditioning for summer, and heated seats for winter. Then I can go home. For now, though, I'm happily stuck in the UK and this feels like a little holiday. Maybe I needed this bit of distance to get perspective, or to try and find it. Am I taking my writing career to another level, with the award of recognition and a seat in a private booth? Or is this the siren calling my Swan-sea song. I've raised my profile to this level and the view ahead is hazy.

Keeping with the theme of mystique and beauty, in the afternoon we go to the Gower Peninsula. A windswept spit of land, west-coast rugged and Welsh-uninhabited. In a pub beer garden we take our first selfie – one of us looks gorgeous, I'm pretty sure I can crop myself out of this picture. On the way back we pass a place of bracken and rocks. Apparently, this is where King Arthur pulled his sword, Excalibur, from the stone, and the bog nearby is the underwater realm where the lady of the lake lived. Of course, this is also claimed to have occurred else-where but it's hard to find facts in fiction. It all seems perfectly believable on this golden autumn evening, lost in sleep deprivation, deep in thought, deciphering the differences between the language of love and longings of lust. Her hippy looks clash with her intellect and the victim of the collision is coherence. There is something I'm still not understanding.

Tonight I can take in the interior. Her mother is an artist. In the sprawling three-story house all walls are adorned with paintings of a distinct style. There is a bohemian décor and the bay windows merit their name, a full panorama of Swansea Bay. I could sit on the window seat and watch for hours. Red wine and art deco, close encounters propped up by stuffed cushions on threadbare couches. It's got a class of specific priorities, not materialistic modern but comfortable individualism. It's the perfect place for a sordid affair or a filthy fling, but we are both single, available and, apparently, finding a mutual fondness for this temporary attachment.

The libido has landed and tonight, with less riding on it, consciousness isn't affecting confidence. Scared stiff was never a dictum relating to sex.

* * *

I'm looking up at a vaulted ceiling, at the shadows cast by the sun rising out of Swansea Bay and shining through the window. I could pretend in a room like this. A role-play life of gin-and-tonic decadence, unimportant obligations, filling a day with idle chatter and flamboyant behaviour. 'Oh, you simply *have* to visit Mumbles dharrling, there's an adorable boutique on the front with the quaintest evening wear you ever saw.'

'What? Mumbles? Are you 'avin' a larf?'

I'm talked into staying another night – it took less time than the kettle did to boil. There is talk of Gdansk as a birthday destination, she has family there. So we are making plans for my fiftieth then? A two-night stand with holiday romance potential. The chatter is becoming one-sided, I can't work out if it's nerves, alcohol or her excessive intake of caffeine and sugar. I take water up to bed; her, a two-litre bottle of coke. I have chai in the morning; she, three spoonfuls of instant and an equal amount of sugar in a cup, and then another cup, and then another. There appears to be no comedown as she's permanently topped up. She's high-functioning, has a doctorate it turns out, and perhaps that's why I can't grasp what she's talking about half the time. Like a radio in the background, I'm beginning to tune out. Is the honeymoon over? Can I fart in bed now? Because I've been holding it like the Hindenburg.

Steak, champagne and candles, at the kitchen table, the heart of the house, my treat, for her hosting and Mum's housing, she's not coming back yet, is she? Oh, you already told me. Shall we go to bed? I really need to get some sleep.

* * *

The morning is dull, my breath is beefy but my elbow is feeling better, thankful for the hiatus from my single-handed love life. Sex, sausage sandwich and some Saturday morning rock radio. It's with open awkwardness and inward relief that I gather my belongings and pack the bike. I think we both need a break, not me and the bike, I've missed not riding it, but as for Lilly it's been intense. To instantly move into someone's life for three nights is something I've never done before. It's been full on. Where shall we go from here, I wonder. All I know for now is that I need a breather.

Ahh, the bike – goodbye my lover, hello my love, how did you enjoy Wales? Pounding round the Brecon Beacons, clinging to a costal road, delving deep into a Welsh valley, or slowing for slag heaps and mineshafts depicting a pit on the outskirts of a coal-based community? No, none of that, the poor thing was chained up and abandoned for three nights, like factory gates at the weekend. Well, you are free now, and tomorrow you are going to be on TV. We arrived here on fumes and are leaving feeling empty. I fill up the tank and calculate 52 miles per gallon – very acceptable, and not a drop of oil burned.

After I cross the Severn to England, I stop to put on waterproofs: insulation from the cold wind, not protection from the rain. By Swindon I'm daydreaming, at Reading I'm warmer. The mid-lane cruisers are out in force today, did something happen while I was away? Is this a new fashion or has there been an amnesty? I undertake because I'm not moving out to the fast lane on a plodding single. I consider the bike show. £3,000 for a lousy location. I'd have to sell forty-five books a day, one every ten minutes, to break even, and that's only the pitch fee. I've got to get there, stay there, shop, cook and eat there. It can't be done. I get the finger on the M25. I don't know what the fuck for – in Kazakhstan they waved and pointed phones, here I get attitude from an arrogant passenger. Get back inside ya circle, London boy. What was I thinking about again? Oh yeah, rip-off England. Man, Bulgaria seems like a dream, such a long way away. 263 miles, a five-hour ride. It'd be quicker to fly to hers from home.

Back at Mum's I'm instantly bored. I can't face TV or the laptop, and certainly not Facebook. It's a topic Lilly talks about too much. She's an administrator on some community group and the job comes with a lot of virtual abuse from the keyboard-warrior fraternity. That's why she doesn't use her real name, I'm still not entirely sure what it is, and it's a bit late to ask. So have I got a girlfriend now? I wonder if I have … and what she's called.

* * *

I can wake up at dawn on any morning except the one I'm obligated to. I've got to look good, the bike's gotta look bad. I'm not even sure if I'm going to be part of the feature Adventure Bike TV are doing on the KLR. I wash my hair anyway and put on my helmet before it's dry, never a good look.

We are meeting in an airfield. I'm not exactly sure why, I'm just happy to take this road to the show. I'm dead on time. There are a lot of other bikes around. My heart sinks a bit, I thought it was going to be an exclusive. I see the producer, who is also the cameraman, the sound crew, the interviewer, the narrator and the editor. Tom *is* Adventure Bike TV. This ain't *Top Gear*.

He already seems to be set up. I see a camera on a tripod and he beckons me to ride over towards him. He seems a little … I don't know, has he changed his mind? I feel like I've been asked to stand on the big 'X' on the floor where the cage will drop or the trapdoor will open. This isn't what I was expecting, why am I on camera before I've even taken my helmet off? He says he's not going to do a feature on my bike. For my birthday, Adventure Bike TV have arranged for me to attend 'Wheelie School'.

My first thought is, what about my tennis elbow? My second is, let's make good TV. So KLR, it seems we will share the spotlight. I'm introduced to the instructor and other pupils. I'm quick to make it clear this was a surprise, that I'm not special and just happen to have a camera following me around like a puppy dog.

There are eight other pupils, three groups of three. We gather in a circle and the instructor tells us what the day will consist of. I'm trying to pay attention but I'm very aware there is a camera three feet from my face. Haven't you got a zoom on that thing, Tom? A zoom yes, but not a boom mic, so suck it up, birthday boy.

Once I've signed and waived any rights for recompense away, the lesson begins. We start on quad bikes. It's a simple technique, throttle at half revs, move forward and at the line dab the clutch – the front wheels come up, easy. Except it's not easy, it just goes against all instinct to pull in or even 'dab' the clutch without throttling back. There is enough time between tries to watch the others and mentally try and rewire a thirty-five-year habit to not disengage the clutch when the engine is revving. I just can't do it, no one else can either. I think that is why we start on quads, to break a habit of a lifetime we have all adopted to increase our life expectancy and that of our bikes.

When I do get it, just like we were told, up come the front wheels. OK, now I've got the knack, let's see how high I can get it. I'm feeling reckless, I'm broken already, I've got all my protective gear on and what can really go wrong? On one run, I manage to physically force instinct and not throttle back. The quad goes up, right up, I think I'm scraping the wheelie bars on the back of the bike. We are all riding on the runway, but one of us is looking at the sky. When I get back to the start everyone comments on my smile. I can't hide that.

I'm not one for recurring dreams, but I have, for as long as I can recall, dreamed I was the wheelie king. I've done a few spectacular ones in my life on two wheels, or one wheel as the case may be, but they have mostly been accidental. One of the most memorable was on the way to Live 8 in London to see what was to be the last time the four members of Pink Floyd ever performed together. I had my favourite ex on the back; the Triumph Sprint never handled better than when she was pillion. Leaving the A12, I got stuck at the lights and Drob and another mate were off up the slip road to the M25. I was so excited for the day to come, I couldn't keep my throttle hand from rocking as I waited for the lights to change. On green, with a fist full of revs and apparently the right clutch control, we left the line like a drag race, up to the redline, into second with G-force acceleration, and then third as we passed a blur of two parked bikes on the hard shoulder – oh, they waited. I felt fists banging on my back and eased off the throttle. There was a gentle bump as the front wheel made its first contact with the motorway. Seeing Roger and David share a stage for the first time since I was at the performance of 'The Wall' at Earl's Court was unforgettable, but the memory of that day which still induces goose pimples is the power wheelie. And, best of all, it wasn't in my head. I had witnesses.

I've got photographic proof today too. After lunch we are given the wheelie school's own stunt bikes. Four-cylinder machines with two sensors on the back, if the first makes contact with the ground two cylinders cut out, and if that doesn't bring you back down, the other one will cut the engine completely, so basically, it's unflippable. I have not ridden a four-cylinder since I went to Alaska, and that wasn't exactly a sports bike. The only time the front wheel was off the ground was when it was on its centre stand. Having got to grips with the clutch dab, I've got another instinct I need to suppress. I seem to have what in the past has been a healthy respect for a borrowed bike. Revving the bollocks and riding the clutch on someone else's machine seems disrespectful. When, in reality, the disrespect is not doing what I'm here to learn. It's OK I can wheelie it a bit, but the sensor takes the vertical out of my front-wheel elevation, and I want to see the sky again. The last part of the day is to take our own bikes down the runway if we want. Oh yes, I want. First, the instructor takes my KLR out. I think after that Welsh trip I can call it run in now. It takes him a couple of runs but he gets it up beautifully. That's what I want to do. He comes back with advice on how to get the front wheel in the air as opposed to the overland that it's more used to. I thought, when I first got the bike all those miles and years ago, that a big single would be the perfect wheelie bike, but KLRs are not geared like that and, much as I've come to love it, that initial realisation was a little disappointing, like when your date can't get a babysitter.

So with a different technique to the one I've been practising all day, I attempt the grand finale. Both panniers are attached and I've got GoPro cameras on me and the bike. I'm riding it harder than I ever have, the 685cc conversion and the Italian exhaust pipe harmonise and pulsate with throbbing encouragement. I rev it harder than I was advised, keeping my right wrist wound back and ridged.

Over the line, grab in the clutch and release. Wahey, here we go, keep on the throttle, right foot over the rear brake in case I go too far. It's bloody spectacular. Apparently, they all cheer, but I don't hear it.

Summing up the day like any TV feature would, the instructor says he's never seen anyone make so much progress, which is a lovely way of saying how useless I was to begin with. Tom says I seem fearless. 'Does anything scare you?' he asks.

'Only commitment,' I reply.

'I'm cutting that out,' he says.

I do a few more runs, but nothing comes close to that first one. I summarise the day to camera ending with, 'I can still get it up at fifty.' Oh cringe, that's TV folks, it's a wrap.

House of the rising scorn

I've got a message from Ivo this morning – when am I coming home? I still don't know.

OK, I've got three major decisions to make. Do I get a stand to myself at the nine-day motorcycle show? Do I buy a pick-up truck? This dictates when and how I will get home. Finally, should I get an investment house to rent out?

Right, if I don't get a truck, I still have transport in Bulgaria. That pitch at the bike show will just be solitary isolation and utter frustration. I email the show and ask them to put me on the waiting list for a better position. I call the magazine again; they still don't answer and won't return my calls.

A coach house has come up on Rightmove so I make an appointment to view it. My research shows it's worth the asking price. It should be easy to rent and sell, in the current climate at least.

Lilly is suggesting Split now – not that we break up, but as a birthday destination in Croatia. I associate the place with narrow streets and oppressive heat, getting stuck in the old town on the same bike that performed the best accidental wheelie ever. Cobbled dead-end alleys and an overheating engine. Anyway, we've left it too late now. Short-notice short-haul flights take the value out of a city break.

After lunch I take Mum to town and put last week's show money in the bank. 'Do you want a personal loan at 3.9%?' asks the cashier obediently. No, I want an investment at that rate. We view the coach house. It's OK, which only shows that I've managed to lower my expectations over the time I've been back here. The agent is very keen to show us the back garden. A five-foot-wide strip that runs the length of the house and contained by a fence the other side of which is an abandoned factory which will inevitably become more high-density housing. There is even a storage cupboard under the stairs; to keep the mower in? Or shall I just hang some scissors inside the door? But then, being shrouded in permanent shadow, I doubt anything will grow anyway. A five-foot-wide garden? 'Adequate dustbin space' might be a more accurate description. The rental return is attractive, but it's still a horrid little house cramped between concrete and overbearing shadows.

An American pick-up truck has just come up on eBay so we go and look at that. Like the house, it's OK, plain white, no air conditioning and only two-wheel drive. It's cheap enough but has no 'wow factor'. I blame wheelie school: I need adrenalin, if it doesn't make my heart beat faster my wallet won't come out my pocket. Bad pitches, cramped coach houses, nondescript pick-ups. Everything is a compromise.

In the evening Lilly agrees that something closer to home is more feasible, but whose home? What starts with a B&B in London turns into two nights at a Thames-side hotel. I look at some gigs in London – yeah, why not? This birthday is going to occur whether I like it or not; I may as well spend it in the capital, get something bubbly, lock the door, turn off the phone and forget the future.

It's just a zero, it's nothing

Tuesday 13th October

50th minus 3 days

This damn birthday. I generally don't even pay that much attention to dates. I don't celebrate Christmas and bank holidays mean nothing when you are self-employed. But birthdays with a zero are significant. Thinking back, I recall them all: on my tenth, the five-speed racer and the first time I felt the effects of alcohol from my parents' home-made white wine; my twentieth, rushing back from Luxembourg in the truck to catch my first love with another man; my thirtieth, the wild joint party with a marquee and a band pitched in the garden of that other man; my fortieth, the canal boat trip with some significant others and other significant absentees. And now this. It's got to be memorable. I should be careful what I wish for, but the half-century has to be recognised. Inevitably, the date is arriving, and I'd better grab at something or it will pass in front of the laptop or inside a bottle and nothing good will come. So perhaps this fling thing, whatever it is, is an attraction with an attachment, although the need was there before.

I go for a long walk on the beach that leads to the village I grew up in. Although every sight has a memory attached, I'm trying to focus on the future, not revisit the past. The tide comes in as I turn and follow my footprints back. I think of those rich Americans I used to work for, their unnecessary neuroses. I could see through their concerns like a tunnel. They found worries in a charmed life, it was ridiculous, almost a guilt-driven need to not enjoy their life of leisure and luxury. In my own modest little way, I've found an enviable future and that should be my focus. I'm putting needless trauma into this transition. October air is

344

good for the soul, it stimulates the mind. The walk is thera-peutic, but I need to go further if I want to find clarity.

The estate agent calls about the coach house, I make an offer of indifference that would only be accepted by the desperate. There is no counter offer, I don't care. They will get their asking price, but not from me. I'm feeling apa-thetic about everything now: house, bike show, birthday. I'm too concerned about doing the wrong thing and I've not done anything. I've thought too much, acted too little and now I'm treading water. The tide is going out and tak-ing time with it.

He's only an old rocker but I like him

As if I had asked the universe, my desire has become available. A pickup truck has just come up for sale on eBay. A fifteen-year-old green American 4x4 with LPG and air conditioning. It's way more than I want to pay, so flippantly I throw out a low offer and get a fair, reduced counter offer. It's still too much, but it does tick every box, except for the heated seats.

A messenger romance is like reading a horoscope: between the lines I can read what I want because the words are not exactly working for me. Two more nights together ought to dispel any illusion.

An adventure motorcycle podcast wants to do an interview with me on my birthday. Hmm, that could go either way. I've worked with them before and I think it's safe. They'll save me in the edit.

The B&B idea that turned into Thames-side decadence has morphed into a three-star hotel near Hyde Park. My bathtub fantasy with a London cityscape view is going to be reduced to a shower cubical in a converted cupboard.

I'm going to go and have a look at the pick-up. It's only just over an hour's ride away and the helmet time will be good. I love October, not just because it's my birthday month but because the weather is invariably bright, full of clear, fresh, colourful days. Every birthday for as far back as I can recall, my parents would recount how, after my birth, my father, who had taken two weeks off work, would hang my terry towelling nappies on the line and every day was dry and sunny. I heard somewhere it's a recognised meteorological phenomenon. St. Luke's Little Summer it's called: two weeks of spectacular weather in October.

It's pretty obvious this is the right house, a fifteen-foot-long Ford F150 in British racing green dominates the driveway. The owner is an older guy and an Americana enthusiast. In his garage is a Ford Model T hot rod and the walls are adorned with US licence plates, beer signs and Elvis pictures. He's selling the pick-up for two reasons: he's got nowhere to keep it under cover and he says it's too good to leave exposed to the imminent British winter; but also because his wife has just had a stroke. Oh, he's not playing the guilt card, but still it puts an air of awkwardness into the sale. They may have to sell up and move to a bungalow as she can no longer manage the stairs.

The guy is a total fanatic and young at heart. I can see this is a blow for him and he can see I see it. He lightens the mood with a meticulous tour of the truck. It's immaculate. He says it's too good to use as a work truck, and I don't have the heart to tell him that's exactly my plan for it. From the carpets in the footwells to the engine compartment, it's spotless. Strange to see they still put cassette players in a 2000 model though. I can't fault it, which is annoying as I want to knock the price down. He takes me into the conservatory to show me his folder of paperwork. The photos of it in the US, the importation papers and receipts for the UK-fitted LPG system. There are two fifty-litre tanks under the bed where the spare wheel would go. He leaves me to peruse the paperwork as he has to attend to his wife. I go back and look at the truck undistracted. It feels right, sitting behind the wheel I can't help but smile. It's outrageous. It's got bling without being ostentatious, chrome running boards, a checker plate tool box and bed cover. It's almost impractical. It's perfect for me.

I can't make him an offer. He says he has already had one. *I know*, I think to myself, *that was me*. Now though, I'm serious. It's definitely got the wow factor, got the pounding heart-V8-throb with a modest 5.4-litre engine. I know better than to ask the mpg. If you're buying a big, fat American

V8, fuel economy should not be a concern. Anyway, it runs on half-price LPG, so that's the environment respected.

I tell him I have to think about it, not in a limp-wristed excuse-to-leave way, but a genuine consideration about making such a big purchase.

And think about it I do, the whole ride back. This isn't a pick-up truck, it's a sign. Life is fragile. He's just an old rocker, got his life-long lusts, his cars and memorabilia, his garage was a shrine to his rock and roller days and day-dreams. And then, all of a sudden, his Judi has a stroke. Pop goes the dream; the reality of carer means rails on the wall and a ramp over the doorstep.

I've moved to my paradise, but how long will it last? There is room in my life for this pick-up truck, and a need too – materials will have to be transported. But practical-ities aside, it's important to me to have a life that raises my heartbeat. Every coach house I look at is killing me a little on the inside. I escaped the UK property market, I liber-ated myself from the rat race, and I'm not about to buy back into the confines of obligation. And, while I'm think-ing freedom thoughts, fuck the bike show. I've been look-ing at it with the same needs I've had for the last four years. To sell, promote, network, elevate my status – but that's all over. It stopped when I moved to Bulgaria. I've glided to a halt, wound down the last of the shows. That wanker in the van was my last interaction. I have to re-mind myself I've retired; I don't need to do this anymore. Everything happens for a reason and that old Teddy Boy has just shown me what's important. I've got myself a new life, now I need to drive that truck to my new home and live it.

Floppy 50th

Thursday 15th October

50th minus 1 day

I imagine I'll be spending much of the weekend in my birthday suit, so I take it into the shower and do the best I can to not make it look like it's been dragged around the world for most of its life or been filled with the forbidden fruits I've found along the way. 'Lived in' is the way an estate agent might describe it.

The train to London takes me past the Olympic development. I'm not a regular commuter but, from 2007, when it was announced that London would be hosting the 2012 Olympic games, I watched with irregular intervals the complex take shape, and with it my excitement rose as London created its third Olympic stadium (the first being White City for the 1908 games and Wembley for the 1948 tournament). This was likely to be the only one the UK hosted in my lifetime. I was unable to get tickets for any of the events, but I was there to watch the marathon runners go down the Embankment. In the three years since London hosted the world's athletes, the place seems to have been a permanent building site. I'm sure you could fit a lot of coach houses in that space.

I get to Victoria station just in time to meet Lilly, only I'm in the wrong place. It's incredible that even with mobile phones it's so difficult to find each other. I bet if I'd posted my status on Facebook, she'd have found me, but I'm staying off that completely. Despite the frustration in trying to connect, I love the way she looks when I get to lay eyes on her again. Definitely a thumbs up. She tells me her period has just started. I'll take the thumb back down, I think.

It's only a ten-minute walk to the hotel and we chat away as we head in totally the wrong direction. I get us back on track and again we go wrong. The walk through Hyde Park I had planned turns into a rush-hour cab ride, nothing moving but the meter.

The hotel is a major disappointment, little more than a converted mid-terrace house with a demoralised receptionist and indifferent attitude. Be sure to leave your excitement in the lobby. Faded paint, stained and foot-worn carpets, stair rails of disease, dust sheets draped over mismatched hallway furniture and neglected paint brushes hardened by mistreatment, damp patches on the walls and peeling plaster – how the fuck is this place a three-star hotel? I open the door into a room that reminds me of the movie *Sid and Nancy*, the portrayal of how Sid Vicious and Nancy Spungen spent the last of their heroin-addicted days together in the Chelsea Hotel. Only this room doesn't have as much space. It's cramped and the filthy high-level window looks out on to a ledge of cigarette butts, a rubbish-covered flat felt roof and the walls of cramped surroundings. The decor is dark, there is just enough space to shuffle between the side of the bed and the wall to the box bathroom, where you bang your knees on the shower screen when you sit on the toilet. I'm feeling deflated, I paid over £200 for this. We could have flown to Gdansk for less.

Come on, let's go and get a drink. There is a pub within sipping distance. I order some insipid lager and the disappointment slips away a little. I've booked us tickets for a gig in Kentish town, and once in the vicinity we try to get food in a pub. The queue for the bar is three people deep, so we opt for overpriced drinks that we have to drink standing up, being buffeted by the pushing passers-by before going into the venue.

The audience is predominantly single middle-aged men. On any other night, I'd fit right in. The sound mix is awful and the lyrics unintelligible, but we find a dark corner and move our bodies in a grinding foreplay kind of way. Fuck this, let's get out of here – so this is what a gig with a girl is like. I bet the aficionados in the audience frown at our premature evacuation. We jump in a cab and go straight back to our squalid little room. But nothing's happening, have I put myself under too much pressure to perform? Is this the middle-aged changes, the male menopause? Come on, it's not hard. So much for my cringe-inducing wrap-up on Adventure Bike TV.

With humiliation and hunger, I hit the streets and bring us back some KFC. It's awful: a smoked salmon and cream cheese bagel would taste like cardboard and goldfish in a room like this. I should never have agreed to that interview tomorrow, it's on my mind. At 4 a.m. we stop talking and trying. I'm fifty. How very depressing.

My 50th Birthday by Graham Field

Friday 16th October 2015

We exclude ourselves from the all-inclusive breakfast. Perhaps I was just tired. This morning we have lift off and now the pressure is off, so am I, let's do it again. I throw on some clothes and walk to the main road. Beyond the KFC I find an off-licence and get a bottle of chilled cava. As I go to put my new card in the machine, the cashier shows me I only have to wave it in the vicinity of the reader. My first contactless purchase. I go back to the room for more contact. You'll never guess how I just paid for this? Apparently, I'm a little behind, talking of which ... Between the romantic interludes is chatter, her chatter, non-stop chatter, no chance of an awkward silence here, and then like a looped tape she tells the same story again. Was she not listening? It wasn't that interesting the first time, like 'Ummagumma'.

We play music on our phones: me, Led Zeppelin; her, Halestorm. I ask, 'So are we in a relationship now?'

She says if that's what I want then she wants it too.

'OK,' I say, 'I'm ready to take things to the next level. What exactly is your name?'

Hmmm, it's going to be hard to remember her new moniker, and it's such a faux pas to call your lover by the wrong name, but Lilly has kind of stuck now. I think I'll go and get more cava. I wave my card at the machine. I love this, there's no need to remember a PIN anymore, but I must try and retain the name of my girlfriend.

I've got a two-bottle buzz when Adventure Rider Radio call for their interview. Although I hadn't anticipated it, obviously, the interviewer asks where I am. I mean, the whole focus of the show is travel. So when I say I'm in a London hotel, predictably (although not to me), he asks if I'm alone. No, I'm with my girlfriend, and now within just a few hours of becoming aware that I officially have a girl-friend I've just bloody announced it on his show. An hour and a half passes and I'm not sure I admit to anything more, he's already got his exclusive. Women around the world will be throwing themselves under buses now.

Speaking of which, perhaps we ought to think about venturing out. It's getting dark and we've not had break-fast yet. However, clearly the impending pressure of the interview was the problem, because now it's over there is a release. I've got my wanton ways back and I want my after-show party.

Lilly, as I will continue to call her, spent the interview with earbuds and Facebook. She brings up the subject of announcing the 'is in a relationship with' topic on her fa-vourite social media site. I've always believed that a sign of a healthy relationship is there's no sign of it on Face-book. I come out of the shower to see I've got a missed call from the other Welsh girl. This isn't complicated, we've not spoken in months, but I still feel she should hear the news from me, not via the internet.

I don't have a preference for type of food, only the am-bience of the restaurant. I want cosy. I've just been in the spotlight and now I want a darkened booth to soothe the jagged day of raunch and recklessness. Although, now I think about it, Indian is too heavy, sushi too precise, Chinese too fast, Mexican too carb-orientated, Greek too cheesy, Thai too hot (the bathroom too close to the bed), French too pre-tentious, American too unadventurous. A sexy discreet little Italian would be ideal, eating spaghetti like Lady and the Tramp. We end up on a loud shared bench seat in a Leba-nese restaurant under fluorescent lights.

I've been noticing for the last two days, and only for the third time in my life, that girls are checking me out. I swear this has nothing to do with my looks but the attractive girl I'm with. Although I could be wrong, it seems to me that eye-catching company comes with intrigue. What's this guy got that he can box above his weight? It's like pushing a pram or walking a lapdog, you stop being a threat, and like a missed *Buy it now* on eBay, they don't want it until someone else has got it.

We stop in our 'local' for a nightcap: me a beer; she rum and coke, and more coke. We sit at our table till just past midnight and the sound of her chatter ricochets around the emptying pub. The looped tape plays, another round, I feel my eyes closing, my head bowing, my attentive mask is wearing thin. The landlord calls time. Sweet, let's go to bed.

In the night the fire alarm screams us awake. My instinctive reaction is to stand on the bed and disarm it; hers is to put on my T-shirt, grab her bag and run. Interesting priorities. I look out the window, I can't smell smoke, don't see flames. The ear-piercing screeching stops and silence is sucked into the dark void of our inherent differences. Turns out it wasn't the fire alarm; it was a wake-up call.

END OF PART 1

GRAHAMFIELD.CO.UK

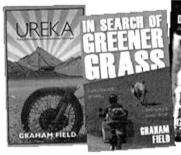

Graham's website has a shop full of temptations for travel lovers and an extensive gallery for readers to follow his stories in photos.

ADVENTURE\BIKE
T E L E V I S I O N

WATCH NOW ON

prime video

patreon

Dear Kaufland

This may seem like a strange request.

I have just completed my fourth book, this one is called 'Near Varna' and is about how I left the UK to live in Bulgaria five years ago.

Kaufland gets mentioned 18 times in my 110,000 word book, as it was a place I went, and still do go to regularly. It became a running joke in the book that I always ended up in your supermarket. But on a serious side as a relocating Brit it was the perfect shop because when I first moved here and didn't have a word of Bulgarian I could pick all I needed off the shelves without needing the language. There was also a variety of products and even some English foods available.

My readers are generally travellers and I hope with this book to widen my audience as it will also appeal to people who have and are considering relocating.

I do say in the book when the name Kaufland comes up at one point that I am not sponsored by this supermarket I just happen to like it however if you see a big red 'K' or an advert in the back pages you will know that they did contribute to the printing costs of the book in exchange for advertising.

I have in my last three books had four or five adverts from companies mentioned, generally smaller businesses, motorcycle part fabricators, internet-based broadcasters etc. (see attached photos) So I was wondering if you would be interested in having a B&W A5 size advert in my new book, I only charge a minimal fee, that helps with the production costs. It would have an impact and would make a great end to a theme that runs through the narrative of the book.

Dear Mr. Field,

Thank you for the submitted proposal and for the interest in cooperation with Kaufland Bulgaria. We have carefully considered the project and after analyzing the elements in it, as well as our current planning, I would like to inform you that unfortunately we will not be able to join it. Our company has a long-term partnership strategy. A strategy that basically has a different focus from your suggestions. Your project is extremely interesting and we believe it will be a great success, but our strategic focuses at this stage are directed to a different topic.

Thanks again for your inquiry.

Regards